ETI DAYAN

ONE OF THEM

My Life Among the
Maasai People in Kenya

The events and characters in *One of them* were inspired by real events and real people; however, the events and characters in the book should not be viewed as an exact reconstruction of these events and/or people. The contents and characters of the book should not be interpreted as possessing direct, comprehensive documentary significance.

Producer & International Distributor
eBookPro Publishing
www.ebook-pro.com

One of Them
Eti Dayan

Copyright © 2020 Eti Dayan

All rights reserved; No parts of this book may be reproduced or transmitted in any form or by any means, electronic or mechanical, including photocopying, recording, taping, or by any information retrieval system, without the permission, in writing, of the author.

Translation from the Hebrew by Yael Schonfeld Abel

Contact: one.of.maasai@gmail.com
ISBN 9798652201685

*This book is dedicated to my Maasai friends who taught me that 'A village without elders, is like a tree without roots'.
And, to Samyan and his family.*

ONE OF THEM

My Life Among the Maasai People in Kenya

ETI DAYAN

Contents

Introduction		11
1	African Princesses	18
2	No'oltwati	38
3	The Cattle Gate Is Not Wide Enough	47
4	Samyan	58
5	What Should I Do Today?	67
6	When the Child Is in the Belly—It Is Yours. When It Is Out—It's Everyone's!	72
7	Black-Ear	78
8	The Water Tank Births a Lamb	86
9	Your Blood Is Happy	96
10	Operation Mom	108
11	Lionesses in the Village	118
12	One Finger Cannot Kill a Louse	124
13	An Old Groom	129
14	Emuyo	142
15	One Round	144
16	AIDS	160
17	The Lion Hunt	164
18	Morans	172
19	The Nose Does Not Precede You	184
20	Maasai Justice	193

21	Children Are a Shining Moon	207
22	Eunoto	217
23	Birth Certificate	230
24	Capturing Flies	232
25	Drought and Tradition	244
26	God Will Help, and If He Doesn't—the White Man Will	250
27	Enkitok Kibor (The White Woman of Ours)	255
28	Water Cannot Climb Uphill	259
29	Life Is a Miracle!	273
30	The Zebra Carries Its Stripes with It Wherever It Goes	284
31	The Zebra Does Not Deny Its Stripes	289
Epilogue		298

Commentary	303
Appendix 1 Where Did the Maasai Come From?	319
Appendix 2 Who Are the Maasai?	325
Appendix 3 The Maasai Social Network	328
Appendix 4 Names, Latin Names and Uses of Plants Cited	334
Appendix 5 Glossary	337
Bibliography	342
Acknowledgments	345

"If there is a place in the world where man may live the legend of his life—Africa is that place!"

(*The Roots of Heaven*, Romain Gary)

Parsae tadamu ena sile
God, remember my debt
esile nemelak nkishu
The cows will not pay it
nemelak enkikuei natudung'uo
The wood I've chopped will not pay it
nemelak enkare naokoki
The water I've fetched will not pay it
nemelak olumbuani atadoikio
Even if I dive to the bottom of the well, it will not be paid
enkerai oltung'ani nalak
Only our children will pay it

(A female Maasai prayer song)

Introduction

The late 1990s. Twilight time. The sun that had blazed during the day produces a breathtaking sunset spectacle.

I'm in Kenya, on the outskirts of the Maasai Mara National Reserve, inside a Maasai village. I'm surrounded by tall, dark-skinned men, wearing red cloaks, holding clubs and strapped with knives. Beside them are women with shaved scalps, wearing multicolored fabrics and adorned with bracelets and necklaces. A few are holding babies. On the sidelines, snot-nosed children clad in rags are huddling, laughing and talking loudly. There's quite a commotion in the air.

Kitipai says, "You saved my wife No'oltwati's life, and therefore from now on, her blood and your blood are one, and you will become a part of our family. We have all decided that your name will be Nayolang." All residents of this familial village, about thirty people are looking at me, a forty-year-old white woman, as they mumble the name four times: "Nayolang, Nayolang, Nayolang, Nayolang."

I'm standing at the center, my gaze roaming over the faces of every person present. I feel the affection radiating from them and tears form in the corners of my eyes. I think of all the events that have taken place and led to me standing here at this moment and still do not know this is one of the crucial moments in a process that will lead to a radical change in my life. Which will culminate in my moving to live in this little village with these people, who have suddenly become my family, among whom I will live for so many years.

∽

About twenty years ago, I relocated to Kenya, to a tiny Maasai village on the outskirts of a substantial nature reserve known as Maasai Mara. The area, known as Osero to the Maasai, consists primarily of a sprawling grassland savanna, speckled with patches of shrubs and veined with a network of riverbeds rich with water, their banks shaded in various hues of green: light orange-green bushes, olive-green vines and dark green trees.

This stretch of land is crossed by a mighty river known as the Mara (Enkepai to the Maasai) originating in a high mountain range called Mao, and flowing—after tumbling down the mountain range to the rolling hills of the reserve—into Lake Victoria, within the territory of Tanzania.

The sensation of happiness emerging somewhere deep within my body and mounting like a wave flooding me, again and again, is not a result of the beauty of the place—there are many more breathtaking places in the world. Here, I can feel an all-powerful wholeness: the hills, arcing with a peaceful softness, blend into the endless sky, the clouds floating slowly in the heavens create various three-dimensional patterns in shades of white and gray, the sparsely scattered trees are shaped like environmental statues, their feet in the flat grassy savanna and their heads brushing the sky. The occasional eagle nesting and the antelopes grazing in their shade illustrate that there's room for everyone within this space. I am engulfed by clean nature, and here, more than anywhere else, I feel an existential optimism. Zebras, antelopes, warthogs, lions, elephants—have all been moving through the savanna for generations now and will continue to do so.

My attraction to the plaines of Africa and to the Maasai Mara

National Reserve did not come as a surprise. I have found that Africa is the closest thing to the formative experience of my life—the Sinai Desert. My love affair with the Sinai Peninsula began during my military service in the Israeli Army, as a guide at Eilat Field School. I had been put in charge of running camel tours in East Sinai. For many days and weeks, I drank in Sinai's untamed expanses from the backs of camels and on foot. The views shifted gradually, from sand dunes to towering granite mountains, from colorful sandstone to broad wadis with scattered acacia trees, in whose shade we sheltered from the blazing sun in the heat of the day. During trips that lasted a week, the only showers consisted of bathing in the freezing bodies of water we encountered in desert oases. Every evening, under a million stars watching us from above, or in the light of the moon illuminating the mountains with a silvery, sensual light, we, the travelers and the Bedouin leading the camels would sit around a flickering campfire, on which a kettle of tea was bubbling, spreading the scent of *habag*, or long-leaved mint, a fragrant herb that added a distinctive flavor to the tea. Conversations and stories stretched on into the night until we collapsed in exhaustion into our sleeping bags. We visited Bedouin tents we came across, breathing in their unique aroma—the smell of smoke typically emanating from campfires feeding on branches of *sich*, the intoxicatingly scented sagebrush plant. We held their children in our laps, adorned our faces with *kuchul*—the blue eye makeup given to us by the women, and made friends with the shepherds seeking pasture for the goats throughout the barren desert while holding on to a transistor radio blasting out Fairuz or Umm Kulthum.

When I arrived in Maasai Mara, I found clean nature and clear air, a blanket of stars and a full moon, goats, and the scents of people, which awakened a hidden yearning within me for a life I'd already had. And besides the expanses of wilderness, this time in Maasai Mara rather than in the Sinai Desert, the people, meaning the Maasai—with the scent of their fires, their snot-nosed children and their herds of goats and cattle—played a significant role in my intense attraction to the place.

My process of acclimation to life in the village was a prolonged one. At first, I arrived for short periods. Later, I extended my stay more and more. Sometimes I stayed in other women's homes, and sometimes in a tent, I set up on the outskirts of the village. Finally, in 2001, I built a house of my own.

During the first weeks, I focused on learning the villagers' names and trying to remember and memorize the vast network of familial and social relationships. I tried to become accustomed to a life immensely different than the one I had come from. No electricity, gas or running water, the constant presence of children and adults throughout the day, the goats that took advantage of every moment of inattention to grab hold of the dish soap and take off, or to bite into the cabbage I had obtained with much effort. I had to get used to walking to the stream to do my laundry and bathe. And also, as strange as it may sound, to living life without a plan: to get up in the morning without knowing what I would do throughout the day, to a social life that begins daily at dawn, ends in the evening, and consists mainly of sitting with the village women in the shade of a tree.

I realized that the curiosity was mutual—up till now, the villagers' only encounter with white people had taken place when casual tourists arrived for a brief visit. Now, however, they had access to a "creature" that could be observed endlessly, marveling at its behavior and choices, and that creature was me.

Me? A creature? Up to this point, I had perceived myself as a normative woman. After my military service in the Sinai Peninsula, I completed my master's degree in African Studies and combined my thirst for knowledge with my love of travel and adventure in my work as a tour guide: in South America, in Yugoslavia, and finally, in Africa. It's true that my backpack was my best friend, but I was, and still am, a product of the society and culture in which I grew up.

Here in the village, I was the odd one out, but despite this, both individuals and society enveloped me with warmth and affection and tried to assist me in fitting in. I often felt like Marcel Griaule, a French ethnographer who, in the 1920s, arrived to live among the Dogon, an ethnic group residing in Eastern Mali. He stayed with them for long periods of time (until his death in the Fifties) and learned their way of life and their elaborate mythology. In one of his books, he wrote that in retrospect, he realized that the society's elders had put him through an "initiation ceremony" of sorts, as he was being accepted into the tribe. As he exhibited increasing seriousness and willingness to learn, additional strata of society were revealed to him—one layer at a time, stretching increasingly deeper.

The first ceremony I attended was a wedding. Several months passed before I could witness a male circumcision, and it was two more years before I could participate in female circumcision, a rite the Maasai know to be subject to severe criticism from Western societies.

This was also true regarding photography: in the first ceremonies, I could only participate as an observer. In the next ones, I could take photos, and later, I was asked to come and take pictures.

Over the years, I became a part of the overall landscape and was no longer subject to any special attention.

The real challenge of living in the Maasai village was watching, observing and learning about a social system different than the one in which I had grown up: the culture, the customs, the dos and don'ts, the manner of thinking—all these were a new, unknown country. Upon first acquaintance, it seemed as if the Maasai worldview—about women, men, romance, love, food, relationships, children and so on—was distinctly different than that of those of us who were products of Western culture. It's hard to find similarities between the two worldviews, I believed, and tried to learn, understand and respect the logic of a society always, or nearly always, different from the one I knew.

"I have a very old relative, about eighty years old. One day I asked him about some custom. He looked embarrassed and went to consult his friends… You see, even someone born Maasai, and who has lived his entire life as a Maasai, still doesn't know everything about our customs." This was the answer I received one day after I asked and asked and asked.

Sure, I understand. I understand you have to be born and to live as a Maasai to get all the tiny subtleties that accompany each family, each custom, each ceremony. I know the extent to which the society is multihued, multilayered and complex. A full life span among the Maasai won't give me the same knowledge that every infant suckles along with his mother's milk.

Nevertheless, over the years, I grew increasingly well acquainted with the fascinating lifestyle of the Maasai, their cultural codes, their rites and customs that have existed for many years and that have succeeded, despite natural disasters, political crises, and other calamities, in preserving the Maasai as a people.

In this book, I hope to open a window onto the richness of Maasai culture. Not merely the overt aspects—rites, clothing or behavior, but also the covert ones—those aspects of Maasai culture that makes its members who they are: the beliefs, the manner of thinking, the laws and the logic behind them all.

I do not aspire to provide a complete, comprehensive or scientific account of the customs of the Maasai people. There is considerable variance in the nature of life in various locations. Each of the Maasai tribes has its own dialect and typical customs (for example, different plants are used in ceremonies), and each family has its own unique traditions. This is even true of families living next to one another (think of the ways people of different ethnicities celebrate weddings; the essential ceremony is the same, but each ethnicity has its own style).

The contents of this book address only the customs and worldview to which I've been exposed first-hand and the ceremonies I've attended as an active participant in a handful of villages, among the Purko* people living adjacent to the Massai Mara Reserve in Kenya.

I'm aware that Maasai in other locations behave, dress, adorn themselves, talk and perhaps even think differently than what is described here. Any mistakes in interpreting customs or the rules governing ceremonies are all mine.

Everything described in this book is true. The characters are actual people. All of their names—other than those who made a point of asking me to mention them by name—have been changed.

---

* Purko: One of the Maasai tribes (sections). At the end of the book is a Commentary chapter, with expansions and clarifications that will assist in understanding the contents of every chapter. Sections in the text further expanded upon in the Commentary are marked with a numbers. The appendixes to this book also include an alphabetical glossary of many Maasai terms.

1

African Princesses

Barsoinkan was the first Maasai with whom I created bonds of friendship. There was a reason for this. He was not only tall and dark-skinned, with bright eyes and a radiant smile, but unlike most of his fellow Maasai, he spoke fluent English, which enabled him to conduct negotiations on behalf of his village about the fee charged for tourist visits to the village.

Like other villages on the outskirts of the Maasai Mara National Reserve in Kenya, this village, a grouping of huts made of cow dung surrounding a stockade for cows at their center, had opened its doors to visits from curious tourists. In their own countries, these tourists had been regaled with the myth of "the noble savage," befitting the tall, thin forms of the Maasai—wearing red robes, clutching spears and capable of leaping to great heights—and they now wanted to "sample" the lives of the tribes. This sampling was usually limited solely to taking photos. Walking through the "town square" that was covered with cow dung, encountering the children engulfed by flies, and entering houses whose walls were made of cow dung deprived even the bravest tourist of the joy of getting to know the locals in depth.

When we got to know each other, the village representative and I, a tour guide who visited Kenya frequently, we agreed upon a fixed fee charged from my tour groups visiting the village, an agreement that served both parties well. I saved time and energy by not having to negotiate anew every time, while he, in a lucrative financial maneuver, ensured his village would receive an ongoing income.

Our friendship grew stronger over the years. I took advantage of idle periods in my working life to meet up with him and realized that my stream of curious questions about his way of life and that of the Maasai people was not diminishing.

On one visit, he greeted me with a big grin. "I'm about to get married, and would be happy if you, Eti—who have known me for many years and invested significant funds in my village, allowing me to save enough money to buy the cattle required for the wedding— could attend the ceremony."

I was taken by surprise. I had known many Maasai over the years and had formed bonds of friendship with many. But I had always felt that despite their pleasant nature, our relationship would hit an invisible wall, which would not prevent them from opening their houses but did prevent them from opening their hearts. I was always invited over to drink tea, to play with the children and to talk to the members of the village, but I stayed out of bounds with customs, ceremonies and events. Was this barrier posed due to the cultural gap, out of fear of the way a white woman would react to the nature of their lives? Therefore, I interpreted this invitation as a change, however minute, in the attitude of Barsoinkan and the rest of the village toward me, which made me happy.

I promised I would attend, gently inquiring (in the spirit of Western attitudes) what gifts I should bring to the wedding, and receiving specific instructions: dresses and fabric for the bride, a jacket for the groom and about twenty pounds of sugar for the village itself, used to brew the local beer.

On the intended day, about two months later, carrying a backpack filled with a sleeping bag, a few clothes and plenty of water, and with the bag of gifts in my hand, I took public transportation to the Maasai Mara National Reserve. I was traveling to a village on the main road, close to the bride's village, where the first stage of the wedding ceremony, the bride's parting from her parents, was set to take place. From here, I knew, the nuptial procession would travel into the bush, a dense mass of shrubs and trees, to the village where the groom's parents resided.

I was excited and nervous.

This was my first time arriving at the village without a tour vehicle, or the tourists who surrounded me and padded my way. I was the only white woman in the public transport truck. I saw the baffled expressions of the tightly packed Maasai men and women slanting looks in my direction and hoped Barsoinkan remembered my promise to attend. I tucked myself against the window, while next to me, on a bench meant for two, sat a man along with a woman holding a little baby in her arms. My curiosity constantly vacillated between the colorful fabrics and jewelry inside the truck and the sights outside. I watched the view shifting from rounded hills sprouting occasional green acacia trees to sprawling plains, which now, toward the end of the dry season, were yellow. Flurries of dust moved swiftly in the wind as it blew, dissipating in the distance. Flocks of sheep accompanied by young children grazed unmolested besides herds of gazelles. The truck occasionally stopped in the middle of nowhere, unloaded cargo and people, and continued on its way.

After several hours, when my body was aching from the jostling and the crowding, and the way became familiar —I identified villages and prominent trees—the truck stopped with a shriek. Outside, I saw Barsoinkan waiting in festive clothes: two red cloaks, new and shiny, were wrapped around his body, tied around his shoulders and clasped around his waist with a fancy, colorful beaded belt, from which a sheath housing a long knife also hung. His short hair was anointed with a red ochre tint. A bundle of *oleleshwa* branches (soft, fragrant camphor) was protruding from under his arm, a local deodorant of sorts. Next to him was another young man, also dressed in ceremonial clothing, a "groomsman" who followed him everywhere and whose role, I was told, was to support and encourage him, and to serve as a witness if something went wrong.

With a sigh of relief, I extracted myself from the crowded truck and descended joyfully on Barsoinkan and his friend while my heavy backpack was taken off the vehicle's roof. After we exchanged greetings, he had an announcement to make: "The bride's father grew sick a few days ago and was taken to the hospital. We Maasai do not celebrate joyous occasions when our family members are sick; therefore, we've put off the wedding until he returns." Since we had to wait, he said, and since I had arrived especially for the ceremony, he and his friends did not want to burden me with the expenses of finding accommodations. Therefore, I was welcome to stay in the village.

I had never rejoiced over a person's illness, but now, due to the father being sick, I'd been granted a unique opportunity to experience village life first-hand, which made me jubilant.

I was brought into a village built as a circle, surrounded by a tall, thick wall of thorny acacia branches. The village houses were built next to this wall of thorns, and beyond them stood another internal thorny fence separating the houses from the central clearing where the cows were kept at night.

I was led by the men to the hut of No'oltwati, a Maasai woman of about twenty-five privileged with attending school in her youth. After graduating from high school, already pregnant, an arranged marriage was set up for her and she was taken here, to her husband's village, about sixty miles from her home. No'oltwati, an intelligent, pleasant and pretty girl, was the only one in the village who spoke English other than Barsoinkan. I was glad of the highly thoughtful decision to "match me up" with an English speaker, a step which ensured many hours of conversation that might satisfy my indefatigable curiosity.

My backpack and I were respectfully led into the dim, smoky hut. The men sat down on the two beds, elevated benches covered with cowhide standing across from each other. In the space between the berths, whispering coals cast a reddish light upon their faces. I sat next to the beds, on a low wooden stool, sipping water and watching them speak their melodious language amongst themselves. After several minutes, Barsoinkan addressed me. "Eti, we've never hosted a white person in our village, and since we want you to be comfortable, we have a few questions. The first: what will you eat during your stay here?"

I knew from books I'd read that the Maasai diet consisted of milk, cow's blood and beef. I was used to milk and beef; however, blood wasn't my favorite food, and I wondered how I could answer the question without insulting them. I paused before providing my answer, then said, "I can eat anything, other than cow's blood." They chuckled and told me that for years now, they did not feed on blood regularly, but rather on *ugali* (a common food in Kenya, made of maize flour and resembling hardened polenta), *chapati* (a sort of pancake made of wheat flour), rice, beans and potatoes.

The men added, "Today, in honor of your arrival—the first white person to stay in the village—we'll slaughter a goat and buy beer!" A real party, I thought to myself, except that I didn't drink beer. I gently declined. Their eyes gaped in amazement. "You are *muzungu* (a white-skinned person) and therefore must drink beer!"

I was amused by their image of me and of white people in general, agreed to compromise on Shandy, beer mixed with Sprite, and a young boy was sent to the store to bring the beverages for the celebration that began that evening and continued on into the night and on the nights to come.

"Okay," the men continued to provide for my comfort. "That boy," they pointed at one youth, "will run to the next village. One man there has a transistor radio, and he'll bring it here."

"A transistor radio?" I asked, baffled.

"Of course," they replied. "You are *muzungu*, and therefore you have to listen to the radio."

I was touched by their concern for me, which extended to the smallest details. I realized that my hosts had perceived my declining of their offers of beer or radio as an attempt to spare the expenses, which clashed with their desire to host me properly. However, I was amazed by how little we knew about one another: they, who briefly hosted tourists in their village every day, and I, who had visited their village and other villages dozens of times.

My hosts turned to me with another riddle. "Where do you prefer to bathe, in the stream along with the other women, or here, behind the hut?" Once again, they gaped in amazement when I told them explicitly that I did not need to shower every day, and even if I didn't bathe, I would be fine… "But you're *muzungu*!" was their reaction, and once again, I could not decline. I compromised on bathing behind the hut, assuming I could discreetly avoid it. The next few days proved me wrong: every night, once darkness fell, No'oltwati produced a large blue basin with a cracked rim, filled it to the brim with water from a yellowish container, stood beside me and made sure I was bathing, while poking through my toiletries kit and inquiring about various objects: tampons, shampoo, a makeup pencil and so on.

The remainder of my first day went by swiftly. The men sat in the shade of the only tree, located outside the village, while the women left to chop firewood, returned and cooked lunch (*ugali* and sour milk sauce). I served as a major attraction for the kids, who fussed over me, groped every part of my body, played with my hair and went through my things.

The lowing of cows returning from pasture rang in the evening. After the cows were put in the stockade at the center of the village, the young girls were sent to close the village gates. They dragged a branch which, during the day, was placed several yards in front of the opening, blocking the village gate. The branch was hard, resilient and knotty so that when the gate was closed, no small animals could pass under it and enter the village. More dry branches were stacked next to this main branch throughout the day, closing the gate at night.

Meanwhile, the women milked the cows, an activity that lasted a relatively long time and ended after darkness had fallen. Each woman went into her hut to make milk tea and cook dinner. I sat in No'oltwati's hut, trying in vain to fight the tears streaming from my eyes due to the thick smoke curling around me. She boiled water, poured in about a pound of maize flour, tore off a piece of paper from the flour bag and used it to hold the soot-blackened pot on the fire. With her other hand, using a wooden spoon, she stirred the paste, which gradually hardened until it resembled a lump of dough. After we savored a meal of *ugali* in sour milk, the party began. One after the other, men and women came in and rejoiced in the beers bought for me.

Only later in the night, when the attendees dispersed to their various huts, did I understand that sleeping in No'oltwati's hut meant sharing the small hut not only with her, but with her husband Kitipai, with their little girl and with another boy. This hut, like every Maasai hut, contained two beds made of woven branches and covered with cowhide serving as a mattress. One bed was smaller, enclosed from every side (other than a narrow opening) with walls made of cow dung, and intended for the mother and her small infant. The protective walls around the bed provided privacy for the wife and husband when they slept together. Across from this bed was a larger, wider one, serving the husband or the older children. No'oltwati assigned me the mother's bed, the smaller of the two, while all the other family members settled down to sleep in the larger bed. Besides us, the residents crammed into the hut for the night also included goats, their kids, and even calves, for whom a separate small room was constructed.

～

Two in the morning. I woke up in a panic. Where was I? I heard heavy breathing near me. Raising my hand toward my eyes, I found I couldn't see it — not an iota of light. The air was stagnant. I tried to turn on the flashlight I had placed next to me, but it wasn't working. I brought my hand up and groped around me. I felt the walls in every direction. Where was I? In the grave? I woke up completely. In utter silence, I worked my way out of my sleeping bag, gingerly brought my feet down to the ground, fumbled for my sandals and made my way out in a state of alarm. I kneeled down next to the hut's external wall, breathing heavily.

The sense of suffocation that had enveloped me dissipated in the soft light of the stars. Somewhere nearby, I heard the breathing and snoring of the cows. The air was standing still. Nothing was moving. Sitting with my back against the wall of the hut, I spent the rest of the night outside, listening to distant growls, to the random chirping of a bird, my eyes peering around apprehensively fearing an approaching animal. Hours later, as the stars grew dim, the sky slipped on a wrap of light blue velvet and dawn was about to break, I entered the hut again and wriggled into the sleeping bag, not wanting to hurt the feelings of my hosts, who might think I had not been comfortable.

A short while later, with the first light of day, No'oltwati blew at the whispering coals to reignite the fire at the center of the hut, put a kettle over the flames and went out to milk the cows. The sweet glass of cooked milk tea I was served a while later helped me wake up into the routine of a new day of waiting for the wedding.

I spent most of the day with the men, most of whom I already knew, under the only tree growing outside the village. They were busy with various small tasks. One was sharpening a knife on stone, and another was carving a wooden club. Four huddled around a wooden board they used for games of checkers. Beer bottle caps competed against Coke bottle caps. I was introduced to passersby who stopped in the shade of the tree, conveying information about what was happening. As we lounged and talked, a scream was suddenly heard from afar. The men tensed at once, grabbing their clubs and spears and running swiftly toward the bush. The shout, I discovered later, had come from the throat of the cow shepherd. He alerted the men that a leopard had attacked the herd and stolen a calf, and they set out to find the leopard and kill it. I met the men again only in the early evening hours, and they told me that the search, which had gone on all day, had ended with no results. The leopard had taken off with its loot, disappeared into the bush and they could not find it.

I moved on to the company of the women. After finishing their morning chores, which included drawing water from the nearby stream in round, yellow five-gallon containers and cooking lunch, they sat down sociably under "their" tree, in the middle of the village, and occupied themselves with various tasks: stringing beads on thin metal wires to make colorful bracelets, shaving the heads of friends and children, and singing songs with the children. To the sound of their gleeful exclamations, I learned the basics of stringing together bracelets and crafted these works of art. The women giggled again and again in response to my odd choice of colors. While laughing, they hinted that they would have picked a different combination.

In the afternoon, my arms and neck itched. Shortly thereafter, my body experienced an allergic reaction and swelled up. I knew that what looked like bites was not caused by insects in the house, as every book about the Maasai way of life stated that the fire burning inside the house, and the thick smoke it created, not only helped in heating (which was very important for people lacking in clothes other than the ones on their bodies) but were intended to keep many pests away from the house: flies, mosquitoes, fleas, ticks and so on. Therefore, I attributed the swelling to being exposed for many hours to the sun and the strong radiation. To protect myself, I put on a long-sleeved shirt—but to no avail. The itching did not stop, and the only relief came courtesy of the breeze, which cooled my body somewhat.

The next morning, the itching became actual suffering. The Maasai Mara National Reserve, with its luxurious lodges, was close at hand, and the thought of relocating there crossed my mind. But meanwhile, I was told that the father of the bride had returned from the hospital and the wedding ceremony would begin that evening.

I let go of tentative thoughts about taking off, and filled with pride when the women invited me, as a "long-time" friend, to go with them to the stream about five minutes away. They tasked me with filling a small water container—merely two gallons, as opposed to the containers they carried, which were twice as heavy. The way to the river was easy and I accompanied them happily, but on the way back, uphill, while they carried the container tied to their forehead with a leather band and walked with ease, I groaned under the weight of the two gallons, which I transferred from hand to hand.

One man, recently married to a loving woman and a new father, offered to take me for a walk in the bush, the thicket of greenery surrounding the village and climbing up the nearby hills. Yesterday, I had noticed that his wife was blowing him kisses, thus becoming the first and only Maasai woman I had seen to this day engaging in public displays of affection toward her husband.

As he walked through the bush, the man exhibited inexhaustible knowledge about the locations of water sources, identifying the ownership of distant herds of cattle, and the names and medical uses of shrubs and trees. At the end of the walk, we returned directly to the wedding ceremony, which was about to commence in the adjacent village. The bride, a girl of about seventeen, had undergone a circumcision ceremony several months ago, becoming a woman according to Maasai belief, and once the wound was healed and only a scar remained, had been matched up with Barsoinkan. Her family had begun the preparations for the wedding, which went on for many weeks, and included making a variety of beaded necklaces and bracelets given to her as a dowry. Once the preparations ended, the ceremony itself was conducted, lasting several days. This was the ceremony whose commencement I was about to witness now.

The first indication that unusual activity was going on was the concentration of men and women near the bride's hut, and in the entire village. The intended groom and his groomsman (who had not left his side for a moment) were sitting outside the village fence along with the father of the bride; from now on, the two families, the groom's and the bride's, would be bonded by a familial relationship.

I greeted familiar faces, found No'oltwati and joined her. She was standing at the entrance to the bride's hut, watching one woman shave the bride's head.

"Why does the bride's head get shaved?" I wondered out loud.

No'oltwati explained this was an important rite serving as an opening to the events of the wedding. "We believe that shaving the head symbolizes shedding one identity and growing a new identity—a rebirth of the soul into a new phase in the cycle of life. That's why we shave a baby's head when it becomes a child, shave the heads of boys and girls before they are circumcised, and shave the head of a bride on her wedding day."

I looked around me. All the women's heads were shaved for reasons of hygiene, but not the bride's. She had relatively long hair, and once again, I required an explanation.

"Look, she was circumcised about six months ago. From that time until the wedding, she'd forbidden to shave her head, so that the length and size of her mane of hair hints to all of us about the interval between her circumcision and her wedding."

I poked my head between the women crowding around the small entrance to the house. The bride was sitting, head bent, on a bolt of cowhide, her face and neck stained with milk. The shaver, a smiley older woman kneeling beside her, poured milk from a *kalabash* (an oblong gourd serving as a container for liquids) into her hand, and spread more of it on the bride's hair. She produced an old-fashioned straight razor with no handle, steadied the bride's head with her large palm, and with her other hand, sheared. The bride whimpered, and the more hair fell from her, the more her crying increased until she was downright weeping. My heart went out to her, but the women around me were giggling loudly.

"She better cry!" they said. "How else will we know she's truly sorry to part from us, her family members and close friends?"

After the shaving, the bride got up and entered the hut along with the women who crowded in. The women around me were sipping homemade beer, and the atmosphere gradually heated up, becoming more and more boisterous. The women aimed their statements at the whimpering bride, who was sitting on the big bed, offering her an array of tips for life: how to be a good wife, how to take care of a husband, of a herd, and so on.

The mother of the bride, sitting across from me, reached under the bed, producing two handfuls of necklaces made of beads both large and small. The necklaces displayed a marvelous variety of forms and a lovely spectrum of colors, indicating a serious investment in the wedding day and many weeks of preparation.

The last rays of sunlight washed us with a golden glow, and the shaven-headed bride put on some necklaces and left the hut for a final stroll through the village of her youth. The crowd dispersed, and the villagers prepared for their nightly routine: the return of the cows from pasture, milking, a final outing to answer nature's call and to close the gates.

The events of the day, including carrying water from the river and the walk through the bush, had their effect upon me, causing me to fall asleep instantly. But not for long. Once again, I woke up scratching my entire body. I turned on the flashlight inside the sleeping bag so as not to disturb my hosts, and was appalled by what I saw: the sleeping bag was teeming with thousands of tiny creatures. Some were the size of a pinhead, black and leaping around, others were whitish, and I also had time to spot reddish-brown insects, flatter and larger. They scurried off, escaping the beam of light. I counted at least three kinds, united by one goal only: to suck my blood.

Once again, I spent the remainder of the night outside the hut, this time to kill off the creatures scurrying around in my sleeping bag, with each successful kill documented on the fabric by a little splash of my blood.

~

The new morning transformed the Maasai women into African princesses in every sense of the word. Most Maasai women are tall, slim and erect. Their outfits include a skirt with three cloth fabrics above it: two solid ones in different, opposing colors (for example, red and green) envelop the two sides of their body, each tied over a different shoulder and secured in place with a broad cowhide belt around their waist, emphasizing their curves. The third, top fabric, adorned with various patterns (such as flowers, stripes or hearts), is wrapped around their back and tied in front, over the chest. Both of their arms are always clad with colorful bracelets, nearly up to the elbow. In their everyday life, which involves going out to the bush to gather wood, cooking over a fire and constantly caring for babies, they wear "work clothes": old cloth bolts, stained and sometimes torn.

However, this morning, and for the first time in my presence, the women were wearing new cloth fabrics in a variety of colors, with beaded necklaces around their necks; some had even gone to the trouble of putting on shoes. They were beautiful. Huddling at the outskirts of the village, chatting and giggling, they were waiting for everyone to arrive to walk together to the next village. The general excitement did not pass me by, and thanks to the women, who produced more fabrics, I was wrapped in a sequined blue skirt, with colorful fabrics above it, tied over my frayed t-shirt, and multicolored necklaces bestowed upon me to complete the look. I felt dressed up and ridiculous, but looking at the pleasure on the faces of the women around me, I played along.

We walked to the bride's house. The village was already in a flurry of activity. Women sat beside the houses, repairing and completing necklaces. The bride herself was ensconced in the hut with her friends. They were sitting on the big bed with a large metal trunk wide open beside them, and after checking and feeling around, each put in her contribution to the dowry, comprised of gifts from her family and all her friends: enamel plates and cups, aluminum pots, underwear, colorful fabrics, pairs of slippers, one thermos, a plastic jug, soap, body lotion, a flashlight. Not a lot, but a whole new world for the bride, allowing her to conduct an independent life in her husband's village.

My impression was this was a sad day for her. Her entire life had taken place in this village and its immediate surroundings, and now she was about to be taken to a distant village and a foreign environment. Therefore, no one was in a hurry. Her mother—who was now supposed to bid her farewell forever—tried to stall and draw out the moment. Finally, due to protests from Barsoinkan, who wanted to get going, the girl came out to the house's tiny foyer, weeping and sniffling, stood still and allowed one woman bearing a baby on her back, to dress her. No'oltwati, who had stayed close by my side, whispered in my ear, "Only a woman who has given birth recently is allowed to dress the bride, so that the good luck and fertility 'pass on' to her."

First, the bride was dressed in a skirt, to which an *orkela*, a swatch of lambskin adorned with beads and dyed with ochre, had been tied. Another *orkela* was tied to the top of her body. Meanwhile, the women around her were busy separating the multicolored necklaces from one another, and arranging them in a particular order clear to them. Finally, a small *kalabash* full of milk, a gift from her family to the groom's family, was affixed to her back, affirming the new familial ties between the families.

The ritual of dressing took about half an hour. The sound of the bride's whimpering signaled to everyone standing outside the house she was approaching. She stood at the threshold of the house, radiant and elegantly dressed and bedecked. We all moved back, clearing the space for two men, her father and his friend, who approached the entrance to the house. Each was wrapped in a new, thick wool blanket—part of the bride price provided by the groom. The two stood before the daughter and began a slow walk, their backs bent, from the entrance of the house to the gate of the village, while sipping from giant *kalabashes*—milk for one, beer for the other—and spitting out the beverages on the ground.[1] The weeping bride—her shaved, jewel-bedecked head bent down—strode behind them, her steps slow and measured. When the two men arrived at the entrance to the village, they stationed themselves across from one another, creating a gate of sorts from the new blankets. The bride stood half-hidden under the blanket gate, receiving her father's blessings. He tucked strands of green grass into her sandals, the belt at her waist and her armpits. Once he was done, the two men turned around and returned home slowly, while she went on, stepping forward in Barsoinkan's footsteps without looking back.

The quiet prevailing during the parting ceremony shattered at once. The women approached her and shouted their goodbyes at her. Her close friends walked close to her. Across their foreheads was a special piece of jewelry made of a swath of leather adorned with cowrie seashells, combined with a thin metal chain with blue beads. The long, kinky hair sprouting above the adornment hinted these girls had been circumcised, and that their own weddings were already on the horizon. They enveloped her in cries of encouragement and consolation, yelling out, "Don't cry," "He'll be a good husband," "He's got lots of cows," and "Come visit." The older women hauled the large metal trunk containing the dowry to the vehicle, along with immense *kalabashes* adorned with beads, and one plastic bowl.

Teary-eyed, the bride climbed into the vehicle—an old, sputtering pickup truck—which drove us to Barsoinkan's village, located inside the bush, about twelve miles from her parents' home. This is not a large distance in Maasai terms, but still separated everything she had known from her new life as a married woman. I sat between the two feeling mixed emotions. On my one side, the bride was constantly whimpering, busy wiping her tears with a handkerchief tied to one necklace. My heart went out to the girl, who, at such a young age, was marrying a man she didn't know, and being forcefully severed from her family. I, too, came close to wiping away a tear, but on my other side sat Barsoinkan and his escort, both giggling and seeming happy.

We stopped abruptly.

The vehicle's passengers exited it, picked branches from a shrub on the side of the road, and used them to decorate the roof and walls of the pickup, which was instantly transformed into a 'limousine.'

In Barsoinkan's village, everyone waited for the trail of dust heralding the vehicle's approach. We stopped near the village. The women closed in around us, helped the girl disembark from the pickup and rearranged her necklaces and other jewelry, which had shifted during the journey.

Now she was ready, the bride strolled slowly toward the village that would be her home from now on. The women from her husband's family huddled around her and then, much to my amazement, I heard the same women tending to her gently a moment ago cry out to her, "Oh no, look what they sent us—a sack of potatoes!" "Can such a young girl really chop wood?" "Oh, she's skinny! She can't carry a container of water!" "We've made a big mistake. And her clothes? It's a disgrace!"

I had never imagined such a reception, and I believed that neither had the bride, as her whimpering now turned into full-fledged weeping. She froze in her place, refusing to move forward. The more she cried, the more the women's cheers increased. Finally, after about five long minutes, one of them tried to placate her. "No, we didn't mean it... We were just joking... Come on, come on. Come to our village..."

But the bride would not relent. She stood motionless, shedding bitter tears and refusing to enter, although the women offered her small gifts such as cups and plates. After several minutes, one of the women approached her and said, "Come here, welcome... I'll give you a goat!" The bride heard this and advanced two steps forward. Another woman stepped toward her. "Come on, don't waste our entire day! I'll give you a calf!" The bride's eyes lit up and she took five more steps forward. The women of her new village continued to offer her goats and cattle as gifts, and she resumed walking, inching toward the village in tiny steps while accumulating gifts from the women[2], who would now serve as her friends and allies throughout her life.

Meanwhile, Barsoinkan and his groomsman were received at the house of the groom's mother. They shed their ceremonial leather, conveyed the *kalabashes* brought from the bride's family to the mother, drank some milk and went outside to their friends, who had arrived at the village and were busy drinking the local beer and dancing.

The bride, accompanied by the rest of the women, stepped in slowly, finally entering the village and the house of Barsoinkan's mother, whom she was meeting for the first time. She sat down on the bed in her heavy jewelry, and a tiny, cute infant was promptly placed in her lap. She held him with one hand while sipping milk from a *kalabash* she held in her other hand.

A woman, standing next to me murmured, "Excellent, the baby's not crying!" and seeing the look of query on my face, explained, "By performing these two actions—drinking our cows' milk and holding a baby from this village—we believe she will forget the place she came from, and become an integral part of our home."

I left the house while the bride remained inside, and did not see her again that day. I strolled slowly between the houses of this village, where I had never been before. The guests, all men, were sitting in groups. The eldest of them sat with Barsoinkan's father, who called me over, and after greeting me with a handshake, sipped from the beer he was holding and splashed it in my face to welcome me. In a different house, I saw younger men, while a third contained young men Barsoinkan's age. All were doing the same thing: drinking home-brewed beer prepared especially for the event. I sat down with the young men and they immediately handed me a glass of beer and urged me to try it. The beverage—a murky yellow, with strange specks floating in it—did not seem especially appealing. I took a wary sip, but my apprehension faded immediately. The beer tasted like extra-sweet lemonade.

Well, it wasn't lemonade! During the late hours of the afternoon, all the attendees were drunk and jolly. They lined up in a long column to take a spin around the cattle stockade, jumping and skipping along after the lead dancer. The revelers growled like wild animals, waved the sticks they were holding, then banded together to leap as high as they could while they danced.

In the evening, after the guests dispersed, the flocks returned from pasture, the village gates were closed and the women finished milking the cows, the entire family gathered together to bestow a new name upon the newly arrived bride, one more stage in erasing her previous identity and establishing a new identity within the new family.

The women debated among themselves which name to propose, and chose the name Nabaru, meaning "she who walked slowly." They repeated it four times. The men now suggested a name of their own, Netaya, "she who will give birth to many children," and they, too, repeated it four times. From now on, those would be the girl's names, while the name she had received as a child was erased. Now, with a new first name and her husband's family name, she would become an integral part of this village.

Although Barsoinkan was busy overseeing the party in his village, during the afternoon hours, he found the time to talk. He said that my condition—my face was swollen, my arms covered with bites—was painful to him, and therefore he had approached a Maasai friend who had built a stone house nearby, with a bed and a mattress, and asked him to allow me to sleep there. He pointed out the house, about 500 yards from his village, and when he noticed my look of hesitation, quickly eased my mind by promising that since I was his personal guest, no one would ever try to hurt me. And so, when night fell, I walked, accompanied by a drunken Maasai holding a container of water (for my bath), to the dream bed in the house of the modern-minded Maasai. The house door actually did not close properly, and the wind slammed it into the doorjamb again and again, but the sleepless nights had affected me, and to the melodious background of the wind blowing outside, I fell into a marvelous slumber.

I returned to the village around dawn.

Barsoinkan and his new wife Nabaru were standing in the cattle stockade. He pointed out the cows he had given her. I counted nine cows, a considerable number. At that stage, I didn't know that the cows were "hers" only regarding milking them and any offspring born to them. Together with the gifts she had received yesterday, they would form her own herd, from which she could bestow cows on her children. However, her husband would retain the sole right to decide about selling them or giving them away.

Later, Barsoinkan explained that giving cows to a woman is highly significant primarily if the husband dies—the woman maintains the right to milk them, and they would allow her to continue supporting herself and her children without depending on anyone. These cows and their offspring would be a form of "life insurance" that the husband bestows upon his wife.

~

The wedding ceremony was over. While the villagers and the many guests were drunk on the bottomless beer served, I was intoxicated with the scents, the colors, the people's thoughtfulness, with the openness and the acceptance enveloping me. Intoxicated with the variety of experiences I had been privileged to go through, with the customs and rites that evoked so many questions in me, still left unanswered. Unfortunately, I had to get ready to go back to my other world, so near and yet so far.

Once again, I was allocated two escorts who helped me carry my backpack and led me through the maze of shrubbery to the main road. They stayed by my side the entire time, and, being protective, refused to leave until I caught a ride to Nairobi, the country's capital.

On that day, I had yet to discover this one-time adventure, the unmediated interaction with the Maasai, would leave its mark upon me as a formative experience, and have such an immense influence on my life.

2

No'oltwati

My relationship with the villagers, particularly with Barsoinkan and with No'oltwati and her family, continued.

One day, No'oltwati told me she was pregnant for the second time. During my frequent visits to Maasai Mara, her pregnancy progressed. She looked like a shoelace with a knot in it: tall and slim, with a tiny bump at her center.

In April, we said goodbye to one another, knowing that the next time we met, she would already be the mother of a new offspring.

I had no idea that our next meeting would be so dramatic.

The encounter began while I was still in Israel. A small note, ragged and torn out of a school notebook, which had traveled from the Maasai Mara Reserve to Nairobi, and from there to Israel told me that "all villagers are doing well, but No'oltwati is ill. Very ill. We took her to Narok [the closest town, about 60 miles from the village] and she received many injections, but nothing did any good…. Perhaps you can help?"

A cry for help from thousands of miles away. How could I ignore it?

Nothing could have prepared me for what I saw upon my return.

Outside the village fence, among the bushes, No'oltwati was lying on a sheet of cowhide, her hands and feet tied up. She was thinner than usual, emaciated, her head shaven, her big eyes protruding and seeming to emerge from their sockets, her fingers as long as wriggling snakes. She saw me approaching, opened her eyes, tried to rise to her feet, to no avail, and cried. She turned both her hands, tied in front of her body, toward me, and yelled in English and in Maa that people in the village had cast a spell on her and also killed her baby. She shouted out, "Why does Eti have to die? When Eti dies, you'll all suffer!"

I moved aside and burst out in tears.

The Maasai, men and women, apparently startled by the sight of a crying *muzungu*, hurried and soothed me. As I stood there, shedding tears, I marveled at the absurdity of the situation: at my feet, lying on the ground, was a woman who looked as if she was about to die, and everyone was indifferent to her, while I, the weepy foreigner, was surrounded by many people trying to console me.

At the clinic, they had been told that No'oltwati was apparently suffering from malaria in which the parasite seizes control of the nervous system, enters the brain, and ultimately kills[3]. No'oltwati was already as good as dead, as far as they were concerned. Everyone was waiting for the end.

From the very depths of my soul, I refused to accept this diagnosis. I refused to agree that just like that, in the bush, a woman would expire with no efforts being made to save her. It was agreed that the next day, we—her husband Kitipai, his good friend Saruni and myself—would take her to Nairobi, the capital of Kenya, to receive a second opinion.

The largest and most well-known public hospital in Nairobi,

Kenyatta National Hospital, was our first stop. It was considered the best facility by those who lived far from the capital.

When we entered the ER, No'oltwati was hanging upon us like a limp rubber doll. Detached from reality, she was mumbling the Kenyan national anthem again and again. The wave of stench that struck my nostrils almost physically pushed me back. Hundreds were waiting for a preliminary exam. The crowding, the smells, and the commotion were unbearable. It was a true emergency—we had to act quickly.

I took advantage of my white skin to expedite the wait. We carried No'oltwati into the examination room. When she saw the doctor, she struck him. The doctor could deal with the beating, but not with a phenomenon he found strange: what did I have to do with this deranged Maasai? When treatment was not forthcoming, I spurred him on: "She helped me two years ago in Maasai Mara. And now I've come all the way from Israel to help her! You're responsible for ensuring she gets good care!"

The doctor came to his senses. When the results of the blood test came back, it turned out she did not suffer from malaria.

Evening came. No'oltwati received a shot of sedatives and was sent to a ward. Physically drained after the difficult journey to Nairobi and emotionally exhausted from our attempts to calm No'oltwati down, we left the hospital.

The next morning, we returned to the hospital and found No'oltwati gone. No one knew to which unit she had been transferred. No one knew on which floor of the big hospital she could be found. We set out on a search, roaming between the different floors and units. This was my first encounter with medical services in a global south country, and I found the sights I witnessed depressing; my dejection increased when we finally found her lying on the floor, sharing a mattress with another female patient. We discovered that no doctor had seen her during the entire night, and even now, it was hard to locate any member of the medical staff. As I stood there, helpless, I saw an angel—a nice young nurse who called me aside and whispered in my ear that if I wanted the patient to recuperate, it would be better to take her to a private hospital.

We signed the release forms and trekked to the next hospital.

Masaba Hospital, a private facility, radiated a calm environment, without the thousands of patients amassing at its doors, and without agitation and noise. We were greeted warmly. The doctor led No'oltwati to the diagnosis room, and about two hours later, we emerged with a definitive answer: she was suffering from post-partum depression, which had grown worse following her baby girl's death, several days after she was born.

The attempt to assign her a shared room with other patients did not end well. She beat them, jumped on their beds and created a major commotion. In her good moments, she was alert, humming the Kenyan national anthem again and again. In her bad moments, she snuck into other rooms and piled up the other patients' possessions in one stack: books, pairs of eyeglasses, thermoses, cups, and anything else on which she could get her hands.

We had her transferred to a private room, where we kept an eye on her. In this room, we greeted a young African lady, dressed in the latest fashion, with light makeup and a stylish haircut, who arrived at the hospital in an elegant black Mercedes. This was the psychiatrist who treated No'oltwati with the appropriate medication.

As an observer on the sidelines, I noticed the existential gap between the two women: No'oltwati, a skinny Maasai from the bush, wearing only two pieces of cloth, and the doctor, a rich, knowledgeable, well-educated woman, a university professor who revealed herself to be a true expert in her field. The two of them, one lying in bed and mumbling meaningless words, the other standing by her bedside and providing me with words of encouragement, presented only two of the many facets of Kenyan society.

The medication made No'oltwati drowsy, and she slept for most of the day. Her husband, Kitipai, stunned by his encounter with the big city and the hospital, never left her bedside, staring at her fixedly. A day went by and then another, with few indications of any change in her condition. I was losing hope, but on the fourth day, Kitipai called out to me, "Look, look, the blood is back in her body!" I looked. I saw nothing other than her dark, thin body lying motionless on the bed. But Kitipai insisted, "She's come back to life! I can see the blood flowing in her veins."

He was right. From that day on, she began to return to her old self, communicated with her surroundings, stopped beating on the people around her, and best of all, uttered two words. A mere two words that conveyed her recuperation: "I'm hungry." We brought her french fries, hard-boiled eggs, bananas, bread, *ugali*. She devoured it all.

The days went by. No'oltwati's condition was improving, but my funds were gradually dwindling. In countries where there is no health insurance, the patient's family must pay for everything: the price of the hospital bed, the doctor's fee, and the cost of the medication we were sent to purchase at the pharmacy. Besides these payments, I also paid the cost of accommodations for Kitipai and his friend, and for myself.

After about three weeks of hospitalization, I agreed with the doctor: we would return No'oltwati home, and I would supervise the administration of medication myself.

It's hard to describe the joy we experienced the closer we got to the village. We felt supreme satisfaction for not having abandoned her to her own devices on her final journey, sprawled out on a pallet of shrubs outside the village. We were ecstatic that she was returning to her family and her hut in a state of health.

We got out of the car.

To my surprise, the reception at the village was chilly. Many days later, I was told that no one had believed she would return alive, and if she did—that she would regain her sanity.

No'oltwati was weak. I hugged her and we made our way from person to person to shake hands, a jubilant smile on our lips and the joy of accomplishment in our hearts.

However, most villagers shrunk away from her.

～

No'oltwati sat down in the shade of the tree and mumbled to herself. I gathered up the women and repeated the doctor's instructions to them: not to leave her alone, to talk to her pleasantly and to constantly encourage her. I asked them to take care to spend time with her. They nodded, but the moment my back was turned, they took off.

I turned to the men: "She can't stay alone! Make sure there are people with her!" I made my request again and again, but once more, the moment I turned my back, they all departed.

I sat down next to her, looking around me at the villagers returning to their own affairs, at the women who had abandoned the shade of the tree and moved to sit in the shade of a house, and found myself unable to understand what was actually going on here. Why was she being received so coolly? Why were these men and women, her friends and relatives, keeping their distance from her? This was a society of courteous, pleasant people!

The moment No'oltwati went into her hut to sleep, I moved over to the men's company and tried to gently inquire why they were shunning her. Gradually, the truth emerged: post-partum depression? What's that? There's no such thing! The Maasai, I discovered, know how to diagnose and treat physical illnesses: a broken arm, malaria, a cold, a stomach ache, and so on. But an illness where a person mumbles strange words, beat on those around her, disengage from reality?

They had never heard of mental illness!

"There's only one reason why she's behaving that way, there's no other reason!" they added.

"What's that?" I asked.

"She's obviously under a spell! Only a spell can make someone behave so strangely. That's why we prefer to stay away from her so that we don't catch the spell."

A spell? What did I know about such things until that moment? Not much. I tried to recall the articles I'd read about African religions. Witchcraft was always brought up in social and religious systems[4], as one of the means society used to discipline people who had veered from the accepted social order, who had evoked jealousy in others and were "punished." I also knew this was never discussed openly. But I still had no idea what they were talking about. Had someone else cast a spell on her? Who? Why on her, of all people?

I knew it was post-partum depression, but how would I convince them? How could I explain the body's hormones?

What should I do now?

I concluded that my only option was to talk to the Maasai in their own language, and therefore I must look for ways to "exorcise" the spell from her. The simplest way would be to summon the traditional doctor, the *oloiboni*, and ask him to conduct the proper rites to undo the spell. But who was he? How would I find him? What would I say to him? I was not sufficiently fluent in Maasai culture and had no choice but to try another way.

As I knew that the Maasai, like other African societies, believe in symbols, which are embedded in their lives in various ways—from head-shaving to their articles of clothing—I decided to make use of such symbols. After Kitipai promised to watch over No'oltwati and give her the medication on time, I flew back to Israel for a week to obtain more money. Far from the village, in a different world, I came up with a plan.

I returned to the village with two articles: one, a rolled-up parchment scroll, tied with a green ribbon, and the other, a 30-oz bottle of a body lotion called 'Life.'

My return to the village was greeted with excitement. Women, men and children huddled around me and welcomed me back. I took advantage of this moment in which everyone was gathered together and asked No'oltwati to come to the cattle stockade in the village, where ceremonies were usually conducted. The two of us stood hand in hand, surrounded by the residents of the village. To create the proper impression, I unfurled the scroll carefully and read its contents out loud: "I am a doctor. Eti has told me of your illness, and I have performed all the necessary prayers in order to remove the disease from your body [I took care not to use the word *spell*]. As proof, I send you Life."

I lifted up the bottle of Life body lotion, showing it to all the attendees surrounding us in a circle. All stared at the bottle as if mesmerized. No'oltwati burst out in tears. She yelled out, "Yes, yes, I can feel that the disease is leaving me!" I made my way among the attendees. Each of them reached out and received a dab of the white lotion to anoint their bodies with the charm, thus ensuring that the spell would not pass on to them. A sigh of relief seemed to echo through the entire village, from end to end. I, too, was charmed by the magic I had invented—as if a new spirit was now imbuing the village.

But it was not enough.

The next day, the two of us walked to two nearby villages. People reacted similarly everywhere: they shied away from No'oltwati, but were curious about me. When we waved the scroll and the lotion around, their reservations dissipated, and all the women approached us. Each received 'Life,' applied it on herself and became instantly protected. Only then, once they were safe, did the women say to No'oltwati, "We heard that you were very sick, so we decided not to come and visit you."

In the next few days, we continued to visit all the villages in the vicinity in an ever-expanding circumference. Slowly, No'oltwati's reintegration process began, simultaneously to my own process of integration.

One day, the men in the family summoned me to the center of the village. Kitipai stood among them, declaring, "You saved my wife No'oltwati's life, and therefore from now on, her blood and your blood are one, and you will become a part of our family. We have all decided that your name will be Nayolang ('she who knows the household members,' or in other words, 'one of us')." All residents of this familial village, about thirty people repeated the name four times: "Nayolang, Nayolang, Nayolang, Nayolang."

∼

The days went by. I spent more and more time in the village. Despite my initial, multi-bite experience, I continued to stay in my friends' houses.

One day, sitting under the tree, I was asked, "Since you're already here so much, why don't you build yourself a house?!"

3

The Cattle Gate Is Not Wide Enough

A house in Maasai Mara?

For many years before this proposal, I had yearned to live here, among the wild animals and uninterrupted nature, even for a short period. It was one of the many dreams hidden within the depths of my soul, of all our souls, while we carry on with our daily routine, knowing such dreams would be tucked away in some side drawer, never to come true.

And now I'd been presented with an offer to make the dream come true.

I realized that the most challenging stage of awareness is converting dreams into reality. It's one thing to think (or say), "Wow, I'd love to live here for a while," a statement I uttered frequently in various places in the world, and it's another to turn that statement into reality. That was even truer when considering moving to a place so different, so desolate, so distant from the way I'd lived. Besides fearing the disappointment I might experience when the dream shattered against the hard surface of reality, I was troubled by the understanding that if I accepted the offer and relocated to Maasai Mara, I would have to overturn the way I lived my life—both by distancing myself from beloved family members and friends and by changing my way of life (I still did not understand the meaning of that term, "way of life").

Yearning and apprehension mingled within me.

Strange as it may sound, my deliberations soon ended, and the exuberance of an adventure sprouted within my soul, spurring it on. However, deep in my heart, I understood this was a far-reaching and long-term change, and that I had other dreams to realize before moving to Kenya. I packed my backpack and traveled for several months to West Africa, and from there to Australia. When I returned, after almost a year of traveling, I was ready for my next adventure, one I hoped would last for a year or two.

I consoled myself, my decision to live in Maasai Mara was not irreversible: Israel was just a five-hour flight away, and the moment I wanted to, I knew I could pack up and leave.

With my backpack, I made my slow way via public transportation, and in the evening hours, I strolled into the village, this time to stay.

During the previous weeks, I had internally debated the question of how to build a house that would be comfortable for a woman arriving from one culture, but would not seem ostentatious to members of the other culture. Happily, during evening conversations by the light of the fire in my hosts' house, I was guided to the answer through a series of questions:

"Are you really going to live in a house made of cow dung, when, after every rain, you'll have to climb up to the roof and apply new sealant?"

"Hmmmm… I'm not sure."

"Are you really going to live in a mud house, which also has to be constantly reinforced?"

"Hmmmm… I don't know."

"Then, let us tell you how you should build the house…" And so, much to my relief, the men, headed by Kitipai, suggested that I build a "modern" house, constructed using local techniques. This solution made me swoon with pleasure. Two days later, I was introduced to the artisan in charge of the construction, who gave me a list of materials.

Early one morning, I took public transportation to the town of Narok, an experience which shook me up, in both senses of this phrase. I traveled in a wobbly combination bus, a truck with a passenger compartment and with no shock absorbers, which was always packed and overcrowded. The upholstery on the seats—for those lucky enough to board in time and find a place to sit—had been worn away long ago. Other than providing rides, the bus also served as the main means of connecting store owners and residents to the town. In the morning, it was loaded with empty crates and containers, and when it returned in the evening hours, plenty of freight was unloaded along with the human cargo: bread, vegetables, sacks of coal, bicycles returning from the repair shop, tables, fuel tanks, beams of wood for construction, cement, and any other required product. The combination bus left Maasai Mara once a day, at about four a.m., and returned every evening. The distance to Narok was about sixty miles, but the drive, beginning with an especially jolting dirt path and ending with a bumpy road just as jolting as the dirt path, lasted two and a half hours in each direction.

To the sound of the children's cheers of joy, I returned to the village in the afternoon hours, this time aboard a rented truck bearing a whole house, or more precisely, everything necessary to build a whole house: beams of wood of various diameters, rolls of chicken wire, sheets of corrugated tin, a tank to gather rainwater, cement, doors, jambs, window frames, nails in assorted sizes, a hammer, a saw and other tools.

I showed up at the village with the overloaded truck but now needed to decide where to unload it. Where would the house stand? The men of the village moved a few paces outside the village fence, pointed at the whole terrain—a hill sloping down toward the river, and said, "You decide. The entire plane is at your disposal."

It was a quandary. On the one hand, I wanted to be a part of the village. But the village was teeming with dozens of children, women, men, cows, donkeys, goats, sheep and dogs—a constant commotion, plus the cow dung scattered in and around the stockade. I wanted to ensure I would be a part of the village, but also that I could rise each morning quietly and peacefully. I wanted to have my cake and eat it, too.

I finally made the decision to build my house toward the bottom of the hill, halfway between the village and the stream.

Kitipai and his friends were there constantly, contributing valuable advice about the directions of the wind and the rain, and therefore, about the best directions for doors and windows to face. But they weren't the only ones present. The villagers hung out by the house, marveling at the way a "modern" house was constructed. I was just as enthusiastic as they were, both because this was the first time I had ever built a house with my own two hands, and because I had never seen a house built in this manner: the construction worker stuck stakes into the ground and stretched ropes between them, thus sketching out the rectangular shape of the house on the ground. We then dug pits along the ropes about seven feet from each other, each about two feet deep. Into the pits, we inserted the wooden poles of the foundation, to which pitch-black used motor oil had been applied to protect them from termites. On these poles we placed the beams of the roof, on which the sheets of corrugated metal were spread out, serving as both shingles and ceiling. Within less than a week, the foundations of the house, including the roof, were standing in place.

After the locations of the windows and doors were defined, we wrapped the outline of the house with chicken wire on both sides of the wood posts, and tossed appropriately sized, locally sourced stones and pebbles from the stream into the ensuing gap, which was as wide as the posts, thus creating the walls.

For the next stage of the work, I needed a vehicle to transport water and sand. We halted the construction while I traveled to the town, and a week later returned with an old 'workhorse,' one of the first models of the Toyota Land Cruiser. It had only three gears, but was roomy, immensely powerful, and had a sunroof allowing unmediated viewing of the local wildlife.

The Toyota was the pride and joy of the village. No one in the vicinity had a vehicle of his or her own yet, and most children, including the teenagers, had never ridden in a car. Therefore, when we began the next stage of the construction, coating the stone walls with cement, and needed lots of water and sand, there were plenty of volunteers eager to assist. Everyone wanted to experience the ride, and I often heard the children sitting by my side mumbling with wide-open eyes, "Yoohoohoo… the trees are moving, the trees are moving!"

We set up the window frames, bought as pre-constructed units, installed the door jambs, and now it was time for the floor: we covered the entire surface of the ground in stones, on which we cast cement and smoothed it out. After installing the doors and the glass panes in the windows, painting, and affixing the gutters that would drain rainwater from the roof into a tank, we were faced with an actual house!

Throughout this time, I was living in the village. At first, I stayed with one woman, and later in a tent, but once I had a car whose seats could be folded down with a mattress placed above them, it became my own private villa. During the day, it transported stones, sand, water and people, while at night it became my dwelling. After a dinner cooked in a hut, I drove the car about 500 yards away, and there I was, alone in the bush, savoring the nocturnal sounds of the cows, the dogs, the jackals, the hyenas, and privacy.

The excitement of building my house seemed to have spread and encompassed the entire village, as within a few days, while the construction was still going on, I saw, not far from my house, the men moving together in a circle, bending down to the ground every few steps as if engaging in a strange dance.

Saruni greeted me with a grin, gestured at the circle created on the ground out of branches, and explained they were preparing to build a whole new village. Such an event, he said, took place every seven years, and the time had now come.

"Why seven?" I asked.

"Can't you see the state that the village is in?" he replied with another question. I had, but taken it for granted: the cattle stockade was so full of dung it was raised about twenty inches above ground level. Now, during the dry season, it wasn't so bad, but in rainy periods the dung became wet goo that flowed out and flooded the clearing where the village's houses stood. On rainy days, the cows had to stand on the wet ground, in mud that came up to their knees, vulnerable to disease. When it rained, walking between the houses of the village entailed crossing a lake comprised of muddy dung, and the sandals of those who bothered to put them on were sucked off their feet in the battle to extract their legs from the swampy muck. The village dwellings also suffered from the effects of the wetness, tilting sideways when their 'foundations' grew loose.

Building the new village was just as interesting as constructing my own home. This was a highly difficult task, in which the division of labor between men and women was defined, requiring intense physical effort.

That morning, the men drew two giant circles on the ground to mark the location of the two thorny fences, the external one surrounding the village houses and the internal one surrounding the cattle stockade. They also planned out the location of the gates in the fence, and the location of the houses between the two thorn fences.

Kitipai explained, "Nothing is random with us. The higher part of the village (if it's built on a slope) or its eastern side always includes the entry gate of the most important person in the community, the village elder, meaning my father's gate. Within the first thorn fence, to the right of the gate, his first wife, my mother, will build her home, while the home of the second wife will be located left of the gate (a third wife would build her house to the right of the first wife, and a fourth wife—to the left of the second wife). Later, clockwise, we're planning to build a gate for my older brother, and his wives will build their houses on both sides of his gate as well. After him will be my gate, where No'oltwati, my first wife, will build the house."

I supposed this predetermined arrangement made sense, as it made it easier for a visitor arriving at the village, at any village, to know how many men lived in the village (based on the number of gates), where the village elder resided, how many wives each man had, and which of each man's wives was the senior (first) one.

"But why do you actually need so many gates?" I asked. "Why aren't one or two gates enough for the entire village?"

Everyone present laughed in response to the question. "The gate," they told me, "is a source of great pride to us. The saying 'the cattle gate is not wide enough for two adults together' testifies to this, as our cows dwell together in a common stockade, but they are not shared! And therefore, every evening, when the cows come back from pasture, each one of them enters through its owner's gate. The same is true in the morning: each cow exits solely through its owner's gate. Owning a gate of our own signals to society we have families and are cow owners!"

During the next few days, all members of the village pitched in vigorously to do the work. The men, whose role was to construct the thorn walls, went out to the woods every morning, chopped down acacia branches and other thorny trees, left them to dry for several days, and then hauled them up the hill toward the new village. My old "wagon" participated in the construction. We tied branches onto its roof and behind it, and used "horsepower" to drag them to the village.

The women's role in building the new village was to establish their own homes. While the wood fence grew steadily higher, they went out every morning to collect branches suitable for construction, meaning relatively straight branches, durable against termites, those tiny insects capable of gnawing through entire houses and bringing about their collapse. After gathering many branches, they moved on to the next phase, sketching out the desired design of the house on the ground—to the right or left of the gate belonging to each of their husbands. The average size of each house was about 13 by 13 feet or 16 feet by 16 feet.

Simaloi, one of the village women, allowed me to participate in her work: she gave me a digging stick with a pointy end, with which I dug pits about four inches deep in the ground around the entire outer circumference of the house. We inserted straight poles in the pits, and Simaloi connected them to each other by tying horizontal poles to their top parts. The ropes used to tie them were made of the outer, green fibers of the leaves of the agave plant. A stable skeleton was thus formed. Between the poles, she threaded dry branches from shrubs, creating walls. From this moment on, the pace in which construction advanced depended upon the forces of nature, meaning the rate at which the cows produced dung. Every morning, the women would rise early and compete among themselves in gathering the fresh "concrete" and piling it in a mound beside the house being constructed. I left this phase of the building to Simaloi and her friends. I didn't feel ready to participate in smearing the dung on the outer walls and the inner partitions. After a month of work, the only task left was positioning the roof.

The women had various techniques for building the foundations of the roof. Simaloi wove the roof out of thin branches, in slow, dense braiding work. The weave lying on the ground grew increasingly larger, and heavier from day to day. Finally, one day, she called us all, men and women, to help her lift the weave off the ground and place it on the skeleton of the house. The operation, conducted with much jubilance, laughter and a major commotion, was not a simple one, but once it ended, we were treated to tea and *chapati* as a token of gratitude. Simaloi was now left with coating the skeleton with branches, with a layer of grass, and finally with a generous layer of cow dung to prevent rain from infiltrating the house. The interior of the house grew gradually darker as the coating progressed.

In constructing the village houses, none of the women exhibited creativity in the design. They perceived the house as fulfilling basic functions only: eating, sleeping and protecting the calves. All activity is conducted outside the house anyway: stringing necklaces and beaded jewelry (under the tree), laundry (in the stream), social encounters (under the same tree), bathing the babies (in the stream or in a basin outside), shaving the children's heads (under the tree), or going to the bathroom (far from the village, in the bush).

The internal structure of all the houses is identical: the only entrance faces the center of the village, leading into a small space where, across from the opening, is a little door leading to a room serving as a stockade for the calves (the calves are vulnerable and a favorite form of prey for predators. The goats and their kids are kept within the house as well). A corridor leads into the interior of the house, with a burning fire spreading warmth and heat, and serving for cooking, at its center. Beyond the fire, on the external wall of the house, are shelves and a place to stack kindling.

On both sides of the cooking nook are two homemade beds. Since every proper Maasai house must have cowhide on the beds, every time a cow is slaughtered, the hide is stretched, processed, and becomes another layer of the mattress. Between the layers of hide, the women conceal money, certificates and other documents. This is their version of hiding valuables under the floorboards.

Other than the single opening serving as an entrance, three more "windows" gape in the walls—small round portholes intended to let in light and air.

The fixed design of the house creates a very cozy environment. Although it is pitch dark, anyone entering can still feel their way around in relative confidence to one of the two beds, or to the benches placed along the bare walls, without stumbling.

∾

Simaloi finished building her home simultaneously to the progress in building my own home. Right in front of my eyes, she built a relatively large house with no financial cost. Building the house required materials from nature, manual labor and time—and she had an abundance of all three. My house, too, was taking shape: rectangular, with two rooms. One room, the smaller one, was designated for my private use. It had a bed and a bathing niche (for bathing with a bowl), its floor equipped with a drainage slot transporting the bathwater into a small container placed outside the house. The other room—intended to serve as a living room, kitchen and sleeping space for both children and guests—also contained another tiny room, designated for my "sister" No'oltwati. Like Simaloi's house, my house also had no electricity, running water or a modern kitchen. However, it was large (compared to the houses around me), had stone walls, large windows and a corrugated tin roof. I innocently assumed that when it rained—that intense downpour that came down for about an hour a day during the rainy season, flooding the soil, carving grooves in the ground and melting every mud wall—the house would be teeming with children and adults seeking shelter.

But reality caught me by surprise: when the rain came, not only did no one seek shelter in my house, in which the rain hammered down on the corrugated tin roof with an immense noise and the cold infiltrated the structure, but I ran to Simaloi's traditional house. There, as in a warm, embracing womb, people were sitting around the blazing fire, drying their wet clothes, laughing, joking or singing, while the pattering of the rain faded into a muted tune in the background.

Interesting, I noted to myself. During the first few nights, I had spent in these houses, I compared the house to a dark, cold grave. A short time later, the house reminded me of a warm, protective womb.

~

For almost six months, I bathed in the stream daily, cooked over a flame and read by the light of an oil lantern. However, one day, I was called up to Nairobi to lead a tour group. While waiting for the group, I stayed at one of the better hotels in the city. I remember as if it were yesterday how it was there, and only there, as I stood at the reception desk next to men in suits and perfumed women in high heels, that I became aware of the heavy scent of smoke absorbed into my body, my hair and my clothes. I went into the room, reached for the switch and... the lights came on. I took off my clothes, went into the shower, reached out for the tap, and a stream of hot water, the first after half a year, washed the smell of the village off me. I stood under the stream, washed my hair carefully, scrubbed my body again and again, and asked myself one question only: *Do you miss this convenience?*

The answer "No!" resounded within me without a moment of hesitation, and that was how I knew that whatever happened—I would survive the life I had chosen.

4

Samyan

The construction of the house was completed. We added a pergola (a shading roof) at the front, and under it laid down three oblong, flat stones in the shape of the letter "U", creating the cooking corner. Beside it, I built a sturdy wooden bench to accommodate guests.

I moved into the small, closed-off room and No'oltwati and her daughter settled into the living space. We purchased an oil lantern for night illumination, furnished the house with a few traditional four-legged stools made of a single log, one low table, and a shelving unit we built ourselves from branches to store pots and plates.

I was immensely grateful to No'oltwati's family—for inviting me to live among them, helping me store and maintain the construction materials, feeding me and taking care of me, and transporting the sand and the water. The house and I both became a shared project taken on by the entire village.

In order to express my gratitude, I declared a "housewarming"—a celebration for the entire village. Dozens of children gathered and came, playing games, engaging in various activities and enjoying experiences previously unknown here: a gunny-sack race, a rally race, a "three sticks" skipping competition, extracting candy from bowls filled with flour, a drawing station, an art and stone-painting station, and so on and so forth… The adults were served tea, biscuits, and *chapati*. The sounds of laughter and excitement echoed until the late afternoon hours.

∼

The emptiness struck me with no warning. While I was building the house and the women were building the village, I got up every morning knowing I had tasks to carry out. And now? Every morning, I woke up to an empty house, standing in a breathtaking landscape, and looked for ways to keep myself busy.

Samyan was the first to break through the feeling of emptiness. He had accompanied me even during my first visits to the village—tall, thin and slightly hunched over, with a broad face and prominent cheekbones. I knew him as an active, jolly boy, and recognized in him an endless curiosity combined with an immense joie de vivre. Samyan viewed me, one who had come from afar, as a trusted source of information about "the world" (everything outside of Maasai culture was considered "the world"). I taught him to ride a bike, explained to him why the size of the moon fluctuated from day to day, what multi-story buildings were, what the sea was, how an airplane flies, and told him about additional wonders of the other "world." He patiently taught me words in Maa and Swahili, two languages I had studied simultaneously, taught me how to recognize fresh elephant dung and which animal made the high-pitched yowls I heard, and mainly, explained behavioral codes —for example, the different ways to greet children, men and women.

Samyan was the first to come and settle in my house.

Only a short while later, Lanoi and Kitapo, two girls of the same age—thirteen or so—from different families came to stay at my house. The two were good friends, but very different. Lanoi,

Samyan's biological sister, also had a broad face and a slightly throaty voice and was very practical. Dreamy Kitapo was a true beauty, slim and petite, with light skin and an oblong face. The two taught me how to live life in a place very different from all that I was used to. How to wash dishes in two bowls without running water, how to conserve water—carried in jerry cans from the stream—by reusing laundry water to wash the house, how to bathe in the stream without polluting it. Absent electricity, how to tend to the oil lantern. Absent gas, how to gather wood, which branches are best for a slow burn, which are consumed quickly, and which mostly smoke and are unfit for cooking. From them, I learned how to light a fire quickly and efficiently, and from which direction I should blow on the kindling, to prevent all the soot from flying into my face. They taught me how to cook the local dishes, *ugali* and *madida* (both made of maize flour and water; however, the latter is softer), *sukuma wiki* (a type of kale) and more. They also helped No'oltwati take care of her giggly five-year-old daughter and watch over her.

The next to join my household was Leporé, about ten years old, another sibling of Samyan's, short, slightly bent over, with cheery eyes and a throaty voice; he was a mischievous, noisy boy who loved to laugh and to pull pranks, happy and kind.

The emptiness I had recently felt was gradually filled up by the need to care for the four children who had transformed from daily visitors to household members. I purchased a large mattress and blankets for them, and the house became their home base. I had become a 'mother' to them.

A mother? When I had decided to live in Maasai Mara, I tried to imagine how my life would look. How I would go out to the pasture with the men and gather wood with the women, how I would witness ceremonies and go through adventures. Children had not been included in the image I envisioned. Up to this point, I had lived without a husband and with no kids.

Friends of the four children, from Samyan, the oldest to Leporé the youngest, came to visit daily. Everyone played with everyone else, drank tea together and told each other stories. I would sit on the bench outside the house and savor their company. Privately, I called the house a "community center." However, children weren't the only ones to arrive; the mothers of the four also came to drink tea with me, to make sure I had no problems lighting the fire, and that I was making *ugali* the way they liked it (I wasn't, and Lanoi quickly took on the role of preparing it). The days flew by, and thanks to the children, my network of relationships within the village were branching out.

One day, when a new bride arrived in the village and, within several days, was assigned children to care for, I suspected that the children's arrival in my home had not been a coincidence, but the Maasai way of welcoming new women. Perhaps they had taken me in the way they took in every woman who came from afar.

As I had experienced first-hand, being responsible for the kids had granted me, and every new woman in the village, an essential significance: cooking, laundry, care, and perhaps most important — the house was not empty. It was full of the voices of children. But that wasn't all: the very act of handing over and accepting children created bonds of friendship between the two families, the one giving and the one receiving, which was especially significant to the newcomer. Many events, I realized, are related to raising children, and therefore, the village "new addition" —i.e., me—was never left out of the loop. I had things to talk about while doing laundry in the river while gathering kindling, or under the tree during the warm hours of the day.

But children were not passed on only to the new women. Infertile or older women, who were no longer bearing children but were still in the prime of life, received kids to care for, as did young women caring for babies who needed some help around the house.

∼

About six months went by. Samyan, who was about eighteen years old and went out every morning to spend time with his friends, brought home a new friend around his own age, Museré, whom I had never seen before. As the Maasai do not like to be on their own—they're always roaming in groups, or at least with another companion—there was nothing unusual about this. Museré, tall, very dark-skinned and handsome, had arrived from a distant region and had been orphaned of both his mother and father. Although he had many brothers and sisters who could have taken care of him, wanderlust had gotten the better of him, and he arrived in the village to find work. My house was a place of shelter and refuge for him, and yet, every few months, he would set out on long journeys from which he always returned gaunter, but enthusiastic and full of tales of adventure. Museré was revealed to possess unique talents. He took care to repair whatever needed fixing in the house, to build furniture from branches, and to harvest honey from the natural honeycombs in the trees.

Museré and Samyan were like a precious gift bestowed upon me. Every two or three weeks, when I wanted to distance myself from the buzzing commotion of children inhabiting the house, we would load the vehicle with a tent, sleeping bags, plenty of meat and water, and set out—sometimes with a few of their friends—to survey our immediate surroundings and spend the night camping. These trips amused me, as my house—which had no running water or electricity, and where the food was cooked daily over a fire—greatly resembled the experience of camping. However, setting out for the bush provided a major advantage: as we sat around the fire, curled up in the Maasai blankets while the rice and meat cooked in the pot and the sweet tea bubbled in the kettle, we could conduct personal, intimate conversations on subjects that would never pass their lips near the village: how do you choose girlfriends? How do the Maasai have sex? How do white guys hit on girls? And how do you feel when another guy is fooling around with your girlfriend?

During a trip, sprawled out by the fire, I watched the four young man-cubs. Only a small portion of their long, skinny legs were covered by their red cloaks, and they wore colorful necklaces around their necks and on their arms and legs. A beaded belt embedded with sequins, from which a long knife hung, affixed the cloaks around their waists. The adornments, and the way they moved, all struck me as very feminine.

Months later, I realized that only men who had stood their ground against lions and elephants, who had gone out to the pasture alone at night or experienced the pain of circumcision at a mature age—men secure in their masculinity, without questioning it—were the men who did not trouble themselves with questions of femininity. But at that moment, I could not hold back from asking them, "Say, does a Maasai man sometimes sleep with another man?"

"Of course," came their reply. "We don't like to sleep alone. We always sleep with other guys."

"I mean, do they touch each other…"

Museré observed me. "Sometimes it happens that a man dreams about his girlfriend and puts his hand on the guy sleeping next to him…"

I debated how to make the question clearer. "That's not what I mean…"

Ruben, a guest, tossed the branch he was holding into the bonfire, straightened and asked me in English, "Do you mean one man shoving his sperm into the other man?"

"That's it," I heaved a sigh of relief.

Ruben translated the question and the answer into Maa, evoking a collective burst of laughter. They all sat down on the ground and continued to laugh, on and on. Finally, Samyan turned amid outbursts of giggles, asking, "Where do you white people come up with these crazy ideas?[5]"

~

On another occasion, as I returned from a short walk, I saw all the letters of the alphabet drawn in chalk on the wall of my house. I addressed the young children herding the sheep and playing around the house in a scolding voice: "Who scribbled on my wall?"

A nice little boy of eight, named Miton, rose and replied, "I did, I wrote it."

Amused by the fact that the boy didn't even acknowledge the rebuking tone, much less allow it to frighten him, I sat him down in my lap and asked, "You did? You herd the sheep all day, every day! How do you know your ABCs?"

Little Miton moved me when he replied, "I really want to learn, so I asked my friends to teach me."

During that period, the early 2000s, the very few children who attended school were usually the "spare" children. The family's priority was to allocate boys to watch the cows, the sheep, the goats and their young. Only the "spare" children could go to school, as long as the family was interested and capable of funding their studies, which cost about thirty dollars a year at the public school, besides the cost of purchasing a school uniform, shoes and a school bag. A similar approach was applied regarding the girls. The first daughter would usually stay home to help her mother take care of the babies, and only "spare" girls were sent to school. Therefore, out of the five children in my house, only Leporé, the third son in his family, attended school.

I went to talk to Miton's father, an elder of our village, over sixty years old, who refused to release the bright Miton from his duties and allow him to go to school, as he did not want to lose a prized laborer. The boy had to watch the sheep!

I showed up at the old man's house every day, until after about two months, he grew tired of me and proclaimed, "Well, if you so badly want the boy to go to school, take him, he's yours!"

And that's how I was lucky enough to end up with a wonderful boy who attended school and became a star pupil.

~

There were now six children in the house. I loved that they took care of themselves, bathing in the stream daily, washing their clothes, helping with lighting the fire and cooking and taking turns washing the dishes. In the unfurnished house, even washing the floor was a game. They would spill buckets of water on the concrete floor and then spin and slide around on it on rags. However, integrating them into the household was not smooth. During one of our first weeks in the finished house, many children came in the evening to spend the night. In the morning, my well-honed sense of smell led me to a gooey puddle of excrement behind the door, indicating one of the children's apprehension about going out into the night and relieving himself there. From that day onward, I established a tough set of rules never heard in the region previously: it was strictly prohibited to smear snot on the walls; no coming into the house through the window when the door was closed; no spitting on the floor; and so on, in the same vein. More children had been candidates for living in my home, but they could not abide by the strict conditions and preferred the convenience of the village houses, without my system of prohibitions. Much to my joy, my kids, who stuck to the rules, felt like an elite team.

And how did I feel? I have to admit that for me, a woman who had chosen not to have kids of her own, the commitment was sometimes tough. Every time I looked at the village women, taking care of their many children and still hosting more children belonging to others in their home, I took my hat off to them.

One day, about a year after I had grown acclimated to living in the village, while the tea kettle was bubbling over the fire and we all huddled around to savor its heat, I wondered out loud: "That boy, the one over there, looks a little strange to me. Every time he herds the goats, he brings me a gift: a log for the fire, a bit of rope he found, a little bracelet… but every time I see him from afar and call out a greeting, he doesn't answer!"

The children looked at me, quizzically. "Him? Do you mean Lemein? He doesn't answer you because he's hard of hearing!"

The next day, I suggested, "Why don't we take him home with us too?"

Lemein, thin and slim with a charming, winning smile, was hard of hearing but loved to sing and dance and was a wonderful addition to the household. Thanks to him, we turned on the radio-cassette player at least two nights a week, conducting raucous dance parties. I watched in admiration, despite his limited hearing, he developed a fluid, agile style. Also, Lemein was blessed with good hands: with his long, beautiful fingers, he repaired watches, sewed torn shoes, and helped Museré with home repairs.

5

What Should I Do Today?

Every day, while No'oltwati made her way up from the house to the village for the morning milking, I imbued life into the coals that had simmered overnight and set a large kettle to brew on the fire. One by one, the children woke up and emerged from the house. Wrapped in the traditional red checkered blanket, with sleep still gumming up their eyes, they found refuge in the warmth of the burning fire. The fresh milk, arriving straight from the cow, was poured into the tea cooking in the kettle. The first sips of the boiling tea warmed us up. Much to their jubilation, I asked my daily question in Hebrew:

"Samyan, what should we do today?"

"Nothing!" he replied in Hebrew.

"Museré, what should we do today?"

"Nothing!"

"Kitapo, what should we do today?"

"Nothing!"

And so the question was passed along from child to child, with them all replying, "Nothing. Nothing. Nothing."

After sipping tea, we divvied up the leftovers from yesterday's dinner among ourselves, and each kid set out to tend to his or her affairs. I was left alone in a house whose construction had ended months ago. All alone. What to do now? Where to go now? How do I get through the day? I tried to keep myself busy: I read books, made beaded necklaces, cleaned windows, tended to the car, but I was all alone! And time—it stretched out slowly. What was going on in the village? I expected to be summoned. But summoned to do what? What were all the other women doing?

I learned from first-hand experience that no one would call me over. Every woman, after concluding all matters pertaining to her own home, came to the tree at her leisure and settled down in its shade. One came, another went, a third stayed, and I, too, could come and sit down in the shade and do… nothing.

That "nothing" made me think. Is being in ("dealing with") the company of others doing nothing? What is the social quotient I need? Why is it that, beyond a limited amount of time spent under the tree, social life seems like a waste of time?

And I initially struggled with that "nothing." This wasn't a week-long vacation, during which I could enjoy lounging on the beach or beside the pool and find pleasure in reading a book. This was day after day for a week, a month, a year, multiple years. A matter of lifestyle.

～

This morning, No'oltwati and I turned to our weekly task, going out to gather wood. Several women joined us, including little Lanoi and Kitapo. Going out to gather wood is always done in a group comprised of five women, and sometimes even more. We all tied straps of cowhide around our waists and held an axe or a *panga*, a thick knife for cutting wood. First, we had to decide on the direction in which we would walk. This depended on the question of where elephants had last been sighted.

My friends, who had been going out to the bush since they were young girls, murmured prayers intended for the wild animals: "We are only women," they said, waving the bands of the thick leather belts around their waists. "We have no weapons, and our intentions are peaceful." They walked through the thicket of trees and shrubs with high confidence and vigor, perhaps because they knew that a lion has never hurt a woman out gathering wood. Occasionally, they might meet one, but when they shifted aside, the lion went its way. However, they sang and talked loudly, making me wonder whether, besides the prayer, this, too, was a strategy intended to keep predators away from the group.

Usually, the women walked about a mile away from the village. This time, we did not go far. We found an area full of dry branches, after which, keeping sight of one another, each of us chopped and collected the wood. Usually, the women gathered the dry branches of the common *olokiordiengai*, or croton bush. It possesses several advantages, the first of which is its resilience against termites (therefore, it is used to build the skeletons of houses). Its second important advantage is that even while parts of it dry up, the plant itself continues to bloom, and therefore, it provides a constant supply of wood, even after wildfires, which sometimes occur, the shrub blooms and flourishes once more.

The sounds of axes and *pangas* were like a sweet melody in my ears. My attempts to strike the same spot on the wood with every swing of the ax failed, and so I focused on collecting fallen, dried branches, which were stacked up on the ground. Nashelu was working next to me: she assessed the dry branch with her eyes, bent it down to the ground, stepped on it with her bare foot, and with a precise strike, chopped it off.

Gradually, each woman formed a respectable pile of wood and tied it up with a cowhide strap. They helped each other heft the load of wood and placed the carrying belts on their foreheads.

We walked back in silence. Bent under the load on their backs, their palms supporting the back of their head, the women progressed toward the village, step by step. I trailed behind, carrying my own pile of wood, shamefully sparse and light, even lighter than those carried by little Lanoi and Kitapo.

∽

On days when they don't go to gather wood, the women go down to the stream, about 200 yards from the village, to bathe and wash their clothes. The banks of the stream are usually steep, covered with thick greenery, and there are only a few places providing convenient access to the water. The stream is about two feet deep, and it flows sluggishly, other than during the two rainy seasons, when its waters rage and foam, overflowing its banks.

As with gathering wood, going to the stream is also a female social occasion. The Maasai community here is more conservative than other African societies. Men have their own bathing place, while women have a separate one. There is no bathing together, or even in proximity to one another.

I have realized that washing in the stream, which necessitates exposing private body parts, also exposes the secrets of women's hearts. There are no men around, and therefore gossip flows like river water: who is whose boyfriend, which woman has lovers, who is serious in their attitude toward them and who wants to have fun.

I knelt on my knees next to them, washed my clothes in a bowl filled to the brim with soapy water, and after scrubbing and wringing, moved the clothes to another bowl with clean water. The women doing their laundry next to me stood with their legs together, unbent and taut, and their back tilted forward at the waist, straight. With their belly touching their thighs like an inverted V, the women stood for quite a while, soaping the clothes and rinsing them. Their flexibility made me marvel. I rose from my crouch and tried to stand as they did. Encouraged by my own flexibility, I survived several minutes of laundry. I then wrung out the rinsed clothing, stacked it in one bowl, and when I tried to straighten up, I felt a sharp, intense pain in my lower back. I had thrown out my back.

With some help from one woman, I managed, with a significant effort, to hobble home and curl up painfully in bed.

6

When the Child Is in the Belly—It Is Yours. When It Is Out—It's Everyone's!

Sinoya, Miton's younger brother, left the village and his mother while still at a tender age. He was sent to live with his older sister, who had married and resided about thirty miles away, and stayed with her for many years. I had never seen him until his father passed away. He had not returned to the village even when his mother passed away two years earlier.

Like Sinoya, who moved in with his sister, in our village, each woman raises other people's children besides her own, often those of family members residing dozens of miles from us.

Girls are transferred to other women when these women need some household help. For example, after a woman gives birth, a girl from another family—about seven or eight years old— is passed on to the new 'mother' to live with her and help with all household chores: fetching water from the river, bathing the baby, massaging his body and keeping an eye on him while the mother goes out to gather kindling. Thus the girl begins training for adult life. The girl will stay with the same woman as long as the woman needs her help. After a year or two, the girl will move on to the house of another woman, in a different village. The process is similar to the boys, who are sent to help families that have no young boys and need a child to go to pasture with the sheep.

~

Maasai society passes children from family to family as part of preparing them for adult life, as part of creating bonds between families, but mostly, so I'd gathered, as part of a deep perception essentially stating, don't get attached[6]—not to an article of clothing, not to a bed, not to a house, not even to a father or a mother. The less attached you are, the less you'll suffer from the sensation of losing a father, a mother, a house, or various possessions.

In that regard, the difference between Western society and Maasai society is extreme: while Western society makes an effort (consciously or unconsciously) to ensure children are attached to their parents, home, friends, bed, clothes or toys, here, in this society with its survivalist mentality, everything is fragile: the rain that came down last year might not arrive next year, in which case relocation might be necessary. The house built four years ago, on a foundation of wood and cow dung, will not last for many more years. There is no personal bed, and the children wander every night seeking a place to sleep. The village will be relocated, and the chance of parents living a long life is slim in a society where the average life span is about sixty years.

Therefore, while breastfeeding babies remain close to their mothers' body day and night, the moment they are weaned and part from their mother (who will soon be pregnant again), society encourages them to be independent and to stand on their own two feet. They are separated not merely from the mother's breast but from her warmth and body. At a young age, they might be passed along to another mother in a different village, and as they arrive at the village, one day they will leave it. On every such occasion, they are instantly separated from "temporary brothers" and from friends they might never see again, and forge new friendships in a new place.

A Maasai child "accumulates" several mothers throughout his lifetime: his biological mother; his father's other wives, who are his mothers; and the additional mothers who have raised him. When the child grows up and becomes a youth who will officially join the protective network of the society through an age group (more on this later), he will be granted a "mother" at any Maasai village.

One of the legitimate and even essential questions asked when a friend comes to visit and introduces me to his brother is, is he your brother from the same mother? From the same father? To my surprise, I have often received a negative response to both questions.

I have to emphasize that every boy and girl knows their biological mother. She is the stable "anchor" allowing them to move through space. They love and respect her, and in the cycle, will return to live with her. This is especially true of boys, who, in their maturity, return to their father's village for their initiation (circumcision) ceremony, and eventually bring brides from other villages to live there. Besides, there are also children who, despite the above statements, are not passed around.

I was impressed by this socio-survivalist logic: in order not to experience deep sorrow if loss occurs, the connection with the biological mother is loosened, but an enfolding network of multiple "mothers" makes sure no child or youth will ever be alone.

※

Nesesyay, the mother of Samyan, Leporé and Lanoi, made colorful beaded anklets for me. When they were almost ready, she asked me again and again whether I intended to sell them to tourists. Wondering at the very question, I replied, "No! It's a gift!"

My answer surprised her. She did not understand my logic. Museré, who witnessed the conversation, showed me a bracelet on his wrist that his girlfriend had made for him, and claimed that if he had the opportunity, he would sell the bracelet, and his girlfriend would make him a new one.

I tried to explain that in our society, people held on to gifts, rather than selling them. This seemed odd to both. "Okay," I sought a compromise. "If I sell the anklets since you made them, I'll give you the money."

She giggled. "You don't understand! The anklets are yours, and therefore, if you sell them, the money will be yours, and I'll make you new ones."

She was telling me in her own way that the mere fact that she had prepared an ornament for me did not require me to keep it. I could do anything I wished with it: give it away or sell it. The moment she finished making the ornament and passed it on to me, she was no longer attached to it.

I witnessed this attitude toward property every time I returned from my journeys in the world (the Maasai perception created a distinction between "us" and "the world" —the latter might be Nairobi or, to the same extent, anywhere else in the world). I always brought back gifts for "my kids": a watch, glittery pens, a handsome new shirt or a Walkman. They were greatly excited to receive the gift, and when seeing their gratitude and their bright eyes, I, too, was moved. But sometimes, I'd see some other young person, occasionally from a different village, with the same object on that very day. At first, I protested. "You gave away the watch?" "Where's the necklace?" Over time, I learned from them: my pleasure came from the very act of giving, and I had been privileged with the ability to give. However, in a society whose people have so little, the pleasure of giving is almost non-existent, and it is a pleasure they wish to experience.

And so my children had fun twice: the first time, through the act of receiving a gift that had value to them, and the second time, through the joy of passing on that same gift to their friends, who savored it as well (and passed it on to others). I learned that the value of an object is in the very act of bestowing it. That in this life, there is no point and no need to get attached to possessions or gifts. I also learned that objects have a "life" of their own, and the moment I bestowed an object on another person, it might break, tear or be given to someone else, and I no longer had any claim to it.

~

Even before I settled down in the village, I had been given a Maasai name: Nayolang. I was doubly moved, both by the very granting of a name and by its meaning. Over time, I discovered that I was not the only one who had received a new name. First names, like possessions, like interpersonal connections, were more fluid in Maasai society, in which a person did not even get attached to his or her first name.

I witnessed this when babies were born in the village. As the new addition was subject to a high risk of infant mortality, the family merely bestowed a pet name that would usually describe the baby: "Whitey" (when the baby's skin was pale), "the Japanese" (if her eyes were narrow), "Donkey Ears" (when his ears were prominent) or "Speedy" (to a baby born prematurely). About two years after the birth, when babies reached an age at which the risk of mortality decreased, they underwent a personal ceremony, the first in their lives: the "naming ceremony." During the ceremony, the baby's head is shaved for the first time in his or her life (a tradition existing in other cultures, in which children's hair may grow until they reach a certain age) and he or she receives an "official" name that will accompany them into maturity.

As I already knew, girls changed their first and last names on the eve of their arrival at their husband's home. Men retain their names until their firstborn, at which stage they will be named after the baby, "Father of...."

The variety of names is spectacular: names with a pleasant sound, names mentioned on the news, or traditional names. In my day-to-day life, I frequently converse with Whitehouse or Tomboy, and with Clinton, Saddam, Livingston or Stanley.

I have never encountered two people with the same name in a village or a region. The reason for this became clear when a young man passed away. In order not to cause his family sorrow by mentioning the deceased's name, the custom was for all people possessing that name in the nearby area to change their names, so his name was omitted from the repertoire of names for many years. The deep main bond that connects a person, like a link in a chain, to his past and his future is his family name: each child belongs to the father's family (patrilineal kinship) and receives the name of the forefather, the progenitor of the dynasty. Therefore, each boy will be "son of" (*ole*) the forefather (similar to a name such as "Ben Moshe," or "Son of Moses" in Jewish culture).

Gradually, I acclimated to the fact that other than the last name, society does not encourage attachment. Not to a house, not to a bed, and not to the property. To what do the Maasai get attached?

7

Black-Ear

Dawn. The sun has just launched its first rays from the distant horizon to the center of the sky. Figures wrapped up in red cloaks emerge, one by one, from the house entrances, each holding a receptacle. They wipe away sleep from their eyes, shivering in the morning chill. Soon, they will begin the milking. The cows huddled together in the village clearing during the night, approach the houses with an increasingly vocal lowing, headed for the small room dedicated to the calves. The first calf is brought out. It suckles on the left teats, while the woman milks the right ones. Each cow has a name, usually a descriptive one: "White Ear," "Brown Blotch" "Spotty" and so on. During the milking, the woman calls the cow, showers her with endearments and sings to her. When the milking of one cow ends, another calf is brought out—and more singing, petting and endearments ensue.

 The men also emerge from the houses. This is the first block of "quality time" with the cows during the day. Wrapped in their red blankets, they lean back against the walls of the houses while the milking takes place, examining the herd. Which cow is teary-eyed? Salivating? Apathetic? Each sign might indicate a disease and will be promptly treated. Medicine and syringes are kept in every house. After the milking, the women return to their homes, rekindle the fire that has died overnight, leaving only fragile embers, and prepare tea with milk. The men herd the cows outside the village fence, separating them from the calves, which will stay near the village. Every man in the village has cows of his own, familiar to him, which will be milked solely by his wives and will exit and enter through his private gate; however, the cows go to pasture in large, familial herds. Each such herd has a shepherd or two, armed with a spear and sticks. All the men accompany the shepherd for part of the way, bid him and the cows farewell, and return home.

The cows! I have a hard time believing it, but I witness it every day. The deepest connection every Maasai man and woman has is not to the house, to the bed, or to their name—but to the cows! I have been living among them for over ten years, and time after time, I marvel at the variety of emotions directed at their cattle. Yes, I have to remember: these cows are not merely food, but also the very definition of the Maasai's individual identity!*

The herd of cows leisurely approaches my house on their way to pasture. The jingle of bells distracts me from any other activity. The cows are thin, always. This is a characteristic of this unique breed, called Zebu[7], originating in India. This breed has a significant advantage: good survival ability, even in barren and semi-arid grass planes. On each cow's back is a hump, a fatty lump serving as a "storehouse" for food when necessary, like the camel's hump. The milk produced by this breed is relatively small, and cannot be compared to the ample milk produced by cows in the West. However, their advantage, is their durability, which allows the economic specialization of pastoral societies in East Africa, including the Maasai. Over time, this specialization was characterized by cultural justification. The Maasai

---

* Read more about Maasai identity in Appendix 2, "Who are the Maasai"

and the cows became inseparable economically, socially, culturally and religiously.

~

Late in the morning. The cows were already out to pasture, the children were in school, and Tabula, one of the village men, drank morning tea with me. As I sipped the hot tea, I had expressed my incredulity at the Maasai's serious attitude toward cows, and he was shocked by my lack of understanding.

"Until not that many years ago," he said, "the milk, blood and meat of cows and other livestock were the main components of our diet. The milk is drunk while it's fresh, mixed in with the tea, or is an ingredient in the children's porridge, or else it's kept in a *kalabash*, and within several days, turns into yogurt, which lasts for quite a while. The blood is drunk fresh, mixed with milk, or stirred thoroughly with a stick, around which it congeals like a lollipop. The meat is eaten cooked or roasted—all parts, including the stomach, the intestines and the bone marrow. An important component in our nutrition is a 'soup' in which cuts of beef, blood and fat simmer in plenty of water, turning into a rich, nourishing stew. However, paradoxically, meat is a resource we're lacking. A plump cow does possess plenty of beef, but as it constitutes value rather than just a food product, we avoid slaughtering it, and its meat is eaten only when it dies or in certain, rare ceremonies. Our consumption of meat comes from the rest of the livestock: sheep and goats. Since they as well have value, we don't slaughter them frequently, either. The constant deficit of meat evokes an immense desire for it in all of us: men, women and children."

We finished our first cup of tea and Tabula continued: "The value of the cow is not merely as food. It also serves additional needs: its dung serves as coating material when building a house; you saw this when we built the new village. Its hide is our mattress, which we place on the elevated pallet (the bed) inside the house. There is no Maasai house without cowhide! The more cows are slaughtered during a person's lifetime, the more layers of hide are added to the bed. These days, there are people who purchase mattresses, but they are placed over the cow hide.

"The hide has other uses. It's used to create the two belts at your waist. The first is the narrow one with the dangling cord, which the bride receives on her wedding day. After each birth, she ties a knot in the cord, and everyone around her can know how many children she has without a single word being uttered. The second belt, about four inches wide, is tied on the waist over all fabrics, and worn only by women who have already given birth. The traditional open sandals worn by boys during their circumcision are also made from cowhide. We no longer use the cows' horns and teeth; however, in the past, the horns have been used as a receptacle for tobacco, fat, and other small objects, while the teeth served as beads, and were incorporated into all kinds of jewelry."

"Tabula," I interjected, "that's all good and well, but are those truly the reasons for your unique attitude toward cows?"

Tabula chuckled and resumed talking. "Hold on, I'm not done yet. Economy and possessions are just one aspect of our attitude toward the cow. The other aspect is its value! It's a resource! It defines a person's wealth! Just as in your society, the considerations in buying a car do not have to do merely with safety and comfort, but are also a declaration of social status, so does the number of cows reflect a person's social status!"

"Hold on," I stopped him again. "There are eleven men in our village. Does the herd that passed through here an hour ago represent the total cows owned by all of you? I would have expected more cows."

He looked at me aslant. "Despite what I just said, we never know how many cows each person has, because we prefer to 'diversify our risk.' Since the cows are so important to us, only some of them are kept at home with us. The rest are passed on to the care of distant relatives, and some of them are kept by debtors for many years. A passerby has no way of knowing how many cows a person truly has. Moreover, out of fear of the 'evil eye,' we don't count the cows! But when they come back from pasture, we'll always observe them, and even without counting, we'll know if one of them is missing. Even if the herd is immense in size! You see, without cows, it's difficult for a person to get married. A father who wants to marry off his daughter will first inquire whether the groom has enough cows to ensure a respectable living for his daughter. And one more thing. The decision on whom the daughter will marry is related to the cows in another way: a sensible person will prefer to marry his children off to families that are relatively distant from his home, and from each other, as the bonds of marriage strengthen relationships of friendship between the families. Therefore, if there is a drought or a plague in one place, someone who is correctly networked can always move his cows to a distant location."

I cut him off for the third time. "In other words, it's a good thing I received cows, sheep and goats as presents! Otherwise, no one would pay any attention to me…"

"You're absolutely right! It's a good thing we gave you cows. We call cow-less people *Ndorobo*, which means 'a poor man with no cattle.' This is a name currently associated with one of our subgroups. Do you know Lekompa? He is *Ndorobo*!"

"Do you mean the man who circumcises all the boys in the area?"

"Right. We don't know what the origin of the *Ndorobo* is. Were they once hunters-gatherers integrated among us? Are they Maasai who, for various reasons, lost their cattle and became hunters? We don't know. But they speak our language, the Maa language. They prefer to live on the outskirts of settled areas, usually near woods or forests. To this day, although some of them already have cows, they sometimes cannot overcome their desire to go out and hunt wild animals, which the Maasai do very rarely, if at all; our pride is focused on our cattle and livestock, which sustain us. When we were children, our parents told us a story about the origin of cattle and about the Maasai's relationship with the *Ndorobo*. Do you know the story?"

Tabula sipped the cooling tea while I moved my chair away from the sun, quickly approaching its zenith.

"In the past, at the beginning of all time, the Maasai did not have any cattle. One day God called Masinta, who was the first Maasai, and told him: 'I want you to build a big, wide enclosure, and when you're done, come back and tell me.' Masinta went to the bush, chopped down trees, dragged them close to his house and began to build the fence. Days went by, and Masinta finished the construction and returned to God to report this. God said: 'Tomorrow, very early in the morning, come out and stand just outside the wall of your house, for I will give you a precious gift—cattle. But you must stand still and stay silent, even if you see or hear strange things.'

"The next morning at dawn, Masinta went outside his home and waited. After some time, the sound of thunder echoed, and a long leather thong dangled down from heaven to earth. Cattle began to descend the rope, straight into the stockade. The earth shifted and groaned so that Masinta's house nearly collapsed on him. Masinta was shaking in fear, but did as God had commanded; he did not move and did not make a sound. However, several minutes later, while the cattle were still descending, Ndorobo, Masinta's partner, popped out of the intensely shaking house. Seeing the countless cattle descending down the rope, he was so surprised that he blurted out: 'Ai ai ai…'

"In response to the sounds, God gathered up the thong and the cattle stopped descending. God thought Masinta was the one who had spoken and scolded him: 'Are these cattle enough for you? I will never give you any more cows. Therefore, love the ones I have given you as I love you.'

"Masinta was very upset at his friend, who had caused the cows to stop coming down to earth, and cursed him: 'Ndorobo! You're the one who cut the divine rope! May you remain as poor as you have been thus far. You and your descendants will forever remain my servants and will continue to live off the wild animals, as you have done to this day. May my cows' milk be like poison in your mouths!'"

A nice story, I thought to myself, wondering out loud, "And what's your relationship with the *Ndorobo* like today?"

"Our attitude toward them is complex. On the one hand, we can't live without them, as they are responsible for the most important rite in a man's life—they perform our circumcisions. We always joke that when they're young, they practice on the genitals of zebras, and only when they are skilled enough do they begin to circumcise our sons. On the other hand, we look down on them because they hunt wild animals, which is only done by the inferior and the poor among us, those lacking cattle."

Tabula rose and departed. While I was cooking lunch, I thought about the relationship between the Maasai and the *Ndorobo*, which I found unusual and interesting. The Maasai had turned the *Ndorobo*, a subgroup among them, into a mirror reflecting what they should not do. Through this segment of the population, the Maasai had created a sharp, clear distinction between the "cultural" world, where people made a living off their manual labor (raising cattle) and the "natural" world, where people fed off what they found[8]. This distinction (based on what they were not—i.e., hunters) had allowed them to consistently dwell in the expanse of the African bush, near wild animals, without hurting them. In addition, the fact that the Maasai have put the *Ndorobo* in charge of carrying out the most important event in a man's life, circumcision, allows the latter not to feel inferior, as it indicates how necessary they are. Also, since the Maasai are a survivalist society, their affinity with the *Ndorobo* opens an additional survival route to them: if, heaven forbid, a plague broke out, or drought occurred, and all the cows died, their bonds with the *Ndorobo* would allow them to obtain food from nature.

The Maasai's special attitude toward cattle stayed on my mind. I recalled incidents when I had witnessed people's reaction to losing a cow devoured by lions or hyenas: some leapt in the air and collapsed on the ground, shaking uncontrollably; others burst out in tears or disappeared for half a day to mourn privately. This was extreme behavior compared to their reaction to the death of a person when everyone had to show restraint and not exhibit any signs of grief.

∽

Twilight time. The sky darkened, and intense thunder sounded in the distance. The sun glided slowly toward the skyline, painting the world in dozens of hues of orange. The cows headed home, the jingle of bells heard far and wide. The men rose at their leisure from their relaxed poses under the tree and walked toward the cows to escort them home.

Occasionally, I would join this evening walk with the cows. Privately, I referred to that time, the last mile on the way to the village, as "the holy hour." The men found time to talk to each other, exchange information and to observe the cows. They would immediately recognize, without counting, if a cow was missing, if one of them were exhibiting weakness as it walked or if one of them was not eating. They knew how to handle such a cow once it returned home.

We approach the village. Next to its gates, the women are already standing, welcoming the cows. Welcoming us.

This herd, which belongs to several families and had been grazing together the entire day, now splits up. Each cow enters the village through its owner's gate. Once the cows have entered, and the goats and sheep are already inside, the village gates, made of shrub branches, are closed. The nursing cows huddle by the entrance to the houses, lowing and calling the calves. The calves are brought out, one by one, and the evening milking begins.

Night falls.

8

The Water Tank Births a Lamb

The months flew by. I allocated each of "my" seven children a cardboard box in which to store their clothes and personal possessions: three t-shirts, one sweatshirt, two pairs of shorts and one pair of long pants. The boys wore sandals made of used, recycled tires, while the two girls wore thong flip-flops. In their personal box, they kept pens and pencils, watch straps, Vaseline lotion, with which they massaged their body after bathing in the stream, and various toys that the tourists visiting the village handed out to the children. Without deciding on this in advance, we all knew that when one of the children's possessions overflowed the boundaries of the box, it was a sign there was "too much," and the child should go through the box and hand out the extras to friends in the village.

∽

I was gradually growing accustomed to life in a place very different from my previous life. I grew used to being a mother of children, but was still dealing with mothering Maasai children: how should

I treat the fact that when I returned from a trip that had lasted a month, they did not jump all over me? That none hugged me, or luxuriated in my hugs? How would I deal with this society being so introverted that public displays of affection expressed weakness? How would I learn to be satisfied with their glittering eyes as the only expression of joy?

My difficulty carrying wood or doing my laundry in the stream, and the children's reserve, all clarified it, that I was not Maasai, but did not leave me as frustrated as the fact that I had a hard time communicating with my friends and my children. Not due to the language barrier, which I was slowly overcoming, but because of the difference between "our" world of imagery and expressions and those of the Maasai. I watched Leporé climbing a tree and wanted to tell him, "You're just like Tarzan," but he had never heard of Tarzan. And the little girl, all wrapped in fabric, ran and rolled in the grass just like Johanna Spyri's Heidi. Miton displayed his muscles like Popeye, Lemein danced like Elvis Presley, and Museré—he was "as handsome as a Greek god."

As a verbal person, I felt a need to express myself beyond basic speech, to express myself as I did naturally in my mother tongue, but I didn't know how and didn't know the proverbs, expressions or the Maasai world of imagery.

About three years after moving to the village, I received a variety of children's books in English from an Australian friend. One evening, I read *Pinocchio* to the children. The next day, as we were sitting around the fire, waiting for the tea to boil, I told them about people who had got to the moon and took a walk there. Lemein interrupted me, saying, "Nayolang, Nayolang, look!"

"Look at what?" I asked.

"Your nose is getting longer!" he replied as the other kids cheered.

I was touched. I realized that on that very day, the children had joined the world of global imagery, and if they wanted, they could communicate with children around the globe.

The repertoire of imagery is different here, as is the accepted terminology. A full moon rose in the east, illuminating the cows and shepherd slowly strolling toward the village in shades of silver. My heart expanded within me in response to what we in the West see as "unadulterated beauty," while here, it was perceived as everyday existence.

When I realized how wide the gap in imagery and terminology was, I examined concepts from my everyday life to see how they were perceived by my Maasai friends. For example, the concept of romance. Could I bridge the gap?

I invited my friend Munkulai to spend the evening with me.

The sun was about to set, and a calm descended upon the earth. We sat outside the house, watching as the clouds assumed shades of orange, while the red ball (image) was kicked (image) to the ends of the earth (image), rolling downward (image), beyond the hill. I sat next to Munkulai, extended my hand toward him, and caressed him, enthusing, "Wow, what a great sunset." While he, Munkulai, gazed at me in bemusement. "Nayolang, it's the sun! What are you so excited about? It'll be here tomorrow, too." (I noted this as a failure.)

We entered my room. I lit candles in the corners of the room and tried to savor the romantic atmosphere. But he noted, "Nayolang, without the candles, we wouldn't see anything. It's not a question of beauty." (Another failure.)

I sat next to him in the darkroom. The shadows cast by the candles flickered on the walls, and a pleasurable sensation mounted within me. It originated in my lower belly and climbed up. I recalled that one moment, ten years ago. I had spent an evening in one lodge in the park and danced with one of the lodge employees, a tall, thin Maasai fellow, possessing a determined expression. To the sound of the music, we approached each other slowly and he took hold of my arms. His touch was so gentle and fluttery that it sent electrical currents through me, remaining seared upon my skin. As the years came and went, despite all the brawny men in our region, who also came and went—that sensation had never recurred.

Now, with Munkulai, I terminated the romance experiment and move on to an experiment in intimacy.

I blew out the candle.

Darkness.

~

The verbal frustration came with deliberations I had not anticipated, which belonged to the realm of finance: although some people around me were a lot richer than I was (the owner of 500 cows, each one of them valued at $300, has property valued at about $150,000!), I was the only one in the vicinity with liquidity, i.e., cash. A sick child has to be taken to the clinic—now! Today is the last day to pay tuition! Someone has to travel to Narok today and needs money! There's a pretty heifer for sale and it needs to be paid for in cash, now! The village wants to bring an *oloiboni* (a traditional doctor) for a blessing ceremony, and money must be procured—now!

In a relatively short span of time, I became the primary go-to person in any quest to seek accessible cash.

The immediate dilemma was practical. Whom to help and when to help, and when not to help. This deliberation led to how to politely say no to some requests, while also maintaining good relations with everyone. This question begat additional ones: Could I build relationships with the people around me that would allow me a place in society similar to everyone else's? What role do other people fill in this society? Was I the only one who got requests for help, or did it happen to them as well? Did other people decline? Was it possible to decline?

Could I live here for the long term without making the people dependent on me?

I knew that the Maasai had gotten along just fine before I arrived, and I hoped to live among them in a way that would ensure that my presence in or absence from the village would not change their lifestyle. Was that possible? And if it wasn't, what could I do to minimize my impact?[9]

Another dilemma concerned the topic of ego. We, Westerners, perceive our society as much more "sophisticated" and ourselves, its members, as having "seen" more, "learned" more, "done" more. How easy it is for us to inflict ourselves, our culture, our knowledge, upon them. How easy it is for us, with our big egos, to ignore the knowledge and life experience of the local people (which are adapted to the environment in which they live), and, as important, to ignore their wishes.

I encountered this conflict of desires during the first rainy season after I settled in the village. I was the only one in the vicinity with a tank to collect rainwater for drinking purposes. The women, including the handful of them who lived in a house with a corrugated tin roof, enabling the gathering of rainwater, went daily to fetch water from the stream, about 200 yards from the village. During the rainy season, my water tank overflowed every day, becoming a place of congregation for the women who arrived to enjoy the extra clean water and the shorter distance from the village. They collected the overflowing water in wash basins, pots, bowls and buckets. On rainy days, soil erosion makes the waters of the stream muddy, and therefore they were especially joyous over the clean water. One day I asked one of them, the owner of a house with a corrugated tin roof, "Why don't you purchase gutters and a water tank? The price of all the required components is less than the price of one heifer! Why don't you sell one heifer and enjoy clean water all year long?"

Her logical answer surprised and amused me: "Nayolang, a heifer grows up to become a cow, which will give birth to more calves and make me rich! But a water tank? Can it give birth to more tanks? And anyway, water is free and plentiful in the stream! When there's extra water in your tank, I enjoy it, while at other times, I'll continue to go to the stream." Different priorities and a different choice than my own.

Another incident occurred years later, once again sharpening my perception of the gap of desires. The members of Samyan's nuclear family relocated to a less crowded site and establish a little village of their own for his father and his two wives, along with Samyan, Museré and their wives. I volunteered for building the new village. Conferring with my two children, we decided on modern residences: two houses with corrugated tin roofs, with a wicker weave on the outside, but whitewashed and painted on the inside.

We completed the construction, bought tanks to collect rainwater, beds, mattresses and so on. In the covered balcony, we installed a cooking nook and built stands on which dishes would be dried.

Two or three months went by, and I noticed that Nesesyay, Samyan's mother, who set out for the bush daily, returned with branches for construction, and piled them up on the outskirts of the village. I looked at her in query and she reacted with a mischievous smile and innocent gazes. Only after the poles had been set up as the foundation of a traditional house did the truth reveal itself: the modern house we had constructed was all good and well, but she wanted the house she had known ever since she could remember herself, the kind she was accustomed to since her childhood: covered with cow dung, with narrow openings for air and light, dark, where each object had a place of its own... If, in retrospect, I felt ashamed for trying to "impose" a house that seemed "better" upon her, I can only imagine her unease regarding me, as she set out to build the house she wanted, kicking my own aspirations aside.

The ego, our constant companion, a product of Western society, gnawed at me often during my first years here, even when I tried to rein it in. I was sitting in the village, telling everyone (with a smidge of pride) how every night, I cooked meals for about ten people, and boasting about the guests, my children's friends, who arrived to shelter under my roof. The women listened before shifting the conversation in a different direction. Over time, I learned: they, with far fewer possessions than I did in their day-to-day life, and more children, hosted strangers every night! They shared not only their small pot of food but their very room with various visitors who dropped in for the night. They did so without feeling "generous" or "noble," without using this or that word intended to empower their ego.

∼

I dedicated quite a while to debating the question of ego from the opposite direction. I realized that in order to live here long-term, I had to accept and respect the people around me the way they were—including their desires, thoughts and behavior, all different from my own. But I wondered, could I relinquish my ego without allowing my own perspective to be subsumed by that of the Maasai? When should I insist on living according to the standards I had brought with me from my own culture, from my previous way of life, and even propose these standards to my Maasai friends, and when would it be right to humbly accept the Maasai worldview and insights?

I had concluded that Maasai insights about "lending children" had proven themselves to be useful. The children created a bridge between me and the villagers, allowing me to actively participate in both day-to-day life and the ceremonies. However, my worldview and acceptance were often challenged. This was particularly difficult regarding the two girls, Lanoi and Kitapo.

Every night, my house attracted many boys and girls who gathered to sleep there. They explained, "Our house is small, and therefore, when our father comes to sleep in the house (he chooses which of his wives to sleep with), we can't stay there. We have to get out and find another place."

My house provided such a place for many teenagers and my children's friends. There was no husband or man there, and I had a separate bedroom. I noticed a recurring pattern of arrival—the first to come were the young girls, Lanoi and Kitapo's teenage friends. Once the girls had settled down for the night, ensuring they were not planning to move on to a different house, the boys followed them there. All , boys and girls, packed in together on the single mattress, about six feet wide, which was placed on the floor. They spooned close to each other, giggled, talked and finally fell asleep.

Fell asleep? For a long time, I couldn't understand why the house was not quiet, and why my sleep was constantly disrupted.

The reason became clear one day, early in the morning. No'oltwati had left for the morning milking and I made the tea. I went into the children's niche and was amazed to find Lanoi sleeping right next to a young man, both naked! I knew the Maasai encouraged children to "have fun" together from a young age. But seeing it with my own eyes? And with *my* girl, no less? All my hypothetical knowledge did not prepare me for seeing it first-hand.

That morning, I walked around, restless. Museré and Samyan picked up on my distress. "Why are you so surprised? Even younger children already fool around with each other."

"Right, I understand, little boys with little girls. But that guy is about twenty, and Lanoi is a thirteen-year-old girl who hasn't even started to sprout breasts yet!"

Samyan replied, "But if she doesn't fool around with boys, how do you expect her to grow breasts?"

"What?!"

He continued, "We believe that a woman's breasts will not grow or develop if a man doesn't fondle them. That's why it's a win-win: the girl wants to grow, to become a woman, and we boys are charged with the pleasant task of 'growing' the girl and making her into a woman. Therefore, the desire to fool around is shared by both sides."

"But these girls are still children! Are they physically ready for this?"

No'oltwati, who had joined the conversation, came to my aid. "No. They don't start having sex with men overnight. The little girls have fun with uncircumcised boys their age, who are forbidden from having sex with a circumcised woman, even if she is their age. Therefore, they fool around with these girls. When the girls mature, and their breasts begin to develop, they stop being interested in boys their age and start looking to boys who are older than them by four or five years. These are boys who have already undergone the circumcision ceremony and become young adults: the *morans*. With these *morans*, true love stories develop, and at the age of fourteen or fifteen, each girl already has a mature boyfriend with whom she engages in full sexual activity."

"In our society," I noted, "children Lanoi's age play 'teacher and pupil' or 'doctor and nurse' at the very most. But sexual intercourse between minors is prohibited, and if an adult is involved, he gets tossed in jail!"

Museré turned with a question. "Maasai society expects girls who arrive as brides in the groom's house to be women in every sense of the word: to know how to manage a household, to cook, to carry water from the river, to gather wood and to be prepared sexually. In a year or two, these girls will undergo circumcision and be married off, sometimes to a man older than them by many years. Would it be desirable for them to arrive at their wedding day without knowing a thing about having sex? Is it better if their husband hurts them?"

∽

What Museré was saying was logical. But I still could not calm down. The gap between the Western worldview, where one principle of law and morality was the prohibition on engaging in sex with minors, and what I had heard today was too large to be contained by a single conversation. As was my custom during times of distress or confusion, I went out for a walk to try and put my thoughts in order: why do I and Western society view sex with minors as an absolute taboo? Who was the "moral authority" who determined the arbitrary age separating what was prohibited from what was permitted? I had to admit that although it is prohibited, having sex with young girls is a fantasy for many men. Why?

But there is more to this—there is a paradox at play here. On the one hand, we claim that sex is the epitome of a couple's intimacy, the "ultimate expression" of the concept of love. However, many Westerners are constantly obsessed with sex, from morning to night: porn sites online, nudie magazines, constant surveys poling: "Does your husband love you?" "How many times a month do you have sex?" and a variety of sex clubs and other temptations.

What is it that prevents us from achieving satisfaction?

Here, light years away and right next to me, is a society that perceives sex naturally. Sexuality is a need, like eating, drinking and sleeping. Children and teenagers grow into sex without cloaking it in intimacy, love or a relationship, and without painting it in an aura of romance. They are not busy with questions of sex from morning till evening. Sex exists, is accessible, and has nothing to do with what I call "church morality" and the weighty baggage that comes with it.

With much effort, I accepted the Maasai perception, even if I could not internalize it.

Until the next challenge, which soon arrived.

9

Your Blood Is Happy

After about two years in the village, I was invited to witness the circumcision of two girls from a neighboring village. Lanoi and Kitapo, the girls in my home, who had started to exhibit womanly breasts, were walking around scowling: *Why are Timanoi and Solvey going to be circumcised before us? We're all the same age. We want to be circumcised too!*

I was amazed. "You want to be circumcised?"

Deep in my heart, I was not surprised by their reaction. I knew this circumcision was the most important and significant rite in the private life of every Maasai, boy or girl. This ceremony, conducted during adolescence (since birth dates were not written down, parents decide on their children's circumcision based on their physical development), transforms the circumcised from boys and girls into men and women. Equally circumcision is the final factor shaping their identity as Maasai, establishing them as full members and partners in Maasai society.

I was also not surprised by my own reaction, as female circumcision, which takes place in many African societies (and in most parts of Africa south of the Sahara), is troubling to those of us who are members of the Western world. The accepted, though simplistic, opinion among Westerners is that female circumcision should prevent women from experiencing sexual pleasure.

Is this the case?

I addressed this question to one of the village's elder women. "Did your family, once, long ago, tell you why the Maasai circumcise girls?"

She replied, "You understand, God had three children; the Maasai is one of them. But we, the Maasai, differ from the other two. Circumcision is a sign of our separateness from the others. We believe that if a woman gets pregnant before she's been circumcised, her baby will be ill or will die! That's bad! You should understand—circumcision is just one of the signs separating us from others. We also pierce our ears, pull out a bottom front tooth, scar our legs, scar our body—all these are intended to distinguish us from others."

When I continued to ask men, women and older people why women are circumcised, I received a variety of answers, starting with the common statement, "I don't know, that's our tradition, starting with our forefathers," and culminating with, "If we don't cut *it* off, it will continue growing" (I was asked often how long *it* was for me), or, "*That* part of the body is obtrusive during birth!"

Studies conducted within other societies indicate that within the African worldview, a newborn is treated as if it is sexually "neutral": every male contains female (the foreskin symbolizes the female vagina, which envelops the male organ during penetration), and every female contains male (the clitoris). Therefore, young boys may participate in ceremonies meant for women only, and girls may be present in ceremonies intended solely for men. When children reach puberty, and a dominant sexual identity develops —girls sprout breasts, while boys grow up to become men—it is society's role to remove the characteristics of the opposing identity: a girl's clitoris is removed, thus turning her fully into a woman, while the boy's foreskin is removed, thus turning him fully into a man.

For the Maasai, circumcision is a condition for acceptance as full members of society.

I tried to appeal to the girls. "Maybe you actually don't want this? Tell me just once that you don't want to be circumcised, and I'll see what I can do."

They blurted out a statement to be repeated numerous times. "Do you think that just because we have a white mother, we're less Maasai?"

I explained to Lanoi and Kitapo what we, in our world, know to be the function of the removed organ, leading to the conclusion that its removal reduced a woman's sexual pleasure.

They scolded me, "But Nayolang, what you're saying is impossible!"

"What do you mean?"

The two spoke out simultaneously. "You know, both before and after girls are circumcised, men are forbidden, strictly forbidden, from touching those body parts. That's our custom, and therefore even if that part of our body is not removed, no man, not even our husband, will touch or play with those areas. It's a taboo!"

Their answer intrigued me. One day, when I was sitting with the women under the tree, I brought this topic up. Nalutori rebuked me: "You don't understand. We really do enjoy ourselves!"

"How, Nalutori, how?"

"It's not the missing part that makes you enjoy or not enjoy yourself. It's the blood! When someone you love comes to you, sings you a song or caresses you, your blood is happy to greet him, and then you enjoy yourself…"

The circumcision ceremony for Lanoi and Kitapo's friends drew closer. As conducting such ceremonies requires the revelers to brew homemade beer and buy food for all the guests who will be attending the ceremony, at a significant cost, parents prefer to circumcise several children together. Here, the father intended to circumcise two of his daughters. Timanoi had started to mature and looked about seventeen, while Solvey, young and physically immature, looked about fourteen. In the week preceding the ceremony, I visited their village, close to our own, every day, and watched the many preparations: the brewing of the traditional beer, the airing out of the *orkela* (ceremonial sheepskin adorned with beads and tinted with red ochre dye), obtaining a metal link chain and cowry shells to create a *segera* (the adornment that identifies a circumcised girl), and coordinating with the person who will perform the circumcision (an older woman from a nearby village) and so on.

Every night, after dinner, young girls and teenage girls arrived at the village. In the darkness, between the houses, they sang and danced, blowing into whistles that spread the sound far and wide. The lyrics of the song, which repeated themselves, urged the ceremony's recipients to be strong and brave during the circumcision, or, in their words, "not to escape the knife," and the loud whistle was intended to "run fear off." As the day of circumcision approached, both the length of the dance and the number of girls gradually increased, all sharing the celebrants' excitement to prepare for the most important rite of their lives, which would signify their transition into womanhood.

The ceremony actually began around noon on the day preceding the circumcision itself. Six women and girls and two men (for each girl undergoing circumcision) went out to the bush to fetch branches of the *Olea Africana*, or wild olive, tree, which would serve as a soft pallet for the girls after they were circumcised. They were gone for about two hours, and returned to the village while singing, their voices heard from afar. After a short rest, the women brought the branches into the house, piling them up on the bed on which the circumcised girl would rest, then covering the pile with cowhide. Each initiate, who had been huddling with their friends outside the village, was called to her mother's hut. They sat down with their mother on a sheet of cowhide in the house's tiny foyer, while the mother shaved their head and dyed it with red ochre mixed with cow fat. Afterward, pleased and cheerful, the girls draped an *orkela* on their back and went out to roam with their friends.

Evening came. More guests converged in the houses of the village. They ate, drank the local beer, sang and enjoyed the shrill of the girls' whistles, which was heard late into the night. Lanoi and Kitapo spent the night at the village where the celebration was being held, while I, in my own home, had a hard time sleeping. I kept imagining, again and again, what their friends were about to undergo in a few hours.

With the first light of day, as the horizon became tinged in dark purple and the first rays of sun had yet to emerge beyond the horizon in the east, I returned to the village. I was too early. Inside the house, on one bed, the girls and their friends slept huddled, covered by a single blanket. Many women were sleeping on the other bed and on hides spread out on the floor. The only ones awake were five men sitting on low stools around the fire, humming drunken songs. I joined them, settling on one of the stools as I continued to think about the girls, still slumbering deeply. How could they sleep?!

The first to shake themselves awake were the women, going for the morning milking. One of them woke up all the girls and demanded that they exit the house. Timanoi and Solvey, the two initiates, were among them, their lower body encased in a skirt and only the *orkela* covering their upper body. They stood outside for half an hour, shaking in the morning chill, which cooled their body, shrunk the blood vessels and ensured less bleeding.

I looked at both. I couldn't help but be impressed by the pride filling them. They looked so peaceful, while I myself felt weak. I was now troubled not by the very act of watching the circumcision, but by the fear I would faint. And so, despite feeling ridiculous, I turned to Kitapo, who had witnessed multiple circumcision ceremonies and knew what to expect: "Please, during the circumcision, look at me, too... And if you see me falling, lay me down and lift my legs up..." A fourteen-year-old girl!

Tradition dictated that the girls' circumcision be held in the calf stockade inside the house. As the girl is compared to a heifer—both have yet to mature or give birth—the symbolism in choosing the location of the circumcision ceremony is obvious. But as the calf stockade is a tiny, crowded, dark room, it must be illuminated. Three little girls volunteered to climb the roof of the house to dismantle a small part of the pallet of weeds covered with cow dung, located over the stockade. They raised the roof until the foundations of the house were exposed, and a ray of light filtered inside like a spotlight.

Timanoi, the older girl, was the first to enter the little room, in which only a single heifer remained. She took off the *orkela* and spilled cold water over herself from a pitcher left outside all night long. I thought about religious purification rituals.

Following her into the stockade were her friends, a few women and some little girls. About fifteen packed into the tiny room. Once she had rinsed herself off, Timanoi put on the *orkela* once more and sat down on a cowhide sheet spread out on the ground where the spotlight of sunshine came in through the ceiling. Placid and confident in herself and in what was about to take place, she leaned back against a thick wooden branch brought in earlier and spread her legs.

The commotion in the tiny room was too intense to bear. The heifer, apparently frightened by the unusual crowd, lowed again and again, the sound merging with the voices of the women talking and laughing. Their patter created an utter cacophony that made me dizzy. I felt as if I was present at the scene of the Binding of Isaac.

The woman performing the circumcision, an older resident of one of the nearby villages, sat down between Timanoi's legs, making sure they were properly spread and firmly held by the two women kneeling on either side of her. She cut with a razor blade purchased a day earlier.

Timanoi cried out.

The more her screams increased, the more jubilant her friends and the women watching the cutting became. They laughed at her while also encouraging her. In the central space of the house, right beyond the paper-thin mud wall, sat more men and women, drinking beer and celebrating the initiation of another girl into the Maasai people. Outside the house, the younger boys tried to peek into the little room to witness some of what was going on inside. It was a true ruckus.

I didn't faint. I overcame the circumcision ceremony. And the yelling. And the association with the Binding of Isaac. I survived.

Toward the end, I felt suffocation in the crowded, teeming room, full of girls and women, and went out. I saw the men walking around smugly and was filled with tremendous rage. I returned to the little room, saw the women exulting in response to the girl's screams, and felt my anger swell: the men were one thing, but these women had lived through this pain. Why didn't they object?

After a few minutes, the cutting ended. A "cheese" made of milk, intended to help the blood to congeal, was applied to the wound. Timanoi rose by herself and walked several steps from the calf room to her bed, onto the pallet of wild olive branches prepared for her yesterday.

Solvey now entered the stockade and poured water on herself.

Outside the house, the gates of the village were still closed, as the cows would not leave the enclosure until the ceremony was over.

While Solvey's circumcision was taking place, several men were running around in the cow stockade to catch one heifer, whose blood would be let so Timanoi could drink it. Two men grabbed the heifer's head and two held its tail. They tied a 'tourniquet' made of a leather band around its neck. Another man aimed a bow loaded with an arrow equipped with a small blade, about half a centimeter long, and shot it at the carotid artery. After several attempts to pierce the skin, a thin stream of blood finally spurted out and was gathered in a *kalabash* held by one woman. When the *kalabash* was full, the tourniquet on the heifer's neck was taken off, the blood stopped flowing, and the animal continued on its way. The *kalabash* was taken to Timanoi, who was already lying in bed. As Tabula had told me months back while we were talking about the cows, drinking blood, once an integral part of the Maasai diet, was today done only in special circumstances: any event involving blood loss (birth, circumcision, injury) required drinking blood ("a blood transfusion").

Solvey's circumcision ended, and another heifer donated blood for her recovery.

While each girl settled down in her own bed and drank the blood, their father's blessing ceremony began outside: his senior wife shaved the sides of his head and dyed his head and those of his other wives with ochre. All the attendees went into the cow stockade in the village. His wife gave him several objects that would testify to his status as an "elder," meaning a father of children circumcised: she slipped a *surutya* (a necklace made of two metal spirals) around his neck and tied a chain of blue glass beads around his head.

The ceremony was over. The two girls had been circumcised, their father had been blessed, the village gates were opened and the cows went out. I glanced at my watch. It was only seven thirty in the morning!

∼

This was the first time since I'd moved in with the Maasai when I felt anger toward everyone, both the men and the women. I walked around restlessly, having a hard time deciding how to express my emotions.

Guests arrived from nearby and distant villages. All helped themselves to food and drink, danced and sang. Friends from various villages huddled in the corners, exchanging information, while the family wives toiled to properly host them all—and I continued to simmer internally. In the evening, I sat down with the young men and expressed my anger.

They looked at me in surprise. "Nayolang, you have to understand. We know that different attitudes prevail these days, but you have to realize that to us, a girl who is not circumcised is not a woman. She's not one of us and we can't marry her!"

I retreated. I went to my house, boiled some tea, and thought to myself: for many generations now, the Jewish people circumcise their men simply because of a short passage in the bible: *"And ye shall circumcise the flesh of your foreskin; and it shall be a token of the covenant betwixt me and you. And he that is eight days old shall be circumcised among you, every man child in your generations... And my covenant shall be in your flesh for an everlasting covenant. And the uncircumcised man child whose flesh of his foreskin is not circumcised, that soul shall be cut off from his people; he hath broken my covenant."* (Genesis 17: 11-14). Or, more simply: a male not circumcised is not considered a member of the Jewish people.

Today, some people justify circumcision for "health" or hygiene purposes, but that is merely a justification, rather than a reason. For us, the Jews, circumcision symbolizes the covenant Abraham made with his god, our god! Circumcision is a cornerstone of Judaism. What would we do if other nations demanded that we stop circumcising boys? Would the Jewish people not fight for this right? History indicates that when other nations demanded that we stop circumcising our boys—we rebelled. The Maccabean Revolt against the Hellenistic Seleucid Empire (from 167 to 160 BC) and the Bar

Kokhba Revolt against the Romans (circa 132–136 CE) both broke out due to prohibitions against the Jewish religion, including forbidding circumcision.

After a night of thinking, I was still besieged by doubts. I wanted to hear the women's voices.

∽

A few days later, I returned to Timanoi, who was sitting with the women. Her hair had begun to grow back, and she seemed pleased. I greeted everyone and initiated a conversation about circumcision. I asked Timanoi whether, when she had a daughter, she would want to circumcise her.

"Sure," she replied.

"And the pain? Will you want your daughter to experience the pain you went through?"

Timanoi said, "That pain is over!"

One woman intervened, asking, "What's it like with your people?"

"We don't circumcise the girls, just the boys."

"So what does a woman do during birth?"

I gazed at her, wondering if I'd properly understood her. "I don't understand."

"With us," she continued, "if a woman wasn't circumcised, no one will help her as she's giving birth. No one will hold her or go near her. She'll be alone."

I realized that initiating a girl into the Maasai people through her circumcision was not an abstract concept, but did have implications for her life in the long term[10].

∽

Since the circumcision ceremony, I had been watching the women, all, in a different manner. I searched them for signs of trauma. But they looked and behaved like every woman in the world: laughing, getting angry or excited, joking, mocking, becoming sad or angry.

I went to a nearby village. Several women were sitting in Nashorwa's house, drinking tea and eating *chapati*. My arrival interrupted their gossip session, but the conversation quickly turned to the subject of circumcision.

"Ai, ai, circumcision hurts," said Njeri. "I cried from the moment I got circumcised until the afternoon…"

"It sounds like it really hurt… Is it like giving birth?" I asked.

"Oh, it hurts a lot worse," she replied.

Nashorwa intervened. "No way, giving birth hurts more." She turned while poking her pinkie into one of her nostrils. "Does that look painful to you? Of course not! But how about now?" She picked up an enamel cup and pretended to shove it in her nostril. "That's what birth is like! And it hurts!" I burst out in uncontrollable laughter.

Njeri returned the conversation to its course. "Nothing hurt me like circumcision did."

I interjected, "And you'd still want to circumcise your daughter?"

As I asked the question, I realized that thus far, internally, I had not distinguished between the actual pain of circumcision and the mutilation caused because of cutting off the clitoris. I was put off by the more trivial matter, the pain, which, according to Maasai perception, even if does exist, is not a significant consideration. The scars adorning their body, piercing the ears at a young age, pulling out the lower tooth with a knife and no local anesthetics—those had made these women resilient.

Njeri replied, "I would."

"Why?"

"It's our tradition, our customs…"

"And why did you invent a custom like that?"

The three women looked at me in puzzlement as I continued.

"Look, every part of the body has a role: the nose, the ear, the mouth, the eyes, and that part as well... So why is *it* the one you've decided to remove?"

"What is its role?" Nashorwa asked.

"To make the woman enjoy having sex..."

Nashorwa was surprised. "Hey, but we do enjoy it! Very much!"

"Well, then, just imagine how much you'd enjoy it if it hadn't been cut off."

Sialoi asked, "How?"

"Oh, it feels so good, that women who haven't had it cut off scream with pleasure..."

They all burst out in laughter that fed upon itself, freeing us of our embarrassment. Nashorwa was the first to calm down. "Could that be the reason that our men go to hang out with girls from other tribes? Is it really 'tastier' with them?"

∼

I continued to seek my place in society. I continued to deliberate on how to deal with worldviews, perceptions of the body and a society so different from my own. Until, one day, I received a message from my mother: her curiosity was increasing. She wanted to see the place where I lived with her own eyes.

10

Operation Mom

From the moment my mother announced her upcoming arrival, we in Maasai Mara launched "Operation Mom." Some "modern" items needed to be purchased for the house to make her stay easier: "regular" chairs besides the traditional low stools, a table, forks and knives (we had been using spoons), a pillow for the bed, a duvet cover and so on. I drove my car to Nairobi, about six hours away, and loaded it up with indulgent food items that could be found only in the major cities. In those days, no one in Maasai Mara had ever heard of such indulgences, much less seen them: broccoli, cauliflower, green peppers, cucumbers, many kinds of fruit and delicacies such as cheese wedges, butter and so on.

～

The drive to Maasai Mara lasted nearly all day. From the airport, in the eastern part of the city, we crossed Nairobi heading west. The city is large and sprawls out over a substantial area. At its center is an impressive cluster of modern multistory buildings towering over wide, clean streets, teeming with modern vehicles. An abundance of trees allows the pedestrians dressed in contemporary British fashion, unsuited to the Kenyan weather—suits and ties for the men, pantsuits and dresses for the women—to walk in the shade.

Once we left the city, the houses grew gradually lower. Jacaranda trees, blooming in shades of lilac, stood next to flame trees with their bright hues of red, and the urban density was replaced by tiny agricultural plots. At the sides of the road were one-story houses with cottage industries, displaying their wares: colorful armchairs, skeletons of iron doors and window frames, tables, doors and jambs, and tiny stalls with a variety of fruit and vegetables.

The road sloped downhill. We passed by a tall, ancient coniferous forest. Then, a sharp twist in the road, and the view changed abruptly: an abyss opened up on the left side of the road, and the Great Rift Valley was revealed in all its splendor. We stopped at a viewpoint next to a line of shacks selling mementos to tourists. The narrow, winding road on a downward slope left little space for the people constructing the stores, and they exhibited resourcefulness by sticking posts down the steep slope and building narrow, unstable observation balconies. Many stalls had Italian names—Milano, Rome, Libretto, Napoli— hinting at the events of World War Two, when the territory of Kenya was under British rule, and independent Ethiopia was briefly conquered by the Italians. In 1941, once Italy was defeated, about 35,000 Italian war prisoners were brought here as a work force, equipped with pickaxes and other manual tools, and ordered to pave a road that would lead from the hot, dry valley to the heights of the Rift's eastern cliff, a height difference of about 550 yards! A tiny Catholic church, with an orange tile roof and a bell tower, standing at the bottom of this road, is the only remainder of the hard labor invested here, linking Nairobi to the southwestern part of the country to this day.

The view of the sprawling valley, with its scattered mountains towering to the sky and volcanic mounds, is breathtaking. The road was full of trucks, and we maneuvered between them, gliding down. With the decrease in altitude, the flora changed. We left behind the thick coniferous forest and the dense greenery for a forest of dwarf acacia trees, about three feet tall, with black spheres growing from their branches. These trees have a unique method of survival: the tree itself grows these spheres to lure in and invite certain stinging ants to settle. The ants dwelling within these hollow spheres benefit from a ready-made home, enjoy the food secreted by the tree, and in return, protect it when an "enemy," such as an antelope desiring the green, nourishing leaves, wanders by. When the ants sense the delicate nibbling, they burst out of their nests en masse, assault the invader and bite it.

The engine growled and thundered as we climbed up the west bank of the Rift Valley. Massive wheat fields spread out before us, scattered with tall acacia trees possessing widespread branches. Another ascent, and now we were "officially" in Maasai country. The fields were overtaken by a dense tangle of woods. Thin smoke curling upward and the large white sacks beside the road hinted at the occupation of the area's inhabitants: manufacturing coal.

My mother admired the ever-changing views, the wonderful weather and the comfort of sitting in a car making its way between the potholes of the (non)road.

⁓

Narok, a dusty town on a crossroads, serves as the capital and entry point into the Maasai Mara area. Like many towns throughout Kenya, its houses are painted in a variety of bright, loud neon colors, serving as ads for various companies: the bright green was donated by one of the cellular providers, the red-and-blue by a laundry detergent manufacturer, while the shocking red belongs to a different cellular company. The town's paved streets are few, and its beating heart comprises dusty dirt alleys. An entire quarter is dedicated to tiny car repair shops with no clear boundaries, where everyone works alongside everyone else. Repairing cars is highly essential in this region of rough dirt paths, and the few roads deserve that title only due to their glorious past. Narok's market is always overflowing with a variety of agricultural produce: potatoes, cabbage, carrots, tomatoes, onions, bananas, zucchini, green peppers, and more, originating from the fertile high ridge that slopes up gently from the town to an altitude of about two miles above sea level.

Everyone visiting Narok, including my mother, a fleeting guest, feel the Maasai atmosphere unique to it, resulting both from the women's colorful dress and from the variety of products offered for sale there, which are characteristic of their culture: fifteen-inch knives sold in red cowhide sheathes, wooden walking sticks, which are part of every Maasai man's presentation, sniffing tobacco, checkered blankets in shades of red and blue, which serve as outerwear for men, and *eleso*, colorful cotton fabrics adorned with various prints, which the Maasai women wear as an outer layer over the two plain fabric cloaks wrapped around their body.

We stopped at the town and bought *elesos* as a gift for each of the village women. Many Maasai we met waved to us and insisted on greeting "Nayolang's mother." They stopped our vehicle and shook her hand warmly and excitedly, an excitement that spread to her.

We embarked on the last part of the journey, the last sixty miles separating Narok from Maasai Mara. The road became a dirt path twisting among sprawling valleys and low hills covered with greenery. Maasai villages surrounded with a thorn wall blended into the scenery. Herds of sheep and cows leisurely grazed next to gazelles, antelopes and zebras. The rumor of my mother's arrival spread far and wide, and friends from various villages waited for us on the road, urging us to sip some tea before continuing on our way.

In the morning, we went to visit the village women, moving from house to house. In each one, my mother was greeted with warm handclasps and treated to milk tea. I enjoyed seeing how, despite the language barrier, physical gestures proved highly effective, and her communication with the women flourished. She gave out gifts at every house: *eleso* for the women and new shirts in a variety of colors for the kids (back in Israel, she had rebelled in response to my suggestion she bring second-hand clothes: "I'm your mother, I can't come with used clothing…")

Around noontime, as she sat in the new chair and savored the view spread out before the house—giraffes moving sedately in the distance among the acacia trees, to the jangle of cowbells—she received reciprocal visits. One by one, the village women arrived to bring her gifts from among their finest jewelry: beaded bracelets, necklaces, beaded watch bands. The gesture caught her by surprise. Tears of emotion welled at the corners of her eyes due to the heightened attention she was receiving.

All the dwellers of the house treated her with the respect worthy of an honored guest. The breakfasts we toiled over for her were an unprecedented celebration here, and included a fresh salad made with the best vegetables Nairobi offered, bread purchased at a nearby lodge, wedges of hard cheese and avocado. Lanoi, who was about fourteen ran the household as my mother observed in admiration: washing the floor, cleaning, and even teaching my mother to cook the delicacies of the Kenyan cuisine (meaning mainly *ugali* and *sukuma wiki*).

Several days after her arrival, as she sat in the shade of the house watching the children playing , she expressed her wonderment at the fact that the village children constantly walked around in worn rags. "Mom," I replied, "those are the new shirts you bought them…"

She found her stay in Maasai Mara pleasant. The days flew by. She enthused over the rainwater shower (which improved her complexion and softened her hair), the view, the food, but mainly the warmth directed at her from everyone around her, a natural, simple warmth. The sorrow of saying goodbye was evident in her as her visit approached its end. She said, "Now I can sleep peacefully. I can see that people here love you, watch over you and take care of you. You're in good hands." Then she added, "There's just one thing I can't understand: why you chose to live in the Middle Ages…"

∼

In honor of my mother's visit, I brought fruit and vegetables from Nairobi, and every morning, made her a fresh salad. My children marveled to see that her desire for fresh vegetables equaled their desire for meat.

Vegetables are not part of the day-to-day diet of Maasai Mara's residents. Some of the Maasai living in Kenya and Tanzania's fertile planes have adopted the agrarian lifestyle and grow a variety of vegetables and fruit, but here, nothing is grown. The reasons relate not only to the legacy and identity of the Maasai as cattle herders, but to a variety of objective reasons: the soil comprises volcanic ash not sufficiently fertile, and after it rains, the ground dries quickly, sealing up. However, the main difficulty lies in the need to protect the vegetable garden from animals. The domesticated animals (goats) and the wild animals (monkeys or elephants) eat any form of edible plant, and it's hard to stop them from doing so. To cultivate a small vegetable garden, thorny acacia trees must be chopped down to try and create an impenetrable fence. I remember that one time, we grew butternuts. When the fruit ripened, emitting its typical smell, we watched from afar one evening as an elephant approached the village's thorn fence, crossed it as if it were a ribbon of paper, and gobbled down the butternuts and the plants around them. The investment is too large compared to the returns.

But the surprised reaction of anyone present while the salad was prepared or eaten contained another element: their apprehension regarding eating uncooked vegetables. To them, fresh food is dangerous! In a continent where many residents do not have a proper toilet, and urinate and defecate in the fields, plagues such as cholera and typhus break out periodically, because of fruit and vegetables not properly washed, or that were washed with contaminated water. Therefore, the Maasai have learned first-hand: fresh vegetables might cause diseases!

∼

Fresh vegetables are difficult to obtain in the bush. Vegetables arrive via merchants with trucks who leave Narok laden with merchandise and travel throughout the week from one market day to the next. They are not eager to bring products with a short shelf life such as tomatoes, carrots, bananas or various leafy greens (spinach and kale), which become even less durable due to the travails of the road, making them hard to sell. Therefore, products that come to the bush are mainly those with a long shelf life: potatoes, onions, maize and cabbage, and they are the main ingredients used for cooking in Maasai households. Besides these, there are also beans, rice, and maize flour, from which two dishes are prepared: porridge and *ugali*. The difference between the two depends on the proportion of flour to water: a little flour and more water makes porridge, while a little water and lots of flour results in *ugali*.

These products are suitable for a society without refrigerators to maintain freshness. Every single meal is cooked over a fire and eaten the same evening or the following morning.

As I am a product of the Western world, I brought a variety of additional dry foods with me from my travels to the city: lentils, dried green peas, grains of chickpea and so on. I did my best not to repeat myself as I cooked during the week: one day rice and beans, the next day *ugali* with potatoes, the next day potatoes with beans, and the next rice and potatoes. Before too long, during one of the shared meals, when we all were sitting with our heaped plates on our knees, Miton said gently, "Nayolang, we enjoy your food, but we prefer *ugali*! Every day!"

"Every day?!" Their choice perplexed me, as out of all the dishes we could make *ugali* was the least tasty. It is made of water, maize flour and salt and is tasteless.

Miton continued, "We eat in the morning, before leaving for school (he meant five thirty a.m.), and the next meal is at school, around one in the afternoon. It's important to us to eat food that leaves the stomach full for a long time. Food that doesn't let the feeling of hunger in."

"Could you rate the dishes that you prefer to eat?"

"Oh, that's easy: first place, with a serious advantage over any other food, is *ugali*. This is food that sits in our stomach for many hours and creates a feeling of fullness. Second place is rice, and third place is potatoes—they disappear the quickest, until we're hungry again..."

As someone who came from a culture that routinely eats *cholent*, a thick, heavy stew comprised of meat, potatoes, beans and barley that sits in the belly like cement for many hours— invented to provide a dietary solution for the impoverished Jews of Eastern Europe—I understood what Miton meant.

And so, spurred by a single comment, the cooking policy in our house changed, and we transitioned to a diverse menu that included *ugali* with potatoes, *ugali* with beans, or... *ugali* with *sukuma wiki*.

I was afraid that cooking the same food daily would prove oppressive but that was not the case. I felt liberated. Liberated from the need to plan the next meal, from dealing with what we would eat today. The possibilities were limited, the food was monotonous and the children were happy as clams.

Sometimes, at lunchtime, Samyan and Museré came to the house with more friends: one, two or five. I didn't know in advance how many would arrive, and as I was afraid there would not be enough for everyone, I tried to dawdle in serving the food, hoping the guests would take off. One day, when hunger got the better of them, they suggested I serve the food on two plates, with additional spoons for the friends. I felt guilty over the fact that they had to share their food with others and were not actually eating enough. Days later, I asked them about it. They burst out in laughter, and told me, "We go from house to house with our friends, and at each house, share the food prepared for each one of us.[11]"

~

In my frequent visits to my neighbors' houses, I was surprised to see how little they ate. After drinking milk tea in the morning, with milk just sourced from the cow and boiled, full of high percentages of fat and filling, most people did not eat a thing until noontime. Lunch was the first meal, usually *ugali* with milk, and in the evening, another meal was prepared. During times of plenty, more ingredients were added to the menu, such as potatoes, cabbage or beans.

This austerity regarding food does not apply regarding the children. For them, there's always a pitcher at the ready full of *oloshoro*, a liquid porridge made of maize flour, which fills their belly until the next meal.

During my first month in Maasai Mara, I tried to adapt to this dietary regime. The result—the reasons for which I initially had a hard time understanding—was that around eleven a.m., I always felt short-tempered. Of course! I was hungry! I was starving! I returned to a routine of breakfasts, noting my striking failure to grow accustomed to the Maasai diet.

I wondered why the people here ate so little and in such a monotonous fashion, as there was no lack of money (in livestock and cattle). Once again, I realized that their choices regarding what they would spend their money on differed from mine, and did not include "squandering" it on unnecessary food items.

The dietary frugality of my neighbors confronted me with another mirror regarding the cultural meeting between the two worlds. I found I was passing a significant part of my time with people for whom food equaled existence: it was not talked about, but eaten. You eat what you have! Another part of my life was still spent within a sated society, nourished by a plentitude of diverse food, and yet the preoccupation with food still filled up a significant portion of it's time: long articles accompanied by color photographs in magazines, various dining columns in newspapers, a television channel dedicated to food, and so on and so forth. Meanwhile, in my professional life as a tour guide, I frequently met people standing in a hotel across from a lavish buffet, and yet, when they did not see a tomato, they complained that "thereis nothing to eat."

11

Lionesses in the Village

The wee hours of the night.

Samyan woke me up with a yell: "Nayolang, get up! There are lions in the village!"

Usually, I tended to be a light sleeper, but this time, I had not heard a thing. I didn't know what to listen for. I quickly got dressed, grabbed a flashlight, and we burst out into the dark night. Shouting echoed from every direction, including the neighboring villages. I started my vehicle and we drove the few dozen yards to the village. The car's headlights illuminated a large swath of the night, revealing a surreal scene: boys and men, most as naked as the day they were born, carrying spears and running in all directions. I stopped next to a few, and they hurried to climb into the vehicle, confirming what Samyan had heard: lionesses had snuck into the village, attacked one cow and killed it. The men who woke up ran them off before they dissected their prey, and were now in pursuit to chase them away from the village.

The men sat down on the roof of the open vehicle, directing me right and left until the car's headlights picked up the seven lionesses, huddled together and growling at us. Yelling and honking, we ran them off to the other side of the stream separating the village from the nature reserve, and then returned to the dead cow, whose hide was already being stripped by several young men. Others sat on the sidelines, in mourning. No one went back to sleep that night. Once the dissection was over, dawn broke, and a celebration of meat commenced in each of the village's houses.

～

Rare are the nights in which we are not subject to a melodious concert: the growls of lions, the yowls of hyenas, the warning snorts of impalas, the barking of baboons or the purr of elephants. The nights are never quiet, but my immediate contact with wildlife usually took place within my own home, and my adaptation to life in the bush was evident in small yet important details: I took care to carefully shake out each garment I was intending to wear, and my hat and my towel before I used it, as they regularly shed uninvited guests—a wasps' nest, gecko or skink eggs. I blocked the openings of shoes with thick socks to prevent centipedes from settling inside them. Open shelving or even a closet would invite spiders or snakes, and therefore clothes had to be stored inside closed bags. And still, these measures were not always effective—one day I returned from a trip and discovered that a field mouse had gnawed through the fabric of the duffle bag serving as my closet, made her way inside, nibbled all my clothes and created a luxurious nest for herself in which she could give birth to a litter of tiny mice. That was how I learned to appreciate the metal trunk that every bride receives on her wedding day, in which she keeps all her possessions.

Living alongside wild animals and direct encounters with them were exciting and moving, but not always pleasant: Miton, Leporé and Lemein attended a school about four miles from the village. We would wake up at five thirty in the morning, while darkness still engulfed the earth like a thick blanket. They ate a breakfast utterly identical to their dinner, and as the first rays of sunshine emerged beyond the horizon and the air was still cold and saturated with dew, they embarked on a vigorous walk toward the school along with other boys and girls from the village, on a path curving through the bush. At the end of the long school day, they returned home every evening, this time winding their way slowly.

The nature reserve is not surrounded by a fence and the path leading to school passes and winds next to its border. The children often returned home with interesting experiences, including an encounter with a herd of zebras that stopped and gazed at them curiously, watching male impalas engage in a clash of horns, or running into a black-backed jackal that streaked past them holding the remains of a rabbit in its mouth.

Most days, the trek passed safely, but not always.

The school is near a small commercial center, no more than a grouping of one-story houses whose walls are made of wood, stone or corrugated metal. The center offers services to the entire region: repairing cars or bikes, a butcher, a grocery store, bars, a carpentry shop, a welder, restaurants and so on. Every Friday, the little center comes alive for the weekly market day.

Market days are especially popular among women. Unlike the men, who are constantly moving around, for the women, this was a weekly opportunity to dress up in their finery, put on their great assortment of necklaces and embark on a "shopping day": colorful fabrics, food supplies for their homes, some vegetables and beads in a variety of colors to make necklaces. Other than shopping, this was an opportunity (much valued in the era preceding cell phones) for encounters with people from the entire region: women separated from their families when they got married could meet their sisters, who had also married and moved to distant villages, or reunite with other relatives. Here they received notification of relatives ill or had died, or news of various ceremonies that would be taking place soon. Market day was an opportunity for young men to meet their childhood girlfriends, who had moved to other villages after getting married. They huddled in groups at the outskirts of the market, conversing enthusiastically.

The market, in the village square, which is no more than a dirt clearing that stood empty on other days of the week, has a dynamic of its own. The first to arrive are the big merchants. They travel in their trucks from one market day to the next, bearing merchandise from Narok, offering mainly wholesale vegetables and additional products. Side by side, they set up the trucks that serve as the stores themselves, thus creating a barrier on one side of the clearing. Next come rickety vehicles, laden with small vendors, primarily women. Each carries his or her own immense cargo. They unpack the bags, lay out a nylon tarp on the ground, and spread out their merchandise upon it: used clothing, colorful beads, soap, razor blades, assorted sundries, cheap housewares, sandals recycled from used tires, and so on. The last to arrive are Maasai women hoping to increase their familial earnings. They spread out their plastic tarps at the edge of the market, covering it with Maasai fabrics (*eleso*), maize flour, sugar and so on.

Gradually, people arrive at the market as it comes to life. The swarming begins from villages about ten miles away. The travelers are joined by people from villages along the way, dotting the planes in colorful gangs. Finally, around eleven in the morning, everyone arrives at the market.

Market activity reaches its peak about an hour and a half later, as the sun is blazing in the sky. The commotion, the rustle of fabrics and clattering necklaces, the bleating of goats trying to snatch a cabbage leaf or a fallen potato, all fade away around three o'clock. Group by group, the market's patrons return home, carrying their weekly shopping on their back.

On market day, many people walk the paths of the bush. The sounds of laughter and chatter are heard from afar, and the fear of wild animals usually decreases.

But that was not the case on this occasion.

Three frightened girls were the first to return to the village, reporting elephants on the path. They were followed by more people, bearing more accurate information: an elephant had killed a woman. The rumor passed from house to house, from village to village. Much panic ensued everywhere as people huddled in groups, awaiting more information. The woman's identity still remained unknown.

Before too long, Leporé came home, frightened and breathless. "I was there! We were walking, two boys and three women. We boys were walking faster than the women and didn't see the elephants. But the women behind us noticed the elephants and hid in the grass. From behind, more women arrived from the market. One of the elephants let out a loud trumpet and attacked them. All of us saw the herd and began to run…" As he was running, Leporé dropped his school bag, but kept going.

That evening, the mood in the village was dark. The rain drizzling during the day had stopped and the clouds dispersed. A half-moon rolled around in the sky, illuminating the darkness. In contrast to most moonlit nights, the village was quiet. The laughter of children was not heard. No games took place by moonlight. Everything was still. The men and women were ensconced in their houses, waiting for the sound of the motor heralding the return of the reserve rangers' vehicle, which had gone to the site of the incident. It returned after what seemed like an eternity, along with Kitipai, who told us, "Just before it grew dark, we arrived at the site of the encounter. The elephant had cracked open the woman's head, broken her leg, and tore up her stomach with its tusks. Then, when the elephant saw she was 'sleeping,' it broke off a large branch and covered her…

"Elephants," he continued, "know very well when they've done wrong, and they take off quickly, like cattle thieves escaping with their loot."

That evening, elephants were conversation in every single house. One man recounted how, one dark night, when the moon had still not risen and low, dense clouds lurked near the ground, he walked to one of the nearby villages. On his way there, he encountered with an elephant standing on the path. He ran away, with the elephant following. While running, he fell onto the ground and apparently fainted. When he woke up, he found himself covered by a pile of branches that the elephant had dragged over and laid out over him.

I contributed to the conversation, describing how, in a trip I'd taken years ago in Botswana, I set up my tent on what later turned out to be an elephant trail. During the night, I woke up. The smell woke me. A heavy smell. Pervasive. I lay in my sleeping bag and looked up to the starry sky visible beyond the netting that formed the top part of the tent. Suddenly, a massive shadow covered the sky and a trunk was extended forward, roaming and exploring… I held my breath. I watched the elephant sniff and sniff, circling the tent and finally continuing on his way. In the morning, I examined his immense footprints around the tent. I admired the extreme delicacy with which he had paced, not touching a single stake. From that day on, I refused to use the expression "the elephant in the room."

Now, however, I got it—there was no animal, none, not even a buffalo, that the Maasai feared the way they feared this "tank," weighing over five tons. They could sometimes deal with lions and leopards, but there was nothing they could do against elephants, other than being fleet of foot and highly alert.

12

One Finger Cannot Kill a Louse

In a place where elephants, buffaloes, lions or leopards roam free, getting around on foot is not simple. And yet men, women and children do walk around in the bush: to gather wood, to draw water, to go to school or to a ceremony at a distant village. Much to my frustration, I found myself leery.

Despite my apprehension, I occasionally go visit friends in adjacent villages, equipped with a wide-brimmed hat, sunscreen, lots of water and… a shepherd's staff. This stick imbues me with security to the same extent it feels ridiculous —if I faced a lion, buffalo or elephant, what exactly would I be able to do with my staff? Despite all my fears, I find walking alone in the bush a pleasure. In the grassy planes in which the animals are visible from afar, I become joyful and free. However, when my path crosses a thick tangle of shrubs, I feel my adrenalin level rocketing sky-high. My body is taut and alert, my eyes examine the bushes, trying to spot motion, and my ears are open to the sound of branches crackling or a faint purr. I face a constant quandary: should I sing and make sounds to scare away the wildlife around me, or step silently, without making a sound, to avoid possible danger?

One day, walking through the grassy planes, I saw a creature running and hovering toward me like a ghost. I stopped immediately, staring at it. It was a cheetah, gradually approaching me: a long, slim feline body, black spots on its fur, and a small head, with two black stripes descending from its eyes to the corners of its mouth, like a sooty trail of tears.

Should I run? Stand my ground? These questions were hypothetical, as I felt paralyzed. I continued to stare at it until suddenly, when it was just a short distance away from me, it saw me, stopped abruptly, changed direction, continued running and disappeared into the distant thicket.

Another encounter with a leopard, which growled over my head, baring its teeth when I interrupted its afternoon nap on a high tree, convinced me to use the vehicle, which would serve as my legs, allowing me to travel relatively long distances at any hour of the day, fearlessly.

∽

Morning. I started the vehicle and the sound of the engine disrupted the peace prevailing in the village. As I drove, on the left, from the corner of my eye, I saw a man running toward me and waving his arms. I stopped.

"Nayolang, where are you going?"

"Where do you need to go?"

"No, you tell me, where are you headed?"

"To Emarti," I declared a direction.

"Great, I'm coming with you."

He boarded the vehicle and I drove about sixty feet.

And another cloak billow toward me, and someone else was stopping me. And so the story repeated itself and this man, too, boarded the car. And once again I drove forward and yet again I was stopped and asked where I was going. When the fifth person stopped me, I felt my suppressed Western cultural upbringing rising to the surface and rebelling (*What do you care where I'm going?* I thought to myself).

∽

As a Westerner accustomed to privacy, I found questions like 'Where are you going?' 'When are you coming back?' 'Will you meet this person?'—questions asked every day, all the time, by everyone—very troubling during my first year in the village. I never, at any point, drove anywhere alone. The destination did not matter; always someone wanted to come along. Others stopped me to convey news: "Ah, you're driving to Emarti? Tell Lenkiton that his sister who lives in Ololarok had a baby girl…"

Over time, I realized these questions were not nosy, and were not intended to invade my privacy, but to use me, as every person is used, as a conduit to convey information. I myself had noticed how every passerby who wandered past the village stopped in the shade of the tree, relayed general news and passed on individual messages. That I had become one conduit of information regarding ceremonies, births, meetings and so on was a compliment. I had received confirmation that society had worked me into the "social network."

A general look at Maasai society taught me that the "social network" was the most important glue regarding their culture, one that united them and made them cohesive. A Maasai expression states, "One finger cannot kill a louse": several fingers are necessary. Fellowship is essential to existence.

The social network is woven from the vertical threads of the clan (the largest unit in which the members are blood relatives) and the extended family, protecting the individual within the broad framework of familial loyalty and blood relations, and the horizontal threads of age groups and age sets—crossing families, clans or tribes. Every person knows their place in this social network, which defines their relationship with household members, fellow villagers and the entire region*. The knowledge that the network exists instills plenty of security in its members, but also requires a commitment from them. Commitment exists on the family level, in hosting, caring and providing for family members who arrive for a visit and sometimes stay for an indefinite span of time. The commitment also exists on an extended family level: if one boy in the family wants to continue studying and attain higher education, the entire extended family comes to his aid financially. There are also obligations on the clan level: if a person from a certain clan murdered another Maasai, all members of the killer's clan have to participate in paying compensation to the victim's family.

The social network also poses requirements on the regional level: if strangers came to the village at night and stole cattle, all the men in the area will leave their occupations behind and embark on a search that might last several days, until the cattle are found. This is also the case if a lion has eaten a cow. When this occurs, any man who is available—regardless of clan, age group or village affiliation—will set out to chase away the lion.

Within the permanent, elaborate weave of the Maasai social network, every person can embroider extensions that will further enhance the network: choosing a bride for a son will expand a father's social network. Giving gifts—heifers, goats or sheep—to friends and associates will also expand the network.

A Maasai person cannot decide independently which part of the social network he wishes to enjoy, and which part he wishes to relinquish. The social network is a package deal that encompasses all

---

* See Appendix 3 for more information on the Maasai social network.

areas of life and leaves no room for individualism: a person cannot decide to merely "take care of number one" and leave the social circle. He cannot get rich by working hard, and forget about his friends and relatives. The more he has, the more people will come and gather around him: his brothers will send their children to him so he can raise them; relatives will come to receive loans or gifts: a milk cow, money for medical treatment, tuition for their children and so on.

The more a person has, the more the social network woven around him becomes dense and demanding. The less a person has, the more protection the social network provides.

∼

Once again, I faced a dilemma.

In its own way, the Maasai social network had opened a door for me. I did feel flattered, but as an individualist, I also envisioned it as a snare tossed at me. I imagined myself flailing in this web, which would gradually tighten around me until it finally compromised my independence.

13

An Old Groom

The clearness and transparency of the equatorial climate are something that I have experienced nowhere else in the world. The colors are brighter, more diverse. The clouds cruising through the sky are constructed of layers upon layers. Morning after morning, I sit on the veranda and savor being part of the view. Across from me, though hidden from my sight, the stream flows leisurely, and the slope of the hill rises from it gently, speckled with acacia trees, until it kisses the sky at the horizon. On my far left, a line of green hills frames the image.

∽

Several months had gone by since I had first witnessed female circumcision, and preparations for Lanoi and Kitapo's circumcision had begun in the village.

The main thing troubling Nesesyay, Lanoi's mother, was making sure she circumcised her daughter before she menstruated; getting pregnant before being circumcised was a taboo, as only circumcision would turn her daughter into a woman.

During these months, I continued to deliberate regarding female circumcision. I read many studies. Some claimed there was no connection between female circumcision and lack of pleasure during sex, that circumcision caused almost no damage, either in the short term or the long term[12], and there was no correlation between circumcision and complications during birth. I was impressed with an article by an American anthropologist of Sierra Leonean origin who had undergone circumcision[13] at an advanced age and provided first-hand testimony. Why was the Western world so appalled by and opposed to female circumcision? My impression was that most current claims focus on questions of human rights and a woman's right regarding her body.

Why did a woman's rights regarding her body serve as an argument against circumcision, rather than for it? What if the girl wants to undergo circumcision?

Is the claim she is a prisoner of her culture not an expression of cultural arrogance? Who determines what the parameters of human rights are? Isn't it possible that if Africans decided regarding a woman's right over her body, they might determine that plastic surgery—facelifts, Botox and silicon injections, breast augmentation, vaginal rejuvenation and so on—actually constitute mutilation?

On the one hand, I felt that if I, as an individual, and we Westerners demand respect for our customs, including the strange ones (the Jewish custom of *kapparot*, consisting of waving a rooster over the head on Yom Kippur; the Mormon custom of wearing special 'temple garment' underwear under the clothes thought to provide protection from evil), I must similarly respect others' customs, even if I did not agree with them, understand them or accept them. However, I decided that because I was opposed to mutilating the body—any form of mutilation, including tongue or nipple piercing—there was no reason not to express my position, sensitively and at an African tempo.

I knew that for several years now, due to international pressure, the Kenyan government had outlawed female circumcision. The results of the prohibition on circumcision were disastrous: whereas previously, many families had consented to circumcise their daughters under sterile conditions in hospitals, now, when female circumcision had become illegal, it had returned to the bush and to unhygienic conditions. I had heard there were places where the chiefs and the police traveled between villages looking for families circumcising their daughters. In those areas, the girls were woken up during the night and circumcised with only flashlights as illumination, and with no ceremony.

In light of all this, I was afraid that if I stridently opposed circumcision, not only would I invoke the rage of my friends, but that Maasai pride would inspire a contrarian reaction. During the years since I had witnessed the first ceremony, I tried to approach the topic from various directions. At first I talked to the women, but they did not cooperate. They kept saying: *We're Maasai and those are our customs!* When I failed on that front, I moved on to talking to the boys: *How do you feel about asking that your future bride not be circumcised?* As well, my words fell on deaf ears. The circumcision of future brides was out of their hands.

In more recent years, some parents still carried out the full circumcision ceremony, but instead of the circumcision being done by one of the older women, as tradition dictates, they invited a nurse who injected local anesthetic, and cut off only the clitoris, using a sterile knife. Despite the advantages of such a circumcision, it was still against the law, and the nurse was putting herself at risk. I have witnessed such a circumcision, and most women's reaction was still negative: they protested vigorously, claiming that such a circumcision was not valid!

The discussions on the topic and education at school are having an effect, and today, most parents will abandon the custom. The few who are not are generally willing to "merely" cut off the clitoris and the labia minora.

⁓

I realized I had no reason to act against the circumcision of my two girls, for which they were yearning. But I wondered if I could at least ease the suffering awaiting them. I approached the elders. "When you circumcise a girl, is it really important that it hurts?"

Their answer was unequivocal. "It's the circumcision itself that matters to us. If you manage to make it so that it doesn't hurt the girls, that's fine!"

This answer pleased me, and I went off to talk to the women. "I have some medicine that reduces pain. Can I give it to the girls?" They nodded in affirmation. I had received the adults' consent, and one day, as the circumcision drew closer, I proposed to Lanoi and Kitapo, "How do you feel about me giving you a lotion to reduce pain?"

They hesitated: "We don't know… we'll see."

I bought a topical anesthetic cream, and as the ceremony grew near, I showed the two girls how to apply it.

The eve of the circumcision. The girls' heads had been shaved and dyed with red ochre. They had put on the *orkela* and looked very excited in anticipation of the ceremony. In the evening, the two approached me and said, "We debated and deliberated, but now we've come to a decision; although we have a white mother, we're Maasai, and we'll experience the circumcision like Maasai! Like all the other girls!"

My appeals that evening and the morning of the circumcision did not change their mind—the two stuck to their guns.

I stood beside them as the cutting was happening, while they writhed and tried not to scream.

Ten minutes later, when Lanoi was lying in bed, the circumcision already behind her, I asked, "Well?"

She replied, "Ah, if I knew it would hurt like that, I'd have applied the stuff."

I sat next to their beds, each in the home of her biological mother. I stroked them and consoled them, but even with all the pain, I already perceived a new spark in their eyes, a glimmer of wild pride, of a new power: *We did it! We passed the difficult trial! We're women!*

The cream did not help Lanoi and Kitapo, but the rumor of its existence spread like wildfire. Before too long, mothers invited me to come to the ceremony and give their daughter the miracle cream that dulled the sensation of pain.

～

Lanoi and Kitapo recuperated quickly. The wound was rinsed daily with a tincture of healing plants prepared by the village women, and then an antibiotic lotion was applied. The combination of traditional and modern medicine proved effective, and within a week, the two looked cheerful, happy and proud.

The girls stayed close to each other during the day, their foreheads adorned with a special tiara made of cowhide with cowrie shells (called *segera* in Maasai, a name also applied to the tiara itself). Delicate metal chains, about two inches long, were affixed to the lower part of the cowhide. The tiara declared, for all to see, that the two girls had joined the Maasai people and were on their way to becoming "full-fledged" women.

We knew that the marriage proposals would soon arrive. Kitapo had been promised as a child to a certain family, and all that was left to discover was which of the family members would win her. However, Lanoi was still unattached.

The girls did not look troubled. They knew that the circumcision and the wedding were separated by an interim period of at least six months, during which they were no longer girls but were not yet women. During this interim period, the girls were excluded from normal day-to-day life, and were subject to rigid rules: they had to grow their hair (their heads were shaved nearly at the circumcision, and would be shaved again only nearly at their wedding), and so long as their hair was growing, were forbidden from having sex. The girls had to sleep within the boundaries of the village every night, and during the daytime—always wearing the *segera* on their forehead— could not roam on their own, but had to come with a friend.

Before the women in the family had even had time to rest from the circumcision ceremony and all the preparations preceding it, a new commotion began. They all pitched in to prepare the many necklaces, made of tiny, colorful beads, which would form a part of the dowry given to the departing girl. Every day, I sat with the women and watched their work. Preparing wedding jewelry is not subject to the creativity of the family member making them; the number of necklaces, their shape and the color pattern are all predetermined and fixed (although they vary from tribe to tribe among the Maasai people). The women took out their own jewelry and copied the shapes and styles. On her way to her husband's village on her wedding day, the bride would wear the jewelry, and these necklaces would tell her story: which clan she belonged to, and where she had come from.

This interim period for the girls, and the simultaneous creation of the necklaces, served as an adjustment period for me, as I got used to the thought that soon the two girls, still so young, would have to leave home.

∼

Lanoi and Kitapo's hair grew out, and they wore the *segera* every time they left the house. Two months went by and one day, as we went down to the stream for laundry day, I asked Lanoi casually, "What would you prefer? An old groom who lives nearby or a young groom who lives far away?"

Lanoi replied with no hesitation, "An old groom who lives nearby!"

My initial surprise was replaced with insight: this girl had never left the village, her family, her biological mother and her boyfriends and girlfriends. The thought of moving to a distant place, even a mere fifteen miles from the village of her birth, frightened her.

And as for the old groom—that question was not so significant for her. If a loving relationship formed between her and her old husband, wonderful. But if that was not the case, quickly, after an adjustment period in the village, she would find herself a young lover and have fun with him.

Clearly, her preferences carried no weight in Maasai society, as marriages were always arranged.

For us, secular modernists who venerate individuality, an arranged marriage seems like a severe obstruction of our freedom to choose. The thought that someone would decide for us with whom we would spend the rest of our lives, with whom we would have sex and with whom we would have children, is appalling to us. We wonder about the role of love in such a relationship. But do we also ask this question after twenty years of marriage? How many Western couples hang in there for twenty years of marriage and still be happy? Love and a successful relationship do not always go hand in hand.

According to the Maasai perception, arranged marriage is a social solution that leaves no one outside of society. Arranged marriage allows everyone to be wed; even the less fortunate, even those with various disabilities—people who are deaf, mute or have mobility challenges—have a place in the social order! (The only ones not married off are those who are mentally challenged.) Therefore, without the 'meat market' of repeated blind dates, of frustration and oppression, every Maasai girl who has come of age will be married!

Love, the parents claim, should not be a consideration in choosing a partner. The considerations in picking a groom or bride must be deeper, and address a person's survival needs by extending his or her already robust social network. As a Maasai person's ability to survive depends on his cattle, and as natural disasters, such as drought or various illnesses, can cause a great mortality rate among the livestock, expanding the social network through bonds of marriage with other families in distant areas will enable transferring some cows to relatives in more protected, sheltered areas when necessary.

Arranging the children's marriages, therefore, is an efficient way to expand the father's social circle, thus ensuring his own survival and that of his family and livestock. In addition, marrying into a family with many assets (i.e., cows) is an advantage that might prove useful during times of trouble.

I wondered what the children themselves felt—would they prefer a marriage of love? Samyan made it clear that on this subject, the Maasai worldview differed somewhat from the accepted Western one: in my own house, he had fallen in love with Kitapo, who was a member of a different family and a different clan. I enjoyed watching their friendship, which was touching and joyful.

"You understand, with her it isn't just sex," Samyan said. "Every time we're together, we giggle and tell stories and have a good time."

"Would you like her to be your wife?" I asked.

"No!" he replied firmly.

His answer surprised me. "Why not?"

"A woman has to respect her husband. If I marry my girlfriend, will she respect me? How could I get mad at her on the day when I have to do it?"

Samyan explained another aspect of Maasai perception: the new bride does not just marry her husband—she marries his entire family. The two do create an economic partnership intended to bring children into the world; however, it is not a closed, nuclear family (two-person system), as the bride enters the society of village women, while the man is a part of the society of men, and there are few points of intersection between the two.

～

One morning, Oloyetinoy, Lanoi's father, came to visit me, as he did almost every day. He was around my own age, but the years had left their mark upon him—he was thin, his complexion wrinkled and his ears pierced, with heavy copper earrings hanging from them. He was one of the few people in the region to wear glasses, thanks to a recent trip to the hospital for an eye exam.

Wearing the traditional outfit of two cloth cloaks, he sat down on a bench on the veranda. As he sipped tea, he apologized for staying only briefly, as he was invited to the village across the river, where someone was interested in Lanoi. I offered to go with him, but he declined: arranging marriages is a man's affair! His friend Barguyare soon joined us, and the two set out on their way.

The drunken singing echoing from afar signaled their return as evening was approaching. Oloyetinoy looked radiant, ecstatic and tipsy with beer: "I found a groom for my daughter!" My attempts to discover who the groom was resulted in the same answer, again and again: "Don't worry, he has lots of cows."

This answer worried me.

I turned to Barguyare. "Please, tell me, what exactly happened there?"

Barguyare, a short fellow, younger than Oloyetinoy and married to only one wife, told me: "Ah, we sat in this man's house. He's about sixty and has two sons of marriageable age. We drank lots of beer, talked about this and that, and finally the topic of the marriage came up. I was convinced that he wanted Lanoi for one of his sons, so I asked him which one of the two he wanted her for. The old man told me, 'Oh, I've gotten older, I need a young girl to wash my feet!'"

I listened to Barguyare and felt horrified, as the statement indicated he wanted her for himself. Would the forecast of "an old groom who lives nearby" ultimately come true?

A week later we were told that, under custom, the intended groom was planning to come to our village to continue the discussion, as the final decision regarding the marriage is not made in a single meeting but rather in meetings, the preparations for which include brewing some local beer.

The preparations began at the home of Nesesyay, the biological mother, and the beer was brewed: two five-gallon containers were filled with water mixed with about four pounds of sugar. "Sausages"—aloe roots, used as a catalyst in the fermentation process—were inserted into the mixture. After a week, when the beer assumed the yellowish shade of lemon juice and a sweetish flavor, the old man was invited over.

He and his friend arrived early in the afternoon. Both were wearing traditional Maasai garb: two red cloaks, a checkered blanket in shades of red and sandals made of tires. They were armed, as was customary, both with a long knife worn at their right hip and with a *rungu* (a wooden club with a ball at its end), and a shepherd's crook. As was the custom among the older generations, metal earrings dangled from their earlobes, which had been pierced and stretched when they were still young, swaying as they walked.

We all gathered in the hut: Oloyetinoy (Lanoi's father), Nesesyay (her biological mother), Samyan (her older brother) and I.

For two hours or more, the conversation revolved around the state of the rain, the grass, the cows, the sheep and upcoming ceremonies.

The entire time, the adults held enamel-covered tin cups and sipped beer. Throughout the conversation, the cups did not stay empty even for a moment. They were filled again and again. I saw how, under the jollying influence of the beer, the two families began to establish bonds of friendship.

Finally, the marriage was brought up. The old man declared his intention to marry Lanoi, and proposed that he and his friend leave the hut for a while so we could get to the heart of the matter. Oloyetinoy ran the discussion. He exhibited a remarkably democratic attitude, asking us all, "What do you think?"

"He's not the right guy! He's too old," Nesesyay replied.

"He's not the one! We have to find someone else for her!" Samyan said.

I chimed in. "Ah, no way! My girl deserves a young man. She deserves to be happy, to love. This man is even older than you!"

Oloyetinoy's gaze roamed slowly across the faces of everyone present. He appeared to be considering what we had said. For one long moment, he appeared to deliberate, but suddenly, he barked out: "You're all nothing! What do you understand? He, he's got cows! Lots of them! He, he's a man! That's it. I've made up my mind. He'll be her husband!"

The guests were called in, and much to our chagrin, the old man was told he had won himself a "young woman who would wash his feet."

I felt overcome with sadness. I was enraged at the father who had so recklessly closed a deal that would shape his daughter's life.

I found Lanoi near the hut. I called her aside and shared the news with her. She looked in my eyes and uttered a single statement. "My father knows what's best for me." The tears popping up at the corners of her eyes were the only indication of her emotional upheaval.

I decided not to give up.

In the next few days, I went to talk to various men and women, trying to discover whether the decision as "signed" was still reversible. I received a uniform reaction. "Nayolang, if the deal was sealed, then there's nothing to discuss anymore."

And yet.

The next day, Oloyetinoy arrived to visit me, have a cup of tea and ask how I was doing, as was his habit.

"Nayolang, how are you?"

"Oh, not good, not good."

"Why not good?"

"I'm in pain, I'm in great pain."

"What hurts?"

"My heart!"

This ritual repeated itself, day after day. I did not give up. As I sat in his home, I repeated myself again and again: I was in pain, I felt sad, I could not agree with his decision. Much to my joy, Samyan helped me, expressing his indignation. "Look, my father, it's true that the man had many cows, but his wives come to our village to receive clothes and food donations. He has many cows, but he doesn't take care of his wives. I don't want Lanoi to be his wife. She deserves better."

As the days went by, we saw the father's hesitations increase, and now the only thing needed was to open an escape hatch for him. Samyan provided a solution.

"Father, did you give Lanoi away in return for a bride for me?"

A common custom among Maasai not interested in paying a dowry for a bride is an exchange of daughters. A man hands over one of his girls, receives a girl from the groom's family, and that way, need not pay.

"Yes."

"Father, you know I'm due to marry. Did you check how old his daughter was?"

"No."

"Well, maybe his girl is young, and not right for me?"

A few days later, his father hastened off to the house of the intended groom to check out the bride intended for Samyan. The girl (as we already knew) was too young, and would be ready only to marry in a few years.

And thus a solution was found. Oloyetinoy apologized, gave the groom a cow to compensate him for his trouble and the unpleasantness, and canceled the agreement.

And Lanoi? Six months went by, and she was properly wed to a young groom who lived close by!

14

Emuyo

One evening, I was visited by my friend Saruni, who years earlier had accompanied Kitipai when we took Noʼoltwati to the hospital in Nairobi. After I cooked dinner, we carried a table out onto the grass clearing outside my house, placed the lantern some distance away to keep the gnats at bay, and covered ourselves with the sparkling diamond blanket in the sky. A light breeze was blowing, carrying the distant calls of the hyenas with it. We savored the *ugali*, told each other stories, and finally went to sleep—he in the big room, and I in my own room.

But a strange, unusual murmur troubled my sleep. It was an odd rustle, like dripping water: *dripdripdrip...*

I turned on the flashlight, and... found myself under attack! Through the cracks in the door, through the windows, through the slits in the wooden boards, black ants, about one centimeter in size, were dropping, striding and streaming into the room. They were everywhere. The black swarm covered the floor, the walls, the entire room!

I cried out to Saruni, "Come here, come quick!"

He arrived, observed, and blurted out, "*Emuyo*..."

"What?"

"*Emuyo*, fire ants. There's nothing you can do about them. They're not in the other room. Come sleep over there."

I took my blanket and ran to the big room.

About half an hour went by, and suddenly, I felt something stirring in my hair.

"Saruni, help, they're climbing all over me now, and they pinch!"

And so I learned, first hand, about the carnivorous fire ants that eat flesh, any flesh. They move through the land by creating a long column and advancing unstoppably. Nothing can stand in their way, and they eat anything that crosses their path.

Saruni was surprised to see me so upset. What seemed like a disaster as they pinched and hurt me, filling up the entire house, was perceived by him as a blessing.

"How... how can you claim they're a blessing?"

"When the army of ants enters any house, they consume all the cockroaches and insects inside every nook and cranny, and do so with a thoroughness that no spray can match. When we are privileged with a visit from the *emuyo*, we move the goats out of the house, as they can kill their kids as well. For a night or two, we sleep at the neighbors', waiting for the ants to complete their task of extermination. After a day or two, or a week, when there is nothing left to eat, the ants will leave the house and continue on their journey, and we know that our home is free of insects."

For the time being, we fled the house, with our blankets in hand. We hunkered down in my car, drove about fifty yards, parked and went to sleep. The bemused, smiling faces of the villagers pressed against the car windows at dawn woke us up to the beginning of a new day.

A few days later, I cut my hair short.

15

One Round

"Where's the tea? Tea! I want tea!"

I smiled to myself as I heard Oloyetinoy's hoarse voice in the distance.

That morning, the kettle was already on the fire. I poured some tea into a large enamel cup, sweetened it with four teaspoons of sugar and handed him another cup so he could cool the boiling beverage by pouring it from cup to cup. He clucked in expectation, sucked the tea noisily into his mouth and nodded in approval. "*Sidai, sidai* (Good, good)." Then, with a broad grin on his face, he told me, "It worked out for you after all—Lanoi married an Ilmeshuki."

"Ilmeshuki? Isn't his name Kyara?"

"Yes, his name is Kyara but he belongs to the Ilmeshuki age group."

"What does that mean?"

Oloyetinoy then embarked on what I humorously called "continuing education" —his attempts to explain and teach me Maasai logic. This was not the first time, and I always enjoyed my conversations with him, which were thought provoking and awakened additional questions within me.

"You already know that any son born to Maasai society goes through several stages in the course of his life, from infancy to old age: a baby, a child, a youth, a young adult, an adult, an old man and an elderly man. Each one of these stages defines a man's place in the social order: what roles are given to him (to herd the goats or the cattle, to run with a spear when a lion attacks the herd or to set out to loot cows, to be a groomsman in ceremonies or to serve as a mediator in disputes), how he will greet those older than him, whom he might have sex with, and so on.

"The transition from one stage to the next is usually accompanied by a ceremony: both personal ceremonies, which you've already seen, and collective ceremonies. One of the most important personal ceremonies for every boy is the circumcision ceremony, after which he is transformed from a youth into a man. Circumcision is a personal ceremony, as every family circumcises its own boys itself, in its home, but anyone who has gone through it is privileged with entering the most important Maasai social tapestry, which is the age group. This is a fraternity that includes all the young men circumcised within five to seven years from the time the group was established (meaning the age gap between the first to be circumcised in the age group and the last to be circumcised may be as much as seven years).

"We Maasai are divided into tribes and clans, but belonging to an age group crosses tribe and clan lines. It is so important that the second question (after 'What is your last name?') that someone who meets a stranger asks is, 'Which age group do you belong to?'"

Museré, with his gorgeous smile, approached us and sat beside us on the bench, poured himself a cup of tea and joined the conversation:

"You certainly know what Ilmeshuki means! It's the current age group opened in 1997, to which Samyan and I belong."

"Yes, but is belonging to Ilmeshuki or to any other age group really significant?"

"Oh, it's immensely significant! Belonging to an age group

determines the relationship among men, between men and women, and among women. It also determines many rules of morality."

"Can you give me some examples?"

"Sure, there's plenty of examples: the most important rule is that the mother of a guy belonging to an age group, such as our Ilmeshuki, is considered to be the mother of all young men in that age group. The father of an Ilmeshuki guy is considered to be the father of all Ilmeshuki guys. We constantly make use of this rule: when I set out on a journey that lasts a few days, arrive towards evening at some village and look for a place to sleep, I ask where an Ilmeshuki's house is, and that's where I'll go. In this house, even though I previously knew no one, I'll eat, drink and sleep. My peer's mother will take care of me as if I were her son. Do you understand? Up till now, you thought you were only the mother of seven children, but actually, you're the mother of all the Ilmeshukis, Samyan's and my age group."

"Are there other examples of the importance of the age group?"

"Of course. A father may not marry his daughter off to a member of his age group under any circumstances, as that would be as if the girl married 'her father.' And when a girl gets married and arrives as a new bride in her husband's village, which is far from her home, she knows she's not alone, since every man who belongs to her father's age group is in effect 'her father.' If she gets in trouble, someone abuses her or her husband beats her, she can always turn to 'her father'—meaning, to a member of her father's age group—for help.

"Do you want some more examples? There are clear rules about whom a woman or a man may have sex with. Prohibitions depend on the clan to which the person belongs, but also on his or her age group."

Oloyetinoy took control of the conversation once more. "Belonging to an age group does encompass all areas of our lives, but I think the main reason these groups were formed is that we're a survival-oriented society that has to take care of all its members. While in your society, as you've told us, the familial connection is vertical: grandfather—father—son—grandson—great-grandson, and you can assume, with a great degree of probability, that the elders (grandfather, father) will live to a ripe old age and take care of their offspring, in our society, there is no such guarantee. The mortality rate is high, and a person's chance of living into old age is small. Therefore, we've found a unique way to ensure mutual responsibility between members of society. This type of responsibility is not vertical, but rather horizontal. Do you understand? The age group incorporates loads of guys around the same age, and they create a sense of mutual commitment and responsibility that will last a lifetime. This is a horizontal security net that is essential in a society like ours, where the mortality rate among adults is high, and the life expectancy is relatively low."

∽

As Oloyetinoy talked, I once again imagined the giant spider weaving the thick webs of the "social network" around each individual. A variety of laws and rules ensured the survival of the individual and the survival of society. Nowhere in Maasai country, and under no circumstances, would a person be alone. By belonging to a tribe, to a clan and to an age group, and through the institutions of arranged marriage and wedlock, a man will always belong to a group to which he can appeal in times of trouble.

However, I was missing the women within this social tapestry. "And what about women? Do they have an age group too?"

Museré chuckled. "Every girl who gets married immediately joins her husband's age group, even if he is older than her by many years. And here's another age group rule for you: if she married an Ilmeshuki, then all the Ilmeshuki men are considered her husbands!"

"Wow! What does that mean in actuality?"

"It means that one day, when I get married and a friend who is a fellow Ilmeshuki comes to visit me, I'll leave the house after dinner and find another place to sleep while he stays behind to sleep in my wife's house. But that doesn't necessarily mean he'll have sex with her, and in any case, he can't do so without her consent. Since he's my peer—I'll never ask."

"Damn, I'm lucky not to have a husband here!"

~

It's true that I didn't have a husband, but I did get plenty of offers to 'go steady,' mostly from my age group—those close to me in age. Turoto, married to five women, was an especially tenacious suitor. On one occasion when he came to my house to drink tea and check up on my amenability, I told him, "I need time to think about it."

He was not deterred. "How long?"

I contemplated it and replied, "A year!"

Turoto lives in a village quite close to my home and we continued to see each other often. He did not bring the matter up again. A year went by, and I had forgotten the entire affair, but one day, he showed up at my home. We took chairs out to the veranda, watched the wild animals visible from afar and sipped tea with milk.

Suddenly, he asked, "So, have you thought it over? What do you say?"

I burst out in carefree laughter, and he joined me. "Turoto, with five wives, how will you even have time for me? How can I say yes?"

"I have a lot of stamina," he answered with a sly smile. "You really should!"

"Look," I replied. "I've thought about it, and I don't really want to..."

His face radiant, he looked at me and said, "Oh well, that's fine. If you don't want to be my girlfriend, that's okay, but let's go into the room now and have one 'round.'"

It was the most amusing sexual proposition I had ever received.

Following my amusing encounters with Turoto, I tried to inquire whether this conduct was typical of all Maasai. I asked Museré how a Maasai young man initiates an intimate relationship with a girl. He squirmed. I understood the reason. Maasai men honor women who are older than them, and not every topic is appropriate for an open discussion.

I found a more specific question. "What makes you desire one girl, rather than another?"

He replied willingly this time. "I look at two things in a woman. The first is her teeth. I want her to have pretty white teeth. The second is her ankles—she should have slim, delicate ankles. But the most important thing is the blood!"

"The blood?"

"Yes. Sometimes a girl walks by and I immediately feel my blood heat up and flow faster, and I know that's the girl I want."

I liked his definition of attraction. "And then what?"

"Then," he continued, "when a guy wants a woman, he comes to her hut and talks to her for about half an hour, laughs, tells her stories, and leaves. The next day, he comes again and talks to her for about an hour. After a few days, he asks her if she's interested, and even if she says yes, he doesn't always arrive on that same day."

In additional conversations, other men told me, "Sometimes it takes a year from the moment we start to flirt with a woman until we have sex with her. We're in no hurry. We show the woman that we're serious about her. And besides, she does have a husband, and is not free to be with us all the time anyway."

She has a husband! How did I not think of that! She has a husband. Girls get married between the ages of fifteen and seventeen. The only single girls have not been circumcised yet, and although they may be permitted to *morans*, those boys already circumcised, many treat them as little girls and prefer the company of girls their own age, who are already married.

"Hold on, do men who are married to several women also have girlfriends?"

Museré chuckled in confirmation. "For us Maasai, there is not necessarily a connection between marriage and love and sex. Love or friendship—which, as I understand it, you view as the basis of a couple's relationship—could be a nice addition to such a relationship, but they're not essential.

"Among us, a pregnant woman cannot have sex once she reaches the fourth month of pregnancy or so, and until her baby is ten months old! Avoiding sex is the only form of 'family planning' we know, which ensures we don't have a baby every year. Therefore, there's logic in a man's desire to marry additional women with whom he can have sex while his wife or several of his wives are forbidden to him."

I grew contemplative as I processed this information. Finally, I deduced, "If that's the case, it's not unusual for a married woman to have one boyfriend or more as well."

"Of course! Many of the women here have a boyfriend. Why are you surprised? The woman's marriage was arranged, and she's not always attached to her husband, who might be older than her by many years, truly an old man. So what's wrong with a beloved boyfriend who will warm her heart and her desires? But since she has a husband who's always around, in many cases the boyfriend is an object of fantasies, and the relationship is rarely consummated."

I tried to explain the significance of a committed relationship in the West. "Mostly, we treat our partners as our property (indeed, in Hebrew, the word 'husband' (*ba'al*) shares the same root as the word for 'ownership' as well as 'coitus,' while in Maa, there is no such word; a Maasai woman will call her husband *orpayan lai*, meaning 'my man'), and therefore, we don't want another person fooling around with them. You know, with us, when a man finds his wife in bed with another man, at best he divorces her, but in a worst case scenario, he kills her!"

Museré gaped in amazement. "Because she had sex with someone else? You white people are completely nuts! After all, what a woman has down there is just an orifice. Can that orifice be used up?"

I chuckled in response, immediately linking that non-possessive attitude to the lack of possessiveness regarding objects passed around from one person to the next—pants, a shirt or a watch. That they belong to one person (and everyone knows who that person is) does not mean they are reserved solely for that person.

"Hold on a minute, Museré, does the husband really not care that his wife has a lover? I don't believe it!"

"Of course he cares! The relationship between two people who are not married must be very discreet. The husband isn't supposed to know about it at all! But her women friends usually will know, and in most cases, when the opportunity arises, they'll help her spend time with her beloved: one of them will wait outside and make sure the husband isn't around."

And what happens when the man nevertheless discovers that his wife has a lover? On another occasion, No'oltwati told me the following story:

"Many years ago, there was a woman who had a lover, with whom she would meet frequently. One day, her husband grew suspicious and decided to accompany her everywhere she went. He went with her to gather firewood, walked her to the stream to fetch water, escorted her when she visited friends in nearby villages, and did not leave her side even for a moment. Her lover, who missed her, knocked on the wall of her house one night, and the two set a time to meet at a ficus tree located far from her village. The next morning, the woman told her husband that she was going to visit her parents' home. Her husband, of course, volunteered to go with her. The woman carried an old *kalabash* with tiny cracks in it. When she arrived at the ficus tree with her husband, she pretended to swoon and asked her husband to go over to the river and bring her water. The husband took the *kalabash*, striding determinedly toward the river, but could not manage to fill the cracked container. He lingered by the river for about an hour, while the wife cavorted with her lover, who had been waiting for her, hidden between the branches of the tree.

"Finally, the husband brought the wife water and they continued on their way. A few months later, the husband noticed his wife was pregnant. He knew the child was not his, and after threatening her, the woman told him how she had conceived. She told him about the *kalabash* and about the lover. The husband thought and thought about it and finally said, 'No one should try to fight the inevitable!' Ever since then, Maasai husbands are not interested in the question of whether their wives have lovers."

And yet?

One morning, Oloyetinoy came glowing with excitement.

"Oloyetinoy, what's going on? What's the big deal today?"

"Oh, I caught my younger wife in bed with a boyfriend."

"Why are you so excited, then?"

"Because this is the second time I've seen them! Now he has to pay me a heifer, two blankets, honey... Ah, how I love that woman."

The payment of the "fine" was not immediate. After about two years, Oloyetinoy brewed beer, and invited the lover, who came to his house bearing the possessions. He was welcomed, presented the fine to the homeowner and, as dictated by rule, remained to sleep in his house for one night.

It's nice to catch a lover, but I wanted to get the perspective of the person who had gotten caught. Kitipai had a girlfriend in a nearby village. One day, the old husband caught them together and Kitipai had to pay with a cow. The days went by and the husband passed away. When I heard that the old man had died, I discreetly asked

Kitipai whether now there were no more obstacles, he would resume being the woman's boyfriend. Kitipai replied, "No way. I still love her and I know she loves me. But the cow... Every time I think about spending time with her, I remember that cow... And that cow has already had at least four or five calves, which, in turn, had yet more calves... And all of those could have been mine... So I think it's impossible that we'll go to bed again..."

One day, an Israeli guest came to visit me, and I proposed an exercise: "Stay in the village for as long as you want: one day or a few days, and we'll see if, at the end of your visit, you're able to tell who's married to whom."

I knew with certainty this exercise was doomed to fail.

A married couple or a pair of lovers will exhibit no physical displays of affection, or even any indication they know each other. Not a hug, not a kiss, not a handshake, not a fleeting glance. They can walk past each other with no expression. An absolute introversion, unacceptable to a Western woman like me.

I saw this with Kitapo, who was married off and moved away to live in the groom's village, located not far from my home. There, she received a new first name and a new family name, and entered not an isolated relationship of "couplehood," but rather into the extended family framework. Her husband was a nice young man, and she told me he treated her well and that she loved him. I followed her marriage and relationship from up close, and could discern no external signs of this love.

Throughout the day, every day, Kitapo is with the village women.

They go out to gather firewood and wash their clothes in the stream. They cook the first meal of the day (around noon), and sit in the shade of the tree: stringing beads into necklaces, decorating *kalabashes*, adorning ceremonial hides, shaving the heads of the children or one another, laughing and gossiping.

When Kitapo's husband wants something during the day—to eat lunch, or the soap and loofah to scrub himself when he goes down to bathe in the stream—he goes into the house without looking at his wife, much less calling her. Kitapo follows him with her eyes, rises leisurely and walks toward her home. After he has received what he was after, she returns to the shade of the tree.

The encounters between her and her husband takeplace mostly at the end of the day. The herd returns from pasture to the village stockade, the men roam slowly among the cows, checking for ones that are sick, wounded or weak, while the women are busy milking. Afterwards, everyone goes home to drink tea with milk. Kitapo cooks dinner, while her husband hangs out with his friends, in her own house or in the houses of others. Nighttime hours are the only private time for Kitapo and her husband. While everyone is asleep, they can talk, make love or go to sleep together.

What is the actual significance of marriage? Of a committed relationship? This institution serve both to provide a place for women within a regulated social system and to determine paternity regarding the kids. From her wedding day onward, all children born to Kitapo will be her husband's children, even if they were not born from his sperm. After he dies, if she had more children, they, too, will belong to his family and bear his last name.

Within the framework of the family, both Kitapo and her husband have well-defined obligations, and so long as each fulfills these obligations, life goes on peacefully. With his family's help, the husband builds the village's thorn fence, herding the livestock, providing food for his family, and —slaughtering a goat or sheep when necessary. He is tasked with the "meaty" roles. Kitapo is responsible for the "milk": building the house, giving birth to the children (all of whom belong to the husband and bear his family name), laundry, collecting wood, drawing water, cooking, tending to the calves and kids, and milking.

∼

This division of labor did not seem equitable. Women work hard. In my travels throughout Africa, this was true of all tribal societies. Was this "male liberation"? Why was this the case?

I gradually pieced things together. One day, Oloyetinoy came to visit me around noontime, very hungry. I heaped a plateful of rice and potatoes for him and sat by his side while he ate ravenously. He wiped his lips, looked at me mischievously and said, "Now you're my wife!"

After newlywed Kitapo left her home, she gave a cow to her father so it would be possible for him to eat at her place when he came to visit her. But it wasn't only her father. Even her new husband would not eat the food she had cooked till she gave him a heifer!

Was I understanding this correctly? The new bride has to 'bribe' her relatives so they will eat at her house? Does that sound reasonable?

Cooking for a man, caring for him and doing housework were, I realized, in the woman's best interest! In a society in which a man can marry multiple women and have many girlfriends, women seek a mechanism that will ensure his dependency upon them, a mechanism that will bring him back home, to their house, every day. They like their man to be helpless with household needs, to perpetuate his dependence upon them[14]. They have no interest in "women's liberation" because, in return for these tasks, they receive his protection and commitment toward them!

Was this pattern of behavior exclusive to African women? Once I came to this understanding, I turned my gaze to what was going on in Western societies such as Israel: I saw women who try to instill a helplessness in their talented male partners—a plant manager, a senior military officer, an engineer, a university lecturer, etc. They purchase clothes for them, sew a button on their pants, or pack a suitcase for them. Food, I noticed, was an important way to keep the family close: the preparations for a big family meal such as Sabbath eve dinner might begin as early as two days earlier. The women go shopping and spend time cooking all of their kids' favorite foods, even if these 'kids' were already forty years old.

Both groups of women, I noticed, sought a way to place themselves firmly at the center of family life and to increase their family members' dependency upon them.

I got somewhat swept up in my thoughts, wondering what would happen to the institution of marriage when that center, the woman, would no longer play that role. Was there a different sort of glue to maintain relationships in our society? Modern women—independent career women who leave for work in the morning and heat up precooked meals—sought "liberation" for themselves, but did not consider that they also liberated men from their dependency upon them. The man gets up in the morning, goes to work and eats lunch with his colleagues, men or women. He no longer depends on the family framework to take care of him. Perhaps he no longer needs a wife, either?

∽

Once again, I troubled those around me with the wrong questions. I turned to Kitapo's husband. "Say, are the two of you okay? Do you love her?"

His answer did not surprise me. I had heard it often, phrased in various ways, when I served as the chauffeur of the "newlywed limousine." "When I came to her village and saw my bride for the first time, weeping bitterly, I felt how young and helpless she was. I realized that from now on, she was under my protection, that I had to defend her—and my heart immediately opened up to her."

∽

I popped in to visit Turoto, who lived in a different village with his two brothers and all their wives. Each of Turoto's wives had a house of her own, which Turoto would visit regularly. His desire for multiple wives, he said, stemmed mostly from his wish to have many children. At the heart of this aspiration was the knowledge that the bigger a family is, the more powerful it is. The boys will serve as an auxiliary force to care for the cattle and livestock and will help the parents when they grow older. The girls would assist their mothers when they were young, and when they grew up, would be replaced by the young brides with whom the boys would be matched. Both the boys and the girls would expand Turoto's social network through their marriages.

The popular custom of marrying multiple wives turned the women into a 'limited resource.' But if having multiple wives was so common, the question arose, where were all these women coming from? Or —were there men who stayed single? The answer to this second question was obvious: No! There were no single men. All (other than those who were mentally challenged) got married.

The Maasai attempt to explain the greater number of women compared to men in several ways. One is statistics. They claim that the number of girls born has always exceeded the number of boys[15]. Another reason they cite is that, until a short while ago, *morans*— young men who have undergone the circumcision rite and are in an interim period lasting seven years—often went out on cattle-stealing missions, and many men were killed. Therefore, women have a numerical advantage.

To my understanding, the option of marrying multiple women was made possible by the fact that since ancient times, many non-Maasai women have been incorporated into Maasai society, as they were abducted from their villages during tribal wars; however, today there are no wars, and women come of their own accord, as merchants, from all over the country. They open stores or bars, and soon find shelter in the arms of the local men, an arrangement mutually beneficial. They bring fresh blood to Maasai society, while simultaneously enjoying a man's patronage.

∾

We Westerners are usually appalled by polygamous marriage, projecting our own anxieties upon it—jealousy among the women over the husband's favors, one woman being preferred over another—or bringing in our own cultural values—our perception of committed relationships, perception of intimacy or perception of love. But when we examine polygamy in Maasai culture—in which sex between a husband and wife is not a declaration of love or intimacy (but closer to the biblical commandment to "be fruitful and multiply"), where matrimony should determine to whom the children belong, where a woman may not have sex with her husband throughout her pregnancy and for many months after she gives birth, and where two women (or more) can divide the burden of household tasks between them—perhaps there is nothing wrong with polygamy[16].

∾

And what do the women themselves think about their husband's being married to additional women?

My impression was that most women are indifferent about the prospect of their husband having another wife. Some were even enthusiastic: *great, someone else can share these tasks with me.* In actuality, as in other polygamous societies, there are households where the second wife makes friends with the first and the two become close, while in other households, there is no love lost between the two.

16

AIDS

Miton's mother grew ill.

Several months ago, she had gone to visit her family's village, and since coming back, she had lost weight, lesions appeared all over her body, and she suffered from pain in her sides. Her ability to gather wood or carry water decreased, and she spent most of the day at home, moaning and crying over her bitter fate. I suspected that she had AIDS.

One day, her older son showed up at my house and asked that I drive her to a mission hospital in Tanzania, in an isolated part of the country, on the border with Kenya.

"You know," I told him, "that hospital treats mainly patients with tuberculosis. Your mother doesn't have tuberculosis."

We agreed that the next day, I would drive her to the local clinic for tests, and if nothing was found, we would proceed to the hospital.

At the clinic, I discreetly asked the doctor to test her for AIDS.

The result was positive.

Upon hearing of this, her son begged the doctor not to say anything to his mother, while the doctor implored the son to take her to a particular clinic that treats HIV-positive people and AIDS patients.

∼

A society in which girls are encouraged to have sex so their breasts grow, and the concept of fidelity in marriage is practically nonexistent, provides fertile ground for the spread of sexually transmitted diseases, primarily the one responsible for so many agonizing deaths in Africa.

AIDS as a disease is doubly problematic: first, because the HIV virus does not cause illness. It weakens the immune system, so that ultimately, the body succumbs to malaria, tuberculosis, pneumonia, or any other disease. Therefore, the symptoms of AIDS are hard to identify, and it's typically difficult to convince people of the disease's existence. The second problem is related to the illness's incubation period, which might be prolonged, sometimes up to seven years in which a person is a carrier, meaning he or she is not sick, but can still infect those around them.

For many years, the Maasai were "protected" from AIDS. They had sexual relations within a closed, exclusive society, Maasai with Maasai, and therefore, the virus's infiltration into the society was slow. But in the last two decades, the situation has changed: the lodge employees, absent from their homes for months, find release with the local women; the drivers of tour vehicles also occasionally "sin" with Maasai women. Quite a few Maasai men find girlfriends from different ethnic groups—women who follow the prospering economy to the Mara region, and who open bars or shops.

AIDS was in the air, but I seemed to be the only one who could "smell" it.

I brought up the subject at almost every opportunity, and the people with whom I talked almost always surprised me with their own logic. One day, visiting one of the nearby villages, I sat with seven young men in the shade of a tree. I asked them about two young people who had recently died from a "mysterious" disease that attacked them. They lost a lot of weight and died within three weeks.

"They were in touch with people from Siria (a Maasai tribe)," Kipyiloi replied, "and those people put a curse on them. Their bodies filled with wounds, they lost their strength, grew weak, got thin and died. Suddenly, they were done! But all of that… is because of witchcraft."

I bolted up. "Don't you see? It's AIDS, but when you don't have an explanation, you claim it's witchcraft! So how can you take precautions? How can you understand? Why the hell don't you use condoms?" I went on, pointing at each and every one of them. "Do you have condoms? And you? And you?" None of them did.

Sanguya stopped me. "And what if we want kids?"

"If you want kids, then, and only then, do you not use a condom."

Now Ruben leapt up. "Well then?!"

"What do you mean, 'well then'? Sleep with your wife without a condom, and when you go to your girlfriend, take a condom."

"But what if she wants kids?" Ruben asked.

"Your girlfriend wants kids?" I protested. "Is it okay for her to want kids with you?"

"Of course!" he replied. "You don't understand! When I have a girlfriend who loves me, she wants me to make her a kid to remember me by."

At home, I tried to convince Museré to go get tested. Like Samyan and the rest of the young men, he firmly refused. "If I know that I'm 'positive,' my life will be over. I couldn't be happy."

"Hold on a minute," I stopped him. "And if malaria is found in your blood, would your life be over then, too? Why do you prefer not knowing over knowing and taking care of the problem?"

"That's how our minds work here in Africa. It's a fact! You see…"

I tried again. "Look, Museré, before I got tested, I lived in a state of uncertainty. I preferred to get tested and know that I might be HIV-positive than to live with uncertainty. Can you honestly say that you don't think about AIDS at all? Even when you see the sick people around you?"

His reply was unequivocal. "I can live with not knowing, but not with the thought that there's a disease in my body that could erupt at any moment."

I persisted. "You realize that if you're a carrier, the disease will manifest whether you know about it or not! Don't you prefer to fight it? Why is it that when an elephant or a lion shows up, you Maasai don't close your eyes, and actually go out to fight it, but when a disease that could kill you shows up, you'd rather ignore it?"

Finally, I invited representatives from a non-governmental organization acting to increase awareness of AIDS to come visit us and discuss the topic with the men and the women. After the meeting, which came with party games and demonstrations, they deposited boxes of condoms for free distribution with me and three other people. Two days later, as I was kneeling to blow at the smoking fire, a young man sat down on the bench and said, "Now we know why you invited them and why they left the condoms with you… It's because **you** have AIDS!"

~

I had hoped the meeting helped in raising awareness, but one day, when I asked Saruni whether he used condoms, he answered me seriously: "If I go to a woman and want to put on a condom, she'll ask me, 'Why are you putting that on? You think I'm sick? If that's what you think, go away and don't come back…'"

But the box of condoms remained in my house, and over time—thanks to education in the schools, and propaganda on the radio and on TV—it gradually emptied, hinting at a change in attitude.

17

The Lion Hunt

Kitapo and Lanoi had gotten married, and I was left at home with five boys. One evening, as we sat around the fire waiting for the rice to cook in the pot, I suggested, "Why don't we bring home two more girls?"

The five boys protested at once: "We don't want girls!"

"And who'll help me with the cooking? With the cleaning?"

"We will," they replied as one.

From that day on, I called them "the team."

This team comprised three young boys still uncircumcised, Miton, Leporé and Lemein, and the two teens, Samyan and Museré. I took care of the younger boys, but the older ones took care of me. Although the two had never gone to school, they had tremendous knowledge about the natural life around us, and miraculous survival instincts and spatial orientation. I went out for long journeys on foot with them and their friends, learned how to identify animal tracks, the names of various plants and their beneficial uses. Thanks to them, I experienced quite a few adventures.

One day, Samyan and I drove to visit friends at a village located some distance from our own. We drove slowly on the uneven, bumpy path connecting the two villages. During the rainy seasons, this soil, nicknamed "black cotton," becomes muddy and boggy. Vehicles lose control and slide from side to side on the "cotton," their wheels leaving deep furrows in the ground. Driving during the rainy season requires much concentration so as not to sink into the mud or fall into the ruts. As I drove this time, I was grateful that the rainy season was behind us. The slow pace in which the vehicle drove over the potholes allowed us to watch the animals that crossed our path, grazing and ignoring us: Thompson's gazelles, impalas and zebras.

We found our friends in the village's "living room," the shade of a long-branched acacia tree. We greeted them and sat down on large stones whose location migrated along with the shade, as did our own location.

Usually, every gathering of Maasai from different villages begins with fresh news updates: cows that had contracted foot-and-mouth disease, an upcoming wedding ceremony, who has given birth, how the grass was doing… I sat quietly and savored the rhythm and nature of the conversation: the listeners do not look at the speaker. While he or she speaks, they are busy with various activities, such as sharpening a knife with a stone, carving a shepherd's staff, extracting a thorn from a foot, and so on. Often, they even sit with their back turned to the speaker. But they are attentive, interjecting occasional humming sounds, "E-h-h-h," into the conversation. Each person has a different tone and length to their hum, and all the sounds blend to form a special melody. The speaker continues his story, while the "E-h-h-h" sounds indicate that the attendees are listening. Elephants in nature behave in a similar manner: they are constantly transmitting a low-frequency sound, which we humans cannot hear, into the space. Each elephant transmits and listens. When one elephant goes silent, the others know it is in distress. Here, the attendees' murmurs tell the speaker they are listening. The expression *"nako-ta-lelo"* ("and so on") will conclude his speech, signaling to those present he is done talking, and that a new speaker can now take his turn. And once again, the listeners hum as he tells his tale, waiting patiently for him to finish before they respond.

Suddenly—within the melody of the conversation, as if responding to a signal—everyone got up, called out to me, "Nayolang, wait a minute, we'll be right back," ran quickly into the village, and within seconds, they were galloping out again, holding an assortment of weapons—spears, clubs, bows and arrows—and running up the mountain.

"Hey, hey!" I yelled out to them. "What's going on here? Where are you running off to?"

They dismissed me with a wave of their hand. "Wait here, we'll be right back."

As I wondered what was going on, I saw similar scenes unfolding in the adjacent villages. The men, wearing their red cloaks, burst out of the villages and ran up the mountain. I got into my car, started it and trailed along in their wake. A few minutes later, I caught up with the slower runners, huffing and puffing in the back, who accepted my offer and piled into the vehicle. From them, I learned that a lion had killed a cow at pasture, and they were now on their way to hunt it down.

～

The Maasai are not hunters. In their day-to-day life, they live peacefully alongside the wild animals. However, in their experience, when any predator—a lion, a leopard, a cheetah or a hyena—devours a domesticated animal even once, it will now recognize it and its scent as food and as easy prey, and will attack again. Therefore, whenever domestic animals are attacked, the men are tasked with the mission of finding the wild animal and eliminating it before it kills again.

"But how did you know that a lion had devoured a cow? After all, we were all sitting together under the tree, talking…"

The men sitting in the vehicle seemed surprised. "You didn't hear the shout?"

No. I had heard no shout.

⁓

Until that day, I had not properly appreciated the role and place of the men in everyday life. I always saw them sitting idly under the tree. Now, however, the essence of their role in the familial division of labor was becoming clear. They were not only responsible for taking care of the cattle and for building the fences protecting the villages against wild animals, but their main role was to be the ones standing guard at the gate. They were the "reserve forces" always on alert to prepare for trouble. On many nights, as the dogs barked and the cows moved around restlessly, the men stayed awake, spending most of the night circling the village with flashlights and letting out yells and barking sounds to deter approaching predators. During the day, they did sit in the shade of tree—talking, playing or sleeping. But, all their senses were on high alert.

Today, for the first time, I witnessed those sharpened senses—they had heard the shepherd crying out for help.

The dozens of young men ran straight up the wooded slope of the mountain. I drove the vehicle slowly, trying to make my way between the shrubs and trees. We drifted down into the valley, crossed a small ravine, and approached the herd of cows attacked.

Three of the cows lay dead on the ground, all displaying fang marks on their necks. One man inserted the rear part of his spear into one wound to measure its depth. About four inches emerged dipped in blood.

Fifty men, breathing heavily following their run, were already present. But the yelling continued to roll on from village to village, and in the distance, dozens of additional men could be seen moving up the mountain in our direction.

The shepherd, a young boy, pointed at a large, very dense clumping of shrubs. This was where the attacking lion had retreated.

I looked around me. The great majority of those present were adult, married men. They huddled together, discussing the tactics they must adopt to kill the lion quickly and efficiently. If they succeeded, I knew, their return home would be a victory parade accompanied by dancing and singing describing the course of the battle against the lion. The first to impale the lion with his spear would be honored by receiving its mane, and would also win gifts (cows, sheep, goats) from the elders of the surrounding villages. The women would wait for the warriors' parade and would come out to greet them, showering them with milk from *kalabashes*. I yearned to witness this celebration.

We stood waiting for the last of the men, who trickled in one by one. Suddenly, a sharp yell rang out, and a young man who had just arrived fell writhing to the ground. His friends rushed to him and held him as he shook uncontrollably and wept. The fellow had answered the call to come fight a lion that had killed a cow, but only when he arrived had he discovered that the cow was his own. Two more young men also dropped to the ground, weeping copiously, held by their friends until they regained their composure.

A true commotion.

Cows lowing.

Cries of grief from the mourners.

People talking excitedly.

Suddenly, striding in formation like a military unit, about ten young men emerged from the thicket, looking different from the others. They stood out due to their long hair, tinted, as were their bodies, with red ochre. They were wearing only a loincloth, their upper body bare and adorned with colorful necklaces. They held spears with particularly long and thick metal blades, and seemed determined and full of unconcealed pride. I gaped at them, overcome by their masculinity and the intense strength they projected. This was the first time I had seen *morans* from up close.

The *morans* did not pause near us; they walked right by us as if we were transparent and, with a determined stride, entered the thicket of greenery in which the lion was hiding. My friends explained, "They want to be the ones that will kill the lion. They want its head." By "its head" they meant its mane, from which a fancy headdress would be prepared, to be worn by the first man to impale the lion with his spear.

The *morans'* entrance into the thicket provided the signal, and with few words exchanged, the rest of the men surrounded the shrubs from all directions. I immediately identified the brave ones who entered the fray with a confident step, the less courageous ones forming the outer circle, and the cowards who stayed with me as "translators and guides," meaning they sat in the vehicle. They told me, "Now that the bush is surrounded, it'll only be a few more minutes before the lion dies."

We sat in the vehicle. About five minutes went by. A suspicious silence engulfed us. A while later, we heard the young men's shouts echoing from the thicket, followed by the lion's growl—too close for comfort, as for me. After which it grew quiet again.

Another two or three minutes went by. Nothing happened.

I started the car and circled the shrubs. The view opened up, and a strange spectacle was revealed: the lion, a large male with a thick, cascading mane, whose glorious fur was speckled in blood from the stab of a spear, broke through the siege and ran off. Dozens of young men in their flowing red robes, with their spears thrust out, galloped after him.

I followed them in my vehicle, to a distance of about 550 yards. The lion dove into another group of shrubs and the race stopped abruptly. "Now," whispered my advisors, those warriors who had stayed with me and whose main strength seemed to be in their mouths, "the battle will be concluded within minutes, since this bush is a lot smaller than the previous one."

With no advance warning, a chill-inducing roar rang out.

"This is it!" my "translators" declared.

And then we heard a shout—not a growl, but a shout! —immediately followed by another. Within moments, the thicket broke open, and from it emerged men bearing wounded warriors. The first was a *moran* injured at the base of his skull, with blood dripping from his neck and shoulders. The second, an adult warrior, was bleeding from his stomach. The third, also an adult, was injured in his forehead.

I tore cloth into bands and dressed the wounds to stop the bleeding. The injured were loaded onto my vehicle and we set out for the nearest clinic. On the way, I heard about the exploits of the lion, which, at this stage, was wounded, curling up in its hiding spot in the thicket. The first injured person, the *moran*, walked next to it without spotting it. The lion leapt at him from behind, digging its claws into the back of his head. A second young man approached from behind and plunged his spear into the body of the lion, which flipped around and thrust its claws in his stomach (later, I understood that only the presence of additional warriors had prevented the lion from killing him). The third was injured in his forehead by a knife hoisted by a friend standing in front of him.

∽

The young doctor was appalled to see the three wounded men. He swiftly recruited me to serve as a nurse, helped me put on disposable gloves, gave me a bottle of disinfectant and ordered me to prepare the injured for stitches. I made the rounds from one man to the next, but when I approached the *moran* to cut off some strands of his long hair, intending to sterilize and sew one of the lion's puncture wounds, he shook his head from side to side, preventing me from going near him. His friend, standing by his side and supporting him, explained: the rules not only prohibited cutting the *morans'* hair; it was forbidden for women to touch their hair. After some negotiations, two strands of hair were cut off, and while I gently cleansed the wounds, I heard yelling, wailing and whimpering outside the clinic, growing gradually closer. Finally, the door was opened wide, and a group of women, the mothers and wives of the wounded, stormed inside. Once again, I was impressed by the "bushphone," which had transmitted the news of the wounded warriors as it had transmitted the rumor of the dead cows.

By the late evening hours, all the injured men had been treated. We piled into my vehicle and drove the wounded men to their different villages. Only then did I have time to ask about the victory parade.

"The lion did die, but the victory is his. People were injured, and so there is no celebration," they replied in hushed tones.

18

Morans

The three wounded men recovered.

Oldabash, the *moran* injured at the base of his skull, visited my home along with his friends. As I was the mother of two members of Ilmeshuki—their age group—I became their mother.

I savored their presence. They were like a passing breeze, here one minute, there the next, and this youthful spirit infused my daily routine with new life. I never tired of looking at them—wild, free, powerfully built—and of asking them questions.

"Oldabash, how did you become a *moran*?"

"Like the rest of my friends, I didn't have any choice. I was circumcised four years ago, and entered the Ilmeshuki age group. One day, about two months later, three *morans* arrived in our village. They stayed with us for a day and continued on their way. That day, when I entered my mother's home, I found a shepherd's staff covered with ochre leaning against the entrance wall. That was the signal. I knew I had to join them within twenty-four hours; otherwise, my home would be subject to a curse. You can't refuse[17]. The next day, I took the staff and joined them. Ever since then, for four years now, my friends and I roam all the time, and that's how we recruit new *morans*."

"And what do you do all day?"

"Our mothers built a *manyatta* (a village constructed to conduct the age group's collective ceremonies) for us, to which we come at certain times and receive instructions from the elders, our mentors[18]. Besides that, we roam in small groups of two or three guys throughout the Maasai land. When evening comes, we go into one of the villages on our path, and they host us there. In every single village, there are homes belonging to our age group members. But, you know, we're subject to a lot of taboos and prohibitions. For example, we can't eat any food cooked by women or by uncircumcised boys. That's why, when we get to the villages, usually they give us a sheep as a gift, which we take to a nearby river, slaughter, and have a meat celebration, just for ourselves."

"So you eat a lot of meat! I know that's everyone's passion, but regular people only rarely slaughter livestock."

"That's true, but we're not allowed to eat any food that doesn't originate from cattle and sheep. We live off milk, fat, blood and meat only."

~

Oldabash had long hair cascading nearly to his waist. He was proud of it. Long hair was the *morans*' identifying sign and distinction in a society where men's, women's and children's heads were all shaved. The length of the *moran*'s hair demonstrated the long period for which he had been a *moran*, endowing him with respect. Just like the biblical Samson, he believed his hair was the source of his power and allowed no woman to touch it. The *morans* would sit for hours in the shade of the tree, and like in a prestigious hair salon, style each other's hair distinctly: after dividing the hair with a horizontal part (from ear to ear), they took strand after strand and rolled it between their palms into skinny dreadlocks. The dreadlocks closer to the front of the head were tied together in a special adornment over the forehead. The rest of the longer dreads hung over the back, their ends held with a decorated, carved branch, about six inches long.

The hair, permanently tinted red, was the *moran*'s main source of pride. Other than that, he wore the minimum: a loincloth and a blanket. He and his friends made do with the bare necessities required for their existence: a spear, a bow and a quiver of arrows, a small box with ochre powder, and another box containing fat (customarily mixed with the dye to create a paste applied to the body). However, they took care to adorn themselves with many necklaces and bracelets received as gifts from their girlfriends in various villages.

∽

Much to my joy, my house became a way station for the *morans*. My unique status as a woman who is not Maasai allowed them to diverge from the strict taboo on eating with women. Sometimes, they would arrive after a long walk, half starving, asking me to prepare a dish of rice for them. They would seclude themselves in the other room and wolf down the pot in an instant.

The *morans*' visit always carried a whiff of adventure. One day, Oldabash and his friends received a plump sheep from the members of my village and prepared to spend all day eating it. I was invited to go with them to the *orpul*, a place chosen for the slaughter. According to custom, Maasai women are strictly prohibited from being present in the *orpul*, unless they are girls who have yet to be circumcised (i.e., with a "neutral" gender identity). The stream is not far from the village, but the four walked along its bank until they found an isolated location under a thick canopy of shady trees and settled down there.

They were skilled. One of them found and dragged dry logs and branches to start a fire, another brought water in a small pot from the nearby stream. The third cut green branches with his long knife and laid them down as a pallet for the cuts of meat chopped up. The last of them began the slaughter: he leaned his full weight against the sheep, blocking the air passages in the mouth and nostrils with his hand. After verifying that the animal was dead, he gently perforated the main artery and collected the blood in a big cup. He then skinned the animal and carefully peeled off the layer of fat enveloping the sheep's body, until he was holding it in his hands like a woolly white cloak. Meanwhile, one of the other *morans* broke off thin branches and built the fire. He and another *moran* examined the sticks and chose two. One was short, broad and soft, while the other was long, rounded and harder. I was then in for a spectacular demonstration: one *moran* knelt, holding the short stick by both ends on the ground. The other knelt next to him, held the longer stick between his open, taut palms, and rubbed his hands together very fast while rotating the stick and pushing it down. The scent of scorching filled the air, and an ember formed on the softer horizontal stick. The ember was collected and carefully placed on the kindling prepared in advance. Light blowing—and a fire burned.

I watched them, thinking that at that moment, I was observing the very essence of survival ability : these people could sustain themselves with merely a knife and a spear! With the spear, they could kill an animal, while the knife would allow them to prepare "fire sticks," chop kindling, dissect the animal and roast its meat.

∽

I sat down in the shade and continued to watch them, my thoughts drifting to a different survivalist event that had taken place about a year earlier. I had loaded up my vehicle with drinking water, picked up two Maasai friends, and the three of us left on a two-day trip to visit their families' distant villages. My vehicle, that same newlywed limousine, was one of the oldest models of the Toyota Land Cruiser. I loved its two major advantages: a back seat that could be folded back, allowing a mattress to be laid down for sleeping, and a convertible roof for convenient viewing of wildlife. The car, with only three gears but with a powerful, simple engine that could be easily repaired with plyers and a piece of metal wire, was so old it broke down frequently (so frequently that every fifteen miles, I had to lift the hood or crawl under it to tighten screws, free the locked brakes and so on), allowing me to exhibit mechanical skills I never knew I had.

The atmosphere in the vehicle was pleasant. I often embarked on such trips, knowing that far from home, in nature, with only two or three Maasai, a more open ambience would prevail, expanding the topics of conversation.

My friends directed me to a narrow path among the tangled acacia trees, a route unfamiliar to me. The overgrown grass indicated that even cows did not graze here. Immense dead logs lay on the ground blocking the path, branches dangled down from above and scratched the roof of the car, and the orange leaves of the croton shrubs signaled that we were at the peak of the dry season, which made many plants shed their leaves in a "heat autumn." Inside the thicket, I watched the animals we came across: ground squirrels with an impressive fluffy tail crossed the path and rushed to their underground burrows. Dwarf mongooses stood on their rear legs, sniffing their surroundings with their narrow snouts, while dik-diks (small antelopes) stood in pairs under the shrubs, like statues, watching the vehicle as it approached and drove off again. Reddish-brown impalas skipped around with impressive leaps and wagged their short tails in excitement. Giraffes stood still, turned their heads toward us and tracked us from up high.

I focused on the path. Before me was a steep drop into one wadi, on a route furrowed by water. A pit gaped at its center. I switched to first gear and carefully maneuvered the vehicle downward. The rise on the other side did not seem problematic, but the moment the front of the vehicle turned up and climbed a yard or two—the engine died.

I tried to start the vehicle while propelling it back—nothing.

A brief look at the engine revealed no loose cables or hoses. I tried to start the car again, to no avail. I was afraid that the battery might be weak—and if this was the case, we should push-start the car.

But my paralyzed metal jalopy stood immobile in the center of the wadi, solid and determined, with slopes rising on both sides of it; three people could not budge it.

We spent the night in the wadi. We lit a fire, put on a kettle for tea and snacked on a loaf of bread we had taken with us for the trip.

In the morning, one guy set out on foot, carrying a brief letter to the local mechanic. I knew he had a long way to go and we had many hours of waiting ahead of us. Gradually, my hunger increased, and I asked Kitaro, who had stayed with me, "What will we do if the mechanic doesn't make it here today? What are we going to eat?"

Kitaro looked at me, puzzled. "There's plenty of food here. Don't worry."

"Food? Where do you see food?"

Kitaro pointed at a male impala standing motionless, close to us. "That's food! Hey," he leaped up enthusiastically. "Maybe you want some honey?" Without waiting for my answer, he said, "Give me the matches and wait for me for ten minutes." I handed him the matches and he disappeared.

I was left on my own. Heavy silence engulfed me, only interrupted occasionally by the buzzing of the flies and the gnats. I lay down in the shade of the trees, with my ankles crossed, and took great pleasure in my fate. About half an hour went by. From afar, I heard the thicket of shrubs moving and then Kitaro's approaching footsteps. He popped up abruptly from one bush, his face radiant. His hands were full of honeycombs, dripping down onto the ground and creating a sweet path.

When the mechanic arrived toward evening, we were still avidly chewing the honeycombs and sucking out the honey.

There I first learned to appreciate these guys' ability to survive.

~

Now at the *orpul* with the *morans*, I watched as the layer of fat peeled off the sheep was gently placed in a pot on the fire. The slabs of meat were chopped up, and each found its place: the ribs were impaled on a pointy stick thrust into the outskirts of the fire, roasting slowly. Other cuts were sliced into small pieces, like shish kebab, and placed in the pot of fat for prolonged cooking. Bones and other parts were placed in a large pot to be cooked into soup, enhanced with branches and tree bark. The stomach lining, which looked like a thorny balloon, received special treatment: it was cleaned of its contents, washed in water and placed aside. At night, they told me, they wore it like a shower cap to protect their unique hairdos.

The contents of the stomach looked like green grass mush. The *morans* took out their knives and polished them in this goo—they said it protected them from rust.

While the meat was cooking in the pot, the *morans* now turned to pampering themselves. One after the other, they went down to bathe in the river, taking care to move aside to where my gaze could not reach them. After getting clean, they began to "dirty" themselves meticulously and thoroughly: they took out red ochre powder from a small metal box, mixed it with fresh fat from the pot to create a red paste, and painted their body with it. With each other's help, they used their fingers to create patterns of waves and curves over their entire bodies. They applied the rest of the dye to their long hair, shaking it back and forth with pleasure while jumping and letting out growls. They were pleased with themselves and now ready to eat.

The Maasai's favorite food is *menono*, and one of them was now busily preparing it: he removed the fat-filled pot in which the cuts of meat were cooking from the fire. The excess fat, which had turned liquid, was drained, and now, while the meat was still very hot, he poured blood over it. The blood congealed immediately over the slabs of meat, creating a crispy coating. Using a knife, several branches were carved into spoons, and we all descended upon the meal. The meat and fat enhanced the steaming dish, and the blood gave it a subtle saltiness. It was a true gourmet dish.

The *menono* was the opening for a feast that lasted for many hours until all the meat was consumed. When I marveled at the four's capacity for eating, they revealed the secret: the beverage they were drinking between courses—made from the bark of one variety of acacia trees—helped them with rapid digestion of the meat.

At the end of the meal, in the late afternoon hours, we returned to the host village. Sated, pleased and jolly, the *morans* danced.

We all gathered round to watch. They thrust their spears into the ground in one spot, hanging the small metal boxes containing all of their personal possessions—the sheep fat, the ochre powder, beads and fragments of round or polished shells serving as hair accessories—upon them. One of them sang, and the others joined him. The singing sounded like a lion's growl: monotonous yet soothing. They created a half-circle, which other young men from the village joined. Two by two, they entered the circle and leaped. I was thrilled to see how, from a complete standstill, they leapt to a great height, jumping again and again, like bouncy springs. An unspoken competition was taking place among the jumpers—not only who would leap higher, but who would keep doing so for longer. They ended the jumping by quickly tossing their heads back and forth, creating a wave of sorts that propelled their long hair back.

The jumping reminded me of the seemingly odd behavior of

gazelles when encountering a predator: instead of rising and fleeing, the gazelles station themselves in front of the predator and leap in place again and again, as if signaling: *we're fleet of foot and fit, and therefore we're allowing ourselves to expend energy on this ostentatious display. So, if you're seeking prey to devour—look elsewhere.*

The *morans*' ostentatious display was intended for the women and girls watching them. They, too, joined the dance, forming a half-circle of their own across from the men. Their dance included a slight bending of the knees accompanied by a vigorous shaking of their shoulders, and their high voices blended in with the men's low growling sounds.

Evening came. The sounds of the bells from the approaching cows rang out from afar, signaling the end of the dancing and the beginning of evening chores. I said goodbye to Oldabash and his friends, who went on their way, heading for another village and new adventures.

∼

The lifestyle of the *morans*, characterized by freedom, independence, joie de vivre, lack of commitment and a certain recklessness, reminded me of young people who take a "gap year," consisting of a long road trip, or a journey to India or South America, before they head off to college. I'm certain there are similarities between the two phenomena, as in both cultures, Western and Maasai, this is an interim period in which young people are removed from the social order, with its strict laws and rules (in our society—elementary school, middle school and high school, higher education, work, marriage, kids and a mortgage; few evade this social order), as if society is telling these youths: *take a time-out dedicated to going wild and breaking the rules, as when you return, you will be channeled back into a system of laws, arrangements and rules that won't leave you much wiggle room.*

But there is still one difference. Whereas in our society, this interim period usually lasts a year or two at most, the Maasai version involves an interval of seven years. Why?

To discover the answer, I tried to slip on the mantle of the Maasai perception, which, as I'd already realized often, was motivated by considerations of survival. I interrogated Tabula, Oloyetinoi and Saruni, and gradually, I attained a more nuanced understanding of the essence and necessity of the *moran* period, and its lengthy duration.

Maasai logic posits that to survive, i.e., ensure the livelihood of a family and livestock within a life utterly dependent upon the whims of nature, each adult must know where there are springs that can provide water during a drought, where the grass remains green even during dry seasons, what plants are edible and which should be avoided, where distant family members live, which rivers never run dry, and where the cows can be taken to lick salt.

While they are *morans*, society actually forces the boys who, till now, have grown up within the village boundaries, to learn—with their own bodies, senses, arms and legs—lessons in geography, civics, botany, zoology and survival. At the end of this seven-year period, they will acquire all the knowledge that a person living in this environment needs to deal with the forces of nature.

I thought of one more reason, and assumed Oloyetinoi would not acknowledge it. Beneath the surface, a constant tension exists between the different age groups regarding attaining positions of political power. When the men within a certain age group turn forty, a new age group opens, and they become its mentors, which endows them with political power they do not want to relinquish. Therefore, it's in their best interest to extend the recruitment of the boys and the *moran* period much, thus enjoying their own power for a greater length of time. In addition, the time limitation on each age group is a way of neutralizing the inter-generational tension, as everyone knows when their time to ascend to power will come.

But that was still not all. As Oloyetinoi had told me, sending the boys away for such a long period of bonding had additional importance, related to the relatively short life expectancy. Recruiting them into an age group and turning them into a separate, distinct unit for such a long time would bond them to each other with mutual loyalty and responsibility, in a relationship that would last forever. And so, while our society relies mostly on "vertical" mutual responsibility[19] (grandfather, father, son, grandson and great-grandson), Maasai society has created a system of "horizontal" commitments that will accompany its members throughout their lives.

~

I had heard that sometimes, *morans* gather in large groups, collect many sheep and spend long periods of time in the *orpul*. They slaughter sheep after sheep, eat well and go wild. In the distant past, they would invite young girls to come stay with them.

Naseyu had been a *moran* for about two years. I asked him, "Is there truth to the stories about how you used to invite girls down to the bush and party with them?"

"When the *morans* are in the *orpul*, they don't have sex with girls, because we believe that having sex depletes all the power you gain from eating meat. We used to invite girls to the bush to have fun with them: we danced, we sang, we told stories, but under no circumstances did we have sex. At nights, before we went to sleep, we'd gather branches and arrange a soft pallet. The girls would sleep in the middle, while we slept on both sides of them to watch over them.

"But when we sleep in the villages—then we can have sex with almost anyone. Not just girls—the young women like to fool around with us too."

This conversation and additional similar ones revealed another reason why boys at the height of their prowess are excluded from society for such a prolonged period of time: after they are circumcised, the boys are eligible for marriage, and may have sex with almost any woman[20] (both uncircumcised girls and circumcised girls their own age who have gotten married). Therefore, they are potential competitors for their fathers not only regarding their existing wives but regarding their future ones. It's in the fathers' best interest to distance their sons and to postpone the age in which they get married for long, so the fathers can continue marrying additional women with no competition. Therefore, this interim period in which the boys are sent away from the villages for a prolonged duration actually decreases the tension between the young men and their fathers over this limited resource—women! The compensation the *morans* receive—celebrations of meat, almost unlimited sex and roaming the Maasai land freely—will apparently ensure they will not rebel against their fathers.

19

The Nose Does Not Precede You

Day followed day. Some days were cloudy, others were rainy, but on most days, a hot, radiant African sun fiercely beat down upon us. Here, in Maasai Mara, I realized that the familiar units of time—"hour," "day," "week"—were not universal. There are places where hours or days fly by quickly, while in other places, "an hour" lasts quite a while, long beyond its sixty brief minutes. I could feel this most acutely on days when I sat with the women in the shade of the tree from the morning hours on. Time went by at a crawl, with unbelievable slowness. Keeping track of the passing days became impossible. Tracking the days of the week, if it was done, was based on market days in the region's trading centers. The market in Olelemutia takes place in two days? Well today is Sunday.

I thought of Robinson Crusoe (with whom, in my cultural isolation, I sometimes identified); he adapted to a solitary life in nature, but was appalled by the thought he might lose track of time: "After I had been there about ten or twelve days, it came into my thoughts that I should lose my reckoning of time... and should even forget the

Sabbath days.'"

This was the exact sensation with which I was living. Why did I feel so lost without knowing the time?

~

The lack of attention to the hour, the clock, the time, is an integral part of life here.

One evening, in one of the first months after I got settled in the village, a young man showed up at my home and asked that the next day, we drive down to bring a bride to his village. I agreed.

"What time do you want to leave?" I asked.

"Oh… around five in the morning," he replied. I gently declined, and we agreed on six a.m.

As a Westerner who had still not adapted to her new environment, I set my alarm clock, got up half an hour earlier, got ready and waited. And waited. And waited. Finally, the fellow showed up at seven fifteen. A fairly small delay, relatively speaking.

This was not the first such incident. Time after time, I set appointments with people, and was constantly upset when they showed up hours or days later. At first, I was angry at them. Later, I wondered at my own reactions: why was I so dependent on the watch I wore on my wrist? It was obvious that calculations of time in modern society were arbitrary: a day consisting of twenty-four hours, each divided into sixty minutes, and so on. The clock, an artificial creation on which the modern world was dependent, had equalized all dimensions of time. Minute followed minute, hour followed hour, and hypothetically, there was no difference between one dimension of time and the next. There was no difference between day and night,

---

*   Daniel Defoe, *Robinson Crusoe*, https://www.gutenberg.org/files/521/521-h/521-h.htm.

between summer and winter. We have drifted away from listening, both to our own bodies (we don't eat when we're hungry, but when the lunch break is declared) and to nature: in houses air-conditioned, spring does not have the same meaning it has for the Maasai who sees buds blossoming or calves being birthed in their season.

Why did I expect my Maasai friends to subject themselves to the same arbitrary method of measuring time so obvious but so foreign to their own nature? Is the perception of time not unique to each society's culture? For example, in contemporary society, time has become financially valuable in its own right (as reflected in expressions such as "my time is precious," "you're wasting my time," "time-suck," "time is money," and so on). But time is not merely its financial value. Time has value of itself ("time is on my side"). That is why we denizens of modern society must keep time and to save time. Among the Maasai, as I learned the hard way, value is attributed to the activity itself, to social or natural phenomena, and not to abstract time (meaning that value is attributed to the "big rain" that has come down, not to the month when it rained). Thus, for example, no one documents or even remembers birthdays. The value is in the birth itself, not in the time it took place. When I asked a friend about the ages of several girls in the village, she replied: "When I gave birth to Sintoya, Taté had already been weened, and Neshelu was very pregnant with Kitayo…"

But there is one more significant difference: we perceive time as continuously consecutive, as events commencing in the past (most of us count years from the same point, Year Zero), entering the present and continuing on into the future. We perceive time as advancing from the past toward the future, and treat it accordingly. We are all oriented toward the future: we do things now (study, work) due to our thoughts of the future (a better job, accumulating property, saving for the children).

In Maasai society, the present—and it's a good thing we got

there—is the most important thing. Reference to chronological time is irrelevant. There is no "forward." The seasons "move"—rainy season, dry season, rainy season, dry season—while the people "stand still." The people are always here and now, in the present, whether it's rainy or arid. The Maasai also know that the length of each season varies, and therefore the concept of a "year" (in the sense of twelve months) is also meaningless.

∼

I learned more about the concept of the future when Museré, who, at twenty-three was already a mature man, let me know he intended to go on a journey that would last a while.

"Where to, exactly?"

"I don't know," he replied. "Maybe to the Lemek area."

"For how long?"

"I don't know."

"What do you intend to do?"

"I don't know…"

As an inquiring mother, I tried to extract more details from him. "You're setting out just like that? What are your plans? What's your direction?"

Museré did not relent. "Nayolang, how can I tell you where I'm going before I've gone? Don't worry, when I come back I'll tell you everything…"

I persisted. "Look, when I want to go on a journey, I have plans! For example, in a week, I'll go to Nairobi to buy some parts for the car. I intend to stay there for two days and then come back. Sometimes the plan doesn't work out, sometimes it goes off track, but it exists. What can you tell me about your travel plans? Do you have any idea how long you'll be gone?"

Museré briefly lost his composure and said, "The nose does not precede you!" I raised an eyebrow, and he explained, "How do you want me to tell you what's going to happen, when I still haven't left on the journey, and I don't know where my feet will take me, who I'll meet, and what kind of offers I'll get? When I come back, everything will be behind me. Then I'll be wiser, and I can tell you."

I was left speechless. For me, the future existed; it was tangible, planned and known (next year, I'll go for a trip in Indonesia, sign up for a drumming class, and so on). For him, the future contained a general, vague plan. And what would happen there? A person could only know that once the future became the past...

I realized I had not phrased my questions correctly. I now tried to ask in a different manner. "What made you think of a trip to Lemek?"

For this question, he had an answer prepared: "I have a friend who lives in Lemek and I received a message that he wants to see me."

Museré said goodbye to us and set out on his way. I watched him walk off, tall and erect. A knife was strapped to his waist, a shepherd's staff clutched in his hand, and a red checkered blanket draped over his back. That was all.

This time, as always, I marveled at how a Maasai man (or, alternately, a woman—but this was rarer) who sets out on a journey—to see relatives, to collect a sheep as payment for an old debt, to create a marriage alliance, or to sell a cow in the cattle market located a two-day walk away—could simply rise and be ready to go.

"Hey, hold on a minute," I wanted to call out to him, "what about sunglasses, sunscreen, a hat, water, money? Plus a sleeping bag? A tent?"

This ability to decide, to get up and just take off, was an option for Museré thanks to the double social network—his association with an age group and his association with a clan—that shaped Maasai hosting customs. I saw it in action almost every day when visitors stopped by at our village. I knew that around evening time, Museré would pause by one village and stand outside it for a few minutes until people approached him: *Where did you come from? Where are you going? What age group do you belong to? What clan do you belong to? What news from the entire region do you bring with you?* In the conversation, he would discover where in the village he could find a house belonging to a member of his age group, or, if there was none to be found, one belonging to a member of his clan, and head out toward this "relative's" home, a house and people he might have never seen before. At this house, he would be welcomed: he would eat, drink and sleep before getting up the next morning and continuing on his way.

In this manner, he could wander for a prolonged period, knowing he would never find himself without a place to lay his head or enjoy a nourishing meal.

~

The traveler's finest hour is his return from his travels.

The villagers will arrive, one by one, to sit with him and hear about his adventures. The story of the journey may last for many days as the storyteller spares no details: "I started my trip on the day the goat got lost and was eaten by a hyena. The *matatu* (public transportation vehicle) I got on had seven other passengers. Two men and a woman were Maasai, and the rest weren't Maasai. The two men were from that village, and the woman was from another village. The main topic of conversation on the *matatu* was about the ongoing drought, and the two men said that in the hills above their village, there was still green grass…" And so the traveler continues to unfurl his tale. A good storyteller knows how to mesmerize his listeners, imbuing life into his descriptions and varying his intonation in the right places. To his listeners, the story is not merely a source of amusement; they can use it to learn many details about what is going on in the region—will any ceremonies take place soon? Have some good pasture areas been found? And what is the price of cows in distant markets?

∼

I returned from a trip to Lake Naivasha, a freshwater lake about a five-hour drive away from us. I was joyfully welcomed by my household members. We put a kettle for tea on the fire, and as I had learned to do here, I described my journey. The tale went on and on. We finished drinking the second cup of tea, and were still all curled up in blankets around the fire. I continued to describe the lake, the volcanic hills around it, and the mighty Mount Longanot, a volcano towering above the lake from the south. I described the "yellow fever" acacia trees growing to great heights, casting shade over the banks of the lake where hippopotamuses loll about during the day, emerging every night to trample the farmers' fields. I struck the pot with a stick to demonstrate the sounds the farmers make every night to scare off the terrifying invaders, sounds that resembled a dance for the forest gods.

When I finished my story, I asked the people around me, "And what was it like over here while I was gone?"

Samyan volunteered to answer. "You left on Talek market day (Wednesday). And we here sat and sat, sat and sat, doing nothing. The next day we also sat and sat, sat and sat, and did nothing, and on Friday we sat, sat, sat…"

I burst out in peals of laughter and all the attendees joined me.

∼

Nighttime. The blanket of stars envelops the sleeping house, protecting it. An indecipherable mumble from the other room occasionally disrupts the silence. Even a hyena's voice is not heard tonight. The quiet pounds at my temples. I had woken up, needing to go out and use the toilet. My restroom facility is about thirty yards from the house: a concrete surface with a large opening gaping over a pit not particularly deep, surrounded by branches and shrubs. I don't dare walk all the way there. Not in such darkness, where I cannot even see the tip of my own nose. The blackness is absolute. I turn on the flashlight, crack open the door of my room, illuminate the area around the house, and see that my neighbor the porcupine, who visits every night, has come by, eaten the potato peels we threw out, and marked my doorstep with his odorous droppings. I venture two or three yards outside the house and relieve myself. I am extra-cautious because once, I had left the house without a flashlight, walked two or three yards, sat down and heard an elephant's stomach gurgling right next to me.

This night, once again, there is no moon, meaning we are at the end of the month.

Similarly to Jewish culture, the Maasai calendar is based on the lunar cycle (the Maasai word for "month," *olapa*, is identical to the word for "moon"). But unlike the Jewish calendar, the Maasai divide the month into two parts: the first fifteen days are called "white moon" (*oibor alapa*). On these days, the white-hued moon is visible in the sky during the day; this period commences when the moon first "shines" as a thin crescent, and lasts until the fifteenth day of the month, when it rises in the horizon on the east, large and round, just as the sun sets in the west. The days of the second half of the month, in which the moon appears after the sun has set, are called "darkness nights" (*eneymen*).

I initially found this seeming arbitrary division odd. On the sixteenth day of the month, about forty five minutes after the sun sets, the moon also rises looking round, large and radiant, and yet this night already belongs to the "nights of darkness." However, since there is no electricity, once darkness falls, people ensconce themselves in their homes. Therefore, the ascent of a large, round (if slightly flawed) sphere after darkness has fallen is not relevant to them.

The "white moon" nights are the joyful ones. The planes are illuminated with a silvery, radiant light. The children stay outside until late into the night, singing, dancing and playing while the women cook at home. The older boys take advantage of the natural lighting and walk to more distant villages to meet girls and peers their own age. "White moon" nights are considered lucky, and therefore most ceremonies will take place during this period[21].

On the rare rainy "white moon" nights, we may be lucky enough to see a "night rainbow," formed because of the combination of a full moon in the east and rain in the west. The "rainbow" is white and looks like the beam of a spotlight in a rock show.

This night, in which there is no moon, is a quiet night in the village. Each family sits in its home, busy chatting, telling stories and cooking. The men are in a state of alert, as during such times, wild animals please approach the village fence to capture plump prey.

20

Maasai Justice

The cultural gaps were having their way with my household. It had been four years since we moved into the crowded little house, and my relationship with No'oltwati was deteriorating. I felt that despite our frequent conversations about the way we lived our life together, in which each of us had to do her part, No'oltwati was constantly shirking household tasks, and they all fell upon me, from cleaning up to participating, however symbolically, in financial expenses. Once again I was facing a dilemma, as the cost of our groceries was low, and I could shoulder it all But was it the right thing to do? Wouldn't I be encouraging exploitation and dependency?

After several conversations did no good, I privately declared a "sugar war": I would purchase everything for the household—other than sugar, which I could do without, but was essential for the Maasai. With an apathetic expression, every morning and evening for four days, I brewed tea without sugar, amused to see how No'oltwati kept up her resistance before finally contributing her part to the household and purchasing sugar.

Our friendship was quickly withering away, and we were having a hard time getting it back on track.

We divided the kitchen, and under the same roof, established two cooking niches, and each of us cooked for her own children. No'oltwati began to sic her husband Kitipai and his family on me, and they threatened me. Her husband, who was often drunk, would raise and wave his *rungu* at me every time he saw me. One day, I returned home and found another lock over my own lock. No'oltwati had blocked me from entering the house. I felt threatened, assaulted and frightened.

I had lived in the village enough years to know what every threatened woman would do—go to seek advice from the members of her father's or husband's age group. I turned to Turoto, who was a member of my age group, and asked for his protection, which was immediately granted. That same evening, a small council was convened, consisting of him and his peers. I bought them beers, and throughout the evening, they conducted a discussion, after which they turned and said, "Look, according to our understanding, it's true that Kitipai and No'oltwati invited you to live here and build a house, but they didn't expect you to live here for so many years. They thought you'd build a house, stay here for a year or two, take off and then leave them the house. And you? Do you really intend to leave?"

I said I wasn't.

"Therefore," they continued, "early tomorrow morning, go see our chief, whose role is to settle disputes. Describe the chain of events to him, and he'll take care of you."

The chief welcomed me into his home. I described the pattern of harassment to him and asked him to intervene. Much to my relief, he promised that on the upcoming Sunday, he would come to our village, summon both sides and discover what the commotion was all about. He gave me a letter addressed to the local police, ordering them to provide me with any protection required.

On the morning of the trial, several dozen people gathered under the large tree in our neighborhood: most men, the area's police officers, park rangers, and any bored passersby wanting to see a trial involving "the white woman of ours." There were only two women present in the audience: No'oltwati and myself. From somewhere, a chair was brought over and placed in the shade for the chief, while the rest of us all sat on the ground. The hearing began.

Kitipai was the first to speak, and as was the custom during hearings, was the only one to stand up. He began by greeting the attendees before commencing his speech. Holding his staff in his right hand, he stamped it vigorously upon the ground while pacing back and forth every time he wanted to emphasize a point. He talked at length about my friendship with his wife, about the trip to the hospital that had saved No'oltwati's life, and how, following that trip, I was invited to live with them in the village. After he finished speaking, he sat down, and another man stood up. After his opening greeting, he, too, paced back and forth while vigorously stamping his staff on the ground as he talked about my contribution to society: how I had used my vehicle to transport cows that had broken their legs, thus saving their lives, how I had driven many people to hospitals and clinics, and, on a different note, how I had offered my vehicle as a 'limousine' to be used by newlyweds. He described how they had invited me, with much eagerness, to live with them, and how I had found my place among them. As the discussion continued, some speakers rose to object to my presence: *It's true that we invited her and that she helps us, but actually—why does she stay?*

As the discussion continued, I was asked to rise and speak up for myself. I got up, greeted the attendees, and while holding a staff in my right hand, described my relationship with the village, a complex relationship due to the vast difference between the world I had come from and my one. I explained that I did not help because I was "white" or "rich," but because in the society I came from, this was the usual attitude among relatives, and I felt thankful to them for warmly adopting me, and that I saw them as family.

"However," I continued, using imagery from the local repertoire, "I want to tell all of you that I feel sad. I feel sad that people who I thought had adopted me as family, and whom I adopted back, merely saw me as a cow! A cow only taken care of, watched over and cherished as long as it can be milked. But the moment it produces less milk, it is immediately a candidate for slaughter." I took a deep breath and continued. "I moved to live among you many years ago, but during all those years, I made one big mistake. Very big!" I paused for a moment and struck the ground with the staff forcefully.

Everyone sat up expectantly. I stalled to enhance the impression, stamped the staff again, and added, "The one mistake I made was… not taking a husband for myself! In this society, a woman with no husband is, in fact, left to her own devices. She has no support and no protector. Would any of you dare to claim you wanted my house if I had a husband? Oh, I feel so sad…"

~

The hours went by. The sun moved along its path in the sky, and the shade of the tree, and the attendees, moved along with it. Hunger gnawed at everyone, but as in every Maasai gathering, each person felt a need to contribute to the discussion. Time was meaningless. I looked at the chief. Throughout the discussion, he sat in his chair and listened. Occasionally, he huddled with a man or two, but otherwise, he did not say a word. I wondered what he was thinking and when he would rise to say his piece.

Jackson, the local policeman, also Maasai, rose to speak, surprising us all with his passionate message. "I want to tell all of you that

I'm ashamed! Today, I am ashamed to be a Maasai! Among us sits a woman who has helped save lives quite a few times. We invited her to live with us, with no time limitation. She built her home on public land, not on private territory. Since moving here, she has continued to help us! And even now, when some of us are harassing her due to greed—we have not heard her get up and ask for her money back, the money she invested in saving lives. And all of you know that we're talking about hundreds of thousands of shillings! And now, instead of saying 'thank you' again and again, we want to force her to leave? It's disgraceful! This is an attitude that is unworthy of our hospitality as Maasai. This gathering is a chance for us to tell her that we're sorry. That we behaved uncivilly! A chance to tell her she's welcome to stay among us for as long as she likes, and on the day she leaves —she may do so in good spirits and remember us fondly."

Jackson was not the last speaker. The discussion continued, and more men rose to speak.

Suddenly, at a certain moment, everyone got up and turned to leave.

"Hey!" I got up. "What now? What was decided?"

~

I had been present at other trials, shorter or longer than my own, which always ended in an identical manner: at some point, after four hours or four days, an agreement is reached among everyone present. The audience recognizes which way the wind is blowing, all objections dissipate, and the discussion ends. Usually the hearing does not end with a verdict of "guilty" or "innocent," but, a solution is found to which all parties can agree. As always, to this day, I am apparently the only one in the audience who misses the subtle nuances and overlooks the turning point, still waiting for a verdict of "innocent" or "guilty."

The Western method, which requires a majority of at least one vote (or one percent) to reach a decision, is perceived as odd here: it creates an intolerable situation where, after the vote, forty-nine percent of the public might remain displeased—people who still have to live side by side and continue with their daily lives as usual.

The Maasai must reach a unanimous decision, in which all parties are in agreement. So long as there is no agreement, the discussion goes on and on and on. There's no shortage of time. This method of reaching an agreement has an important advantage: no extreme decisions can ever be made. An extreme decision may only be reached when there is a pressure group and a majority. However, when one side has to convince another - that holds very different views - to reach an agreement, both sides have to edge closer to each other in their opinions.

In addition, because there is no verdict of "guilty" or "innocent" in disputes between people, society does not shame the guilty, and therefore, it's easy for everyone to quickly re-establish routine.

In my case, the general agreement was that No'oltwati must leave my home, that I could continue living here for as long as I wanted, and that when I left, I could decide to whom I would give the house.

But I was still wondering about one thing: why hadn't the chief intervened at all?

The answer was clear to everyone present but me.

"Look," Museré explained, "if the chief had intervened in your favor, everyone would have spoken up against him. And if he stood up to speak for the Maasai, you yourself would have objected, claiming he put tribalism over justice. Therefore, he maintained a policy of neutrality, but occasionally summoned various speakers, and used them to shape the climate of the proceedings."

∼

For a long time after the trial, I continued to contemplate the Maasai system of laws and rules, and the manner in which they resolve disputes. Isn't it surprising to see how hundreds of thousands of people conduct their lives under their tradition, with no police, no courts, no organized, formal system of laws, and yet crime rates among them are minute?

One reason for this, I assumed, was the paucity of material possessions. I realized just how meager these possessions were when, one day, I drove a family—a father, his two wives and five children—to a new village. The family's main property, comprised of cattle and livestock—their hide marked with a branding iron[22]—had been sent out that morning with one boy. The family members fit into my vehicle with room to spare, along with all their possessions: the cowhides (mattresses) rolled up together on the roof, three plastic bowls, four pots of various sizes, and two metal trunks containing the private possessions of the two wives. The few houseware items—plates, glasses, spoons and so on—were placed in a big sack, and the children's clothes were crammed into another sack. That was all. Therefore, there is no incentive for theft, anyway.

Another strange reason for the rareness of crime is that the boundaries of permitted behavior are very broad. People may do many things before their actions are defined as a crime. In one village lived a kleptomaniac. Everyone knew him, and every time objects disappeared from one house, they all knew he was responsible. People complained about the inconvenience of things disappearing, but no one bothered to go to the chief or to the police and complain about him. No one saw him as a criminal who should be banished from society.

A very important incentive to preventing crime, stems from highly intimidating penalties for unforgivable crimes. Such penalties have been passed on from generation to generation and continue to be applied today. For example, if people are caught slaughtering or eating a stolen cow, each must pay a fine of five cows[23] to the cow's owner.

If a man is killed in a dispute, the victim's relatives will try to catch the murderer and kill him. Usually, however, the killer escapes, receives the protection of his family members, and once the victim's relatives calm down, negotiations will begin. The fine consists of sheep, and when the offense is murder, the number of sheep must include the number forty-nine[24]. This might be enough for some people, while others might demand 149, or 249! This is a very large fine, and no household can pay it all by itself. Therefore, the killer's clan members must step up and contribute livestock of their own. Thus, a heavy responsibility rests on the shoulders of anyone who "decides" to kill—a responsibility that extends to all his clan members, who must pay for his sin.

"Hold on a minute," I asked Tabula one day. "And what happens when a woman is murdered?"

Eyebrows were raised all around me. "We don't know about any law regarding murdering a woman because… it would never occur to us to murder women!"

And yet? I turned to the elders, who came up with an answer: the murderer of a woman must undergo a purification ceremony. Otherwise, the dead woman's spirit will put a curse on all members of the killer's household.

Similarly to my case, and in nearly all cases, if someone commits a crime, or when a dispute breaks out between people, society will handle the problem within the framework of the family, the village or the region, and avoid involving the authorities.

∼

During my first years in the village, I experienced a small crisis every time I returned from a trip. The transition from the Western world—with its tumult of cars, the pace of life, food, computers, TV, sirens, phones—to the tranquility of village life, the chirping of birds waking me up in the morning and the calm, leisurely awakening, was difficult. The first days after my return would go by immensely slowly, and I would ask again and again, so what now? What should I do today?

Gradually, the slowness would seep into my bones and bring me pleasure, until I returned to the routine of life.

But one topic was occupying my subconscious. Sometimes, I was gone for an entire month. My house stood on its own, outside the village, with no fence or wall. One little lock on the door separated everyone from my immense property (according to Maasai standards). How could it be that no one had ever tried to break into the house? I shared my query with Munkulai, my romantic friend. "I've heard of the heavy penalties for those who violate the social order, but those exist in my society as well, and don't stop people from committing crimes. And you know, after all, we're all human! Sometimes I witness disputes, arguments and fights. Why not thefts, then?"

Munkulai thought it over for a moment, then asked, "And what about the curses?"

"Curses? What do you mean?"

"Look, we believe that a word has power. Thought, too, has power. And the older people get—the more powerful they become. And the elders, if they see someone going off track by behaving shamefully, they will curse him. And then trouble will descend upon him and his household."

∽

Shortly after this conversation, I got to witness how the elders used their power. Sanguya had been drunk for many days now, and two days ago, returned home and beat Nashelu, his second wife. Bruised and weeping, she found shelter in my house, and a few minutes later, Sanguya's mother showed up on my doorstep. After making sure her daughter-in-law was getting better, she shouted, "What happened to my son? Why does he want to beat up us women... I, who went through the pains of pregnancy and labor and the difficulties of raising him... I, who lived with him for so many years... I don't need to suffer anymore! A woman gives birth to many children. Some of them die without us knowing why. But this son, I'm going to kill him myself, and I certainly know why!"

I raised an eyebrow. No'oltwati explained, "You understand, he can't control himself. He's very weak. He doesn't eat. Just drinks all day. It's not right. Therefore, his mother is going to kill him."

"And how is she going to do that? Brew herbs?"

"No! With words! We believe that words are sufficient, and that something will happen to him!"

After that first time, I witnessed the power of the elders again and again. It is surprising to see how the fear of the power of words and the power of thoughts helps maintain a society's system of rules and laws, with no need for police, jail or rehabilitation camps.

Two months went by, and the curse reached my own home.

It was a Friday. Two young men were brawling over a bet during a game of cards. Gambling is not common here, but sometimes, a group of boys get their hands on a pack of cards, and from an innocent game, they move on to playing for money. Violent brawls between two young men are even more unusual around here. One of our two village elders, who noticed the fight, immediately summoned all members of that age group, and ordered them to stop playing cards.

The games stopped at once.

When I asked Trishé and Museré, who had participated in the conversation, about the reason for this blind obedience, they both replied that such a command is a threat of being cursed. Therefore, even if they're in a faraway location, they still could not play. The elders' curse is not limited to the region, but is in effect regarding the deed committed, wherever the young men might be.

The guys found a workaround and played pool. Once again, the old man saw them and yelled at them that pool was like cards, and therefore, anyone who continued to play pool would be "punished."

Nevertheless, the young men kept playing.

~

Night descended on my house. It was a moonless night, and a heavy darkness lurked upon the universe. In the big room, on the mattresses laid out on the floor, Samyan and Miton curled up under one blanket, while Museré draped another blanket over himself. We were engulfed with silence; only the sound of breathing, rising and falling, was heard. Suddenly, I heard a sharp yell and woke up in panic.

"Samyan, what happened?"

No answer.

"Miton, are you up? What happened?"

No answer.

"Museré, is that you?"

No answer.

"Samyan, Samyan, answer me, what's going on?" Had one of them had a bad dream?

Suddenly, I heard a shout. "Nayolang, Nayolang, come quick!"

I swiftly got dressed, turned on the flashlight, ran to the other room, and found Samyan shaking, all frightened. "Something bit me and I'm bleeding!"

I looked at his knee. It was swollen and bleeding. I brought some antiseptic and by the light of the lantern, tried to figure out, based on the wound, whether it was a snake or a mouse. I could not see bite marks on his black skin. I lifted the covers off the bed and looked under the mattress, but the "something" was long gone, and by the faint light of the oil lamp, I could not find it. I believed it was a field mouse that had escaped through a crack in the door.

"Samyan, go back to sleep, but if you feel even a little bit ill—call me immediately," I told him, and turned back to my room.

Even before I lay back down in bed, I heard him: "Come quick, I feel really bad."

I got dressed and started my car. We drove toward the closest clinic, in a nearby lodge. It was 12:30 a.m. according to the vehicle's clock, and the lodge had turned off its generator for the night. We tried to attract the attention of the guard, who was patrolling the grounds of the hotel. After a period of time that seemed endless, the guard finally arrived, opened the gate and woke up the doctor, my good friend Anthony.

By the faint light of a flashlight, Anthony injected Samyan with medication, gave him black pills and sent us home.

I laid out a mattress on the floor of my room, sat down on it and held Samyan in my arms. Within minutes, he vomited black water. For the rest of the night, he tossed and writhed. His leg swelled up and became edematous, and his fear was even worse than the pain he was experiencing.

At first light, during the morning milking, the entire village already knew that something had happened. Samyan's father showed up, followed by his mother, and then the entire population of the village, men and women. I poured tea for everyone, and finally, one of them said, "Nayolang, it has to be a snake!"

"If it's a snake," I said decisively, "then we have to take everything out of the house and look for it."

We found it in the corner of the room, behind a cabinet—a giant viper, about five feet in length, curled up in the corner. Two men beat it with their staffs with all their might. When the snake was dead, they carried it some distance away from the house, piled kindling on it, set it on fire, and within seconds, the snake had returned to ashes and dust.

Throughout this time, Samyan was writhing in pain. Then, while it was still early in the morning, his aunt, who lived about six miles away, arrived huffing and puffing, crying and nearly hysterical. As she drank a cup of tea, she said, "I dreamt at night that one of the children is very sick. I got up, looked in on all my children and then my grandchildren. They were all okay. So I decided to come here and see what was going on with my sister's children." She was shocked by the way her dream had come true and continued to weep until she gradually calmed down.

When the rest of the world woke up, we tried to discover whether the clinics around us had anti-venom serum. They did not.

We returned to the doctor to continue Samyan's treatment, and I felt calmer, thinking that if Samyan was still alive, the worst must be behind us. But this was not the case. Three days went by and his condition did not improve. The village elders prepared a traditional potion for him from what seemed like a chopped stone that was ground to dust. The powder was mixed with water, whose color immediately turned scarlet and its taste bitter.

Samyan's leg continued to swell up. At night, still in my room, he became delirious, sweating heavily and talking in his sleep. One night, I woke up in anxiety; how had I ignored that, other than death, snakebite could have other severe consequences, including gangrene, paralysis and amputation?

I returned to Dr. Anthony once more and we called a snake expert in Nairobi. Anthony talked to him, described the case and the current state of the leg to him, and as their conversation lengthened, I discovered, to my surprise, that even black skin can turn pale... He returned the receiver to its cradle and uttered one sentence: "Take him to the hospital, as soon as possible!"

In Narok, we turned to Dr. Chula, an angel who lives and works there. He saw Samyan, heard the description of the incident, and without waiting even a moment, laid him out on the operating table, grabbed his scalpel and made a cut in the side of his leg. All at once, the pressure eased: blood diluted with white fluid, rotting tissue, pus. I held on tight to Samyan, who was writhing in pain, growling (Maasai do not yell in pain) and biting my hand. However, all of us could see that the swelling was going down.

Samyan lived. Samyan recovered. Today he can run, and a thin scar on his knee is the remaining evidence of the snake bite. Many days afterwards, I claimed that that "midnight kiss" turned him into my prince. But he had never heard of fairy tales or princes. He had heard of elders' curses, and along with the other members of the village, he now takes care to honor the elders' commands.

21

Children Are a Shining Moon

One morning, as I savored an early morning tea across from some scenic acacia trees, watching a troop of baboons strolling slowly toward the stream, two men from a village in one of the distant hills showed up at my house. I invited them to join me for tea, but, breathing heavily, they urged me to put down my cup and hurry off with them, as a woman in their village had been stricken with severe malaria and needed to be quickly driven to the clinic. I put down my cup of tea, boarded my sputtering car, and we set off for the village. There was no access path for a vehicle, so in the places where the terrain was tough to traverse, the two disembarked and, using their long, sharp knives, forged a path through the shrubs. By the time we arrived at the entrance to the village, the sense of urgency spread , and I wanted to hurry into the sick woman's house. However, illness is one thing, but the dictates of good manners are another: one by one, the local men and women approached me and shook my hand in greeting. As I responded, I thought to myself, *these salutations are all good and well, but where's the emergency?* Only after the series of greetings ended did a young woman with long hair, wearing no necklaces, appear in the doorway of the house, flanked by two women supporting her. She was bent over, waddling in my direction in tiny steps, clutching at her stomach as she shuffled toward me.

"What's wrong with her?"

"Malaria!" came the answer.

"Are you sure she's not pregnant?" (Hair on a married woman's head testified to her being pregnant or had recently given birth, in effect signaling to her husband and boyfriends she was not sexually available.)

"Oh, she's pregnant but her time has not come yet. She has malaria!"

The young woman shuffled over to my car. I opened the door for her, but she stopped, grabbed hold of the handle and sat down outside the vehicle. I waited. She lay down on the ground in a fetal position and clutched her belly. The moment the woman lay down, all the men and children drifted away from us, shifting aside. Only women, teenaged girls and younger girls stayed in our immediate vicinity. In retrospect, the signs of what was about to take place were clear, but I did not know how to decipher them.

One of the old women lifted the leg of the woman still curled up in an embryonic position, fumbling under the blanket and the skirt.

I still did not understand what was about to happen.

The old woman called out a few instructions and resumed groping between the woman's legs. And then, in half a minute, a tiny, pinkish baby girl was pulled out! In front of my astonished eyes, a birth had taken place! With no moaning or screaming, while lying in a fetal position, a baby had been extracted from between her legs! A young girl came running from the village, holding a razor blade in her hand. The umbilical cord was cut, the baby was swaddled, and one woman helped the new mother get up and led her toward the car.

I was shaken up. "Hold on a minute," I stopped them. "What's going on here?"

The women looked at me, calm and perplexed. "She's got malaria! Aren't you going to take her to the clinic?"

"Oh, of course I'll take her, but what do you think about washing off her legs (still covered by trickles of blood)?"

"Good idea," they replied, and one girl was sent to fetch a bowl of water.

Meanwhile, I turned to fold down the vehicle's seats, lay out a mattress, and make a bed for the woman who had just given birth. Once again, the women gazed at me questioningly. "Nayolang, what are you doing?"

"Making a bed for the new mother."

"Why?"

"To take her to the clinic."

"Right, but why a bed?"

"She just gave birth!"

"True, but the birth is over…"

I folded the mattress once more, straightened the seat, and with a full entourage—the new mother and two old women gently holding the baby (who was promptly named "Eti," a name she would keep until her marriage), swaddled in blankets—we set off for the clinic.

And indeed, the new mother was suffering from malaria. After being treated, she was safely discharged to go back home.

∽

By now, Lanoi was expecting, and I accompanied her pregnancy. Pregnancy is an integral part of an adult woman's life. From the moment she has gotten married and got her period, if she is healthy, she is expected to become pregnant and bring children into the world, one after the other. The Maasai version of family planning decrees that from the moment the pregnancy is discovered and until the baby is about ten months old, the woman may not have sex. They believe that if the man's sperm (his "milk") enters the woman's body, it will spoil her own milk, and therefore, the baby's food.

The advantage of this abstinence is not just creating a gap of about two years between offspring, but also the interval in which the newborn may breastfeed for as long as it likes, until the first teeth appear and beyond—this in a society that is not familiar with milk substitutes such as Similac and its equivalents. To justify the gap that should be maintained between children, custom decrees that when a woman conceives, she must stop breastfeeding her baby, as the "juices" of pregnancy will affect the quality of her milk.

Although it seems as if Maasai society is sexually liberal, relatively speaking, in reality, an adult woman engages in little sexual activity once she reaches maturity: she is almost always pregnant or breastfeeding. I suspect it is actually these dictates, rather than female circumcision, that are the men's way of ensuring a wife does not stray from the marital path...

Lanoi continued to wear the wide leather belt, the *enkiteti*, over her belly until the fifth month of her pregnancy. Throughout this time, she went on with her life as usual: gathering wood, carrying containers of water from the stream, and taking care of the young children handed over to her when she arrived in her husband's village. She stopped shaving her head and allowed her hair to grow.

When her belly swelled and the leather belt was taken off, Lanoi switched to a special diet that worried me, as instead of being encouraged to eat and grow stronger to prepare for the birth, she was actually restricted to one meager meal a day, consisting of one helping of *ugali*, the popular local dish. I grumbled, but the village women did not understand what my problem was: the birth would take place at home, with no sort of aids, and therefore the women tried to ensure that the newborn would be small and would come out easily.

In the last months of her pregnancy, Lanoi would engage in a form of "colon cleansing": she boiled water in a pot, put a piece of elephant dung in the water (an immense cube, with a diameter of about eight inches) and steeped it. Once the concoction was ready, she strained the liquid, drank it, and then—shoved a finger down her throat and threw up. She thus emptied her stomach and cleansed it using natural means[25].

In addition, in the last months of her pregnancy, she increased the pace of her firewood gathering, collecting a large stock that would last her for about a month after the birth. In every Maasai village, the house of a woman in her last months of pregnancy can be easily identified based on the gradually growing pile of wood next to the house.

When the time a Maasai woman is due to give birth approaches, she is assigned an older woman who watches over her, her diet, and the fetus in her belly. Nesesyay, Lanoi's biological mother, moved into her hut and helped her collect wood and cook, massaging her belly with fat every day to help the baby flip over if its head was not correct.

One day, Lanoi was restless, and we understood that the birth was drawing close. In the evening, after the cows returned from pasture, her contractions began. One woman stationed herself at the center of the village, declaring loudly four times, at the top of her voice, "There is a birth!" In response to this signal, all the women free at the time hurried to gather in her house. The hut was packed with women talking, cheering, yelling and chattering. Lanoi lay in her bed in the dark, moaning weakly. The midwife, one of the older village women with plenty of experience in facilitating births, knelt beside her, waiting for the right moment.

~

I arrived about ten minutes after the birth. The dark house was full of jubilant women, talking excitedly among themselves and to Lanoi. The fire at the center of the house emitted a pleasant heat.

After exchanging greetings, I asked, "Boy or girl?"

"Oh," the attendees' eyes gaped wide. "We don't know."

I could barely contain my amazement.

"We haven't looked yet! We're happy with every offspring born. The moment the baby came out, we swaddled it well, and we're not asking."

Nesesyay melted fat in a pot until it turned liquid. She sat down, hitched up her skirt, took the baby, placed it on her bare thighs, removed the rags in which it was swaddled, scooped up some fat from the pot and massaged its body. Now, by the light of the flames from the fire, we could all see it was a boy. One woman went out to tell Lanoi's husband, who was waiting outside, that he should draw blood from the neck of a calve —an indirect way of telling him he had a baby boy (had the baby been a girl, he would have drawn blood from a heifer). A gourd was filled with the blood, then sent back inside the hut, which had become female turf. Lanoi lustfully drank it down after it was mixed with milk, sugar and redpaprika. Nesesyay passed a swatch of cloth between the women, torn from an old sheet. Each of us tied a knot in it, and finally, the ribbon was tied around the baby's neck as protection against envy and the evil eye.

Meanwhile, one woman placed a pot over the fire, filled with water and… donkey droppings. When the mixture was properly cooked, the donkey dung, like tea bags, was taken out of the water, which was mixed with the blood and milk and drunk down not only by the new mother but by all the women present.

Another woman somehow produced a buffalo horn. She broke up a tiny bit of it, and using a knife, crumbled it into powder, mixed it with fat and scrubbed the baby's lips and mouth with it ("so he's strong as an ox"). When I expressed my astonishment, I was told that when a girl is born, she receives a different powder, made from the spine of the palm branch ("so she's resilient and flexible like a palm").

At a late hour of the night, I retired to sleep in my house. It did not even occur to the rest of the women to go back home, as "children are a shining moon" (I thought of an expression I knew, "children light up a house"). From the moment of the birth, Lanoi was on "birth rest," which continued as long as she was still bleeding. She was prohibited from doing any housework, not even milking. Throughout this period—resembling the period of *niddah* in Jewish tradition, in which a woman must abstain from sex in the days when menstruating—she cannot enter the houses of other women, and her husband is forbidden from entering and sleeping in the same house with her. This is actually the Maasai version of maternity leave. Therefore, Nesesyay now prepared to sleep beside her daughter, while other women settled down to sleep on the other bed.

Throughout the next few weeks, the women took turns assisting Lanoi. They cooked her meals, helped wash the baby and massaged him with generous portions of fat, which was also shoved down his throat to prevent constipation. They helped bring water from the stream and host Lanoi's friends, who were arriving from distant villages.

After about a month, when all discharge had stopped, Lanoi's head was symbolically shaved above her temples in the shape of two horns. That evening, for the first time since the birth, she resumed milking the cows.

Lanoi returned to her usual routine.

~

There are few things more pleasurable than seeing the immense love and devoted care bestowed upon Maasai babies. The women do not part from the baby even for a moment, and if his mother is not holding him, another woman is. About every half an hour, the baby's entire body is massaged with fat, usually accompanied by humming or singing from the masseuse. There are kisses, hugs and lots of tenderness. The moment he opens his mouth to express his protest loudly, the "natural pacifier," the mother's nipple, is inserted inside; it is always ready and waiting for him.

The moment the mother conceives again, she stops breastfeeding her "previous" baby, who is now passed on into the public domain: other women, boys and girls will watch over him. And yet, despite this, or perhaps because of it, it is apparent that even when they mature, Maasai babies suffer no separation anxiety or childhood frustrations over unfulfilled desires.

Maasai mothers are not busy "educating" their kids. It is very rare for them to spank them (raising a thin branch in the air will make a child burst out in tears, realizing he has made a mistake) or yell at them. Children grow up with immense freedom, and with full faith in adults. I couldn't help but be impressed by the mothers' calm and by their lack of anxiety regarding their children. They know with utter certainty that no one will harm their children, young or older. A girl can walk around on her own in the bush while semi-exposed. She can bathe naked in the stream and will never, ever be harassed. It would never even occur to her that harassment is even a possibility.

Children model their behavior upon the adult world. Therefore, starting at a young age, they are full, eager participants in various activities: the boys go out to distant grazing grounds with the cattle, and the girls help run the household, including cooking and laundry. Often, the girls around twelve years old organize wood-gathering trips of their own initiative, including an unofficial competition over which of them will haul more.

But the thing that was most prominent for me was the utter absence of the statement so commonly heard in our society: "Mom, I'm bored…"

I noticed two reasons for this: first, it would never occur to any Maasai child that his mother should be responsible for his amusement or for managing his time. The mother, too, would never consider herself to keep her children busy or entertaining them—reading them books or playing Monopoly with them—or think that they should "do" something during the day.

The second reason is that for these kids, the world is their playground! There are myriad "toys" around them: stones, branches, wild animals, plastic lids, corks, broken dishes, the soles of shoes, ratty pieces of cloth, and so on.

The tiny ones play all day. Their endless inventiveness leaves me ecstatic: they design miniature villages from mud and stones, building houses by bending branches and creating bowers with roofs made of greenery. Inside the houses, they weave beds from twigs, padding them with rags, create cooking nooks in which old tin cans serve as pots and plastic bottle caps are cups, and "cook" food from tiny pellets of dung. They feed "babies" (plastic bottles swaddled in rags) and water the "cattle" (tiny quartz stones). They play hopscotch, jacks (using stones) and jump rope, with a rope they wove themselves. And they sing. All day long, they sing![26]

The older children go out to pasture with the livestock in groups of two or three kids, while constantly playing: they practice hitting targets, throw spears or clubs, chase rabbits, whittle *rungu* (wooden clubs) or shepherd's staffs, and engage in much mischief.

A moonlit night. Dinner was cooking over the fire. As they waited for the meal, the children took advantage of the natural spotlight shining down at us from above to play night games. Initially, the game seemed to resemble Catch, but when I listened to the voices and the shouting, I realized there was an extra catch to this Catch: the game, called 'Park Rangers,' reconstructed their daily experience. Two of the kids played the role of the park rangers. They ran back and forth, holding a band of cloth (a whip) and trying to catch the other kids, the "cow herders." The "herders" caught were whipped and put under arrest, unless they paid a fine (leaves plucked from a tree). The game went on until all the shepherds were thrown in jail and the rangers were replaced, or until dinner was ready.

22

Eunoto

It had been three years since Oldabash the *moran* and his friends had visited my home regularly, and the year began with great excitement: the elders announced that the *eunoto* ceremony, which marks the end of the *moran* period and thus closing the Ilmeshuki age group, would soon take place. In the ceremony, all the prohibitions and taboos applying to the *morans* would be symbolically lifted, and they would return to society as young adults.

The *morans* displayed great urgency: according to tradition, by the time the ceremony took place, they had to kill a lion or a male ostrich and show up with a "badge of honor": a hat made from the lion's mane or a headdress made from the ostrich's feathers. Other than that wretched event that had introduced me to Oldabash, out of all the *morans* who passed through my home, I had not heard of a single one who had taken on this mission, in which, as I already knew, man was not always the victor.

A ceremony, according to my understanding, is an occasion meant to mark an event: the ending of a school year, a promotion, and so on. Here, I discovered, a "ceremony" could last six month and sometimes even more.

In each and every village, women—the mothers of the *morans*—were recruited to depart, along with their small children, for a traditional site whose location had long been established, where this ceremony customarily took place. Their task was to build a *manyatta*, a village serving solely for the ceremony. Once it was built, about 3,000 people would be living there, and their number would rise to about 5,000 during the closing events. As thousands of people have to be fed for about six months, everyone pitches in and contributes. Representatives roam from village to village, collecting money, cows, sheep, goats, sacks of sugar and maize flour from every household, all transported to the *manyatta*. This is an immense logistical operation, and therefore, ceremonies on this scale take place rarely, only four times in a person's life—when the members of an age group transition together from one maturity level to the next*.

The ceremonial *manyatta* of the Purko tribe, the largest of the Maasai tribes in Kenya, is always rebuilt at the same spot on the outskirts of the Mau Escarpment, a mountain range towering to a height of about two miles above sea level. Deep river beds, full of water, cut through a landscape forested with ancient trees that rise to impressive heights. Scattered among the trees of the forest are plots tended by Maasai who, taking advantage of the fertile land, had transitioned to farming many years ago, abandoning the herding of cattle.

I was invited by Oldabash to stay at the *manyatta* until the final day of the ceremony, which was scheduled for about a month later. I loaded my vehicle with food, a sleeping bag, potable water and seven more *morans* who were staying at my house. We drove the bumpy route to Narok, as the *morans*, celebrating their good fortune, laughed, sang, but mostly growled, an indication of the great excitement they were experiencing. About halfway to our destination, I

---

* See Appendix 3.

stopped abruptly. Out of the bush emerged about a hundred and fifty *morans,* their hair and bodies dyed in red ochre. They strode vigorously down the road, waving their staffs and growling, some wearing lion-mane hats on their heads. It was a thrilling sight—the road was full of them! Such excitement! Out of the throng of *morans,* I spotted a close friend, and he joined us in the car.

Although the *manyatta* was located only sixty miles from Maasai Mara, the change in climate and landscape was immense. As I drove, I felt as if I had boarded an airplane and landed in the high, cool plains of Ethiopia: the air was ultra-clear; heavy low gray clouds covered the sky and constant rain drizzled in thin trickles. On days when the clouds lifted somewhat, the forest was revealed in all directions, interspersed with tiny plots of land scattered here and there. It was easy to figure out why this location had been chosen as the site of the ceremony: the forest, butting against the *manyatta,* provided plenty of firewood, and the streams flowing everywhere provided a rich supply of water for drinking, cooking and bathing.

~

As evening approached, we finally reached our destination. Like every Maasai village, the *manyatta* was built as a circle, yet its dimensions were so grand it was possible to drive through it in a vehicle, from one end to the other. It was a breathtaking, colorful sight that filled me with immense excitement. The *manyatta* was teeming with people, particularly the *morans'* mothers along with their young children. At the center of the clearing I saw hundreds of *morans* sitting, dancing or roaming around. I knew many. During the last few years, they had often visited my home to rest before continuing on their journeys. I had spent many hours in their company, interviewed them, taken their pictures and made friends with them. Now, in the *manyatta,* they fell upon me with cries of joy, leading me from house to house to meet their mothers, drink tea and hear their adventure stories.

Unlike a regular village, the houses of the *manyatta* were no more than little crannies providing shelter overnight. They were attached to one another, so that from the outside, the outer wall of the houses resembled a fortified barrier, interrupted every few dozen yards to enable access. A view from the inner courtyard revealed tiny entryways adjacent to each other and nearly converging.

The mother of Tirishe, one of my closest friends, took me under her wing and showed me our "house." The mother, a short, smiley woman, dressed in rags, who had built the house and had been living in it for the last two months with her eight-year-old daughter, welcomed me with a special dish, "rice without"—without salt, without onion, without oil. I ate it with relish. As I looked around me, I was impressed, yet again, by the Maasai's ability to live austerely for long periods of time. Although the structure was small, it was still built in the traditional style: two beds and a cooking space between them. I counted three pots, two plates, one spoon and five cups. I added my contribution to the stock of objects, giving the family a sponge and some detergent to clean the dishes, which had been cleaned with coals. I thought about the possessions I had brought here and felt ashamed. For a trip that would only last twenty-five days, I had brought plenty of luxury items: two plates, two cups, two pots, toilet paper, two pairs of pants, shirts, a sweater, Maasai cloaks, a dress, a towel—and I still felt somewhat deprived.

~

Many *morans* were still absent. They were trying to take advantage of these final days to hunt a lion or a male ostrich. Oldabash told me there were only two occasions when Maasai could hunt wild animals: first, as boys before their circumcision, they were asked to hunt birds, and later, to prepare for the *eunoto* ceremony, they had to try and hunt the most difficult animals to capture, representing the height of power and the height of speed.

The hunt, Oldabash said, had to be carried out with spears. Therefore, to strike his prey, the *moran* had to get close to the animal and only then cast his spear. This hunting undoubtedly demanded unusual bravery, considering the strength of the lion, which could fight back fiercely—a battle that often resulted in injuries, as Oldabash himself had experienced in the hunting incident that had led to our meeting.

Confronting a male ostrich could prove just as difficult—this was capable not merely of running swiftly, but also of landing a kick that could stun a man. To hunt an ostrich, the *morans* had to work as a team. They had to surround the ostrich in a large circle, then gradually decrease its size as they approached their prey. The frightened ostrich would flee in fright in a certain direction. That was the time for the valiant warrior to cast his spear at it and subdue it. Unfortunately, often, the ostrich stunned the warrior confronting it with a kick, and the battle would end with one or more *morans* being injured, sometimes fatally.

The first warrior who impaled the lion with his spear could scalp his mane and make a hat out of it. The first to pierce an ostrich with his spear would gather its black-and-white feathers and here, in the ceremonial *manyatta*, the men from the mentoring age group would create a stunning crown that would surround his face.

The hunting of lions and ostriches is an object of desire for the *morans*. As in the "handicap principle"[27] observed among animals, in which the males try to impress the females with their physical characteristics to win them over, here, too, putting on the lion or ostrich crown results not only in respect and appreciation, but in wealth as well—elders from various villages, proud of these courageous fellows, grant them rewards in a cow, sheep or goat.

Winning the objects of their desire was difficult —I witnessed this about two weeks later, when, at the height of the ceremony, in which over 900 *morans* were present, I counted only twelve lion hats and four ostrich-feather headdresses.

For the women and children, these were days of waiting. Everyone eagerly anticipated the appearance of a slim crescent in the sky, heralding the beginning of the "white nights" in which the final ceremony could be conducted. The *morans* staying at the *manyatta* spent their time dancing, coloring their skin, weaving their hair and slaughtering sheep.

Many sheep were slaughtered every day. Not only were there multitudes of people to feed, but the *morans* were still subject to the laws of taboo, and could not eat any other food. As my daily diet in the afternoon and the evening consisted solely of "rice without," every morning, I invited myself over to join one group of *morans* leaving for the *orpul*, in the heart of the bush. There, far from the eyes of any women, they slaughtered and roasted meat.

∼

The appearance of a white moon in the sky heralded the beginning of the *eunoto*—the last days of the seven-year-long *moran* period. The *manyatta* was more crowded than ever. Not a single *moran* was absent, and many Maasai, both men and women, had arrived to be present for the last stages of the ceremony.

The *morans* were instructed to go out to the forest and each chop a long branch from a juniper tree, many of which grew in the area, peel off its bark, expose the white xylem, and return with the peeled stick. Hours later, each bearing a stick of his own, they danced in the clearing within the *manyatta*. I had never seen this dance before: they held the sticks horizontally, parallel to the ground, and advanced in small steps, occasionally bending or kneeling while bringing the stick closer to the ground. Their gestures reminded me of a male ostrich's mating dance, as it wriggled and exposed it's behind to the female.

Female. Was my association actually a random one? At this stage of the ceremony, they could not carry any weapon: no spears and no arrows, but only sticks. The weapons had not only been their trademark, but also allowed them to move fearlessly through the region and provoke the wild animals and the Maasai herds; however, disarming them had turned them symbolically and temporarily into "women."[28]

The transformation of the *morans* into "women" continued the following day, when they were instructed to put on an *eleso*—the external cloth cover that women wear on their back. Dressed like women and unarmed other than those sticks—nothing could be more humiliating for someone who, only a few days ago, had been a fearless warrior.

The humiliation, I knew, would continue, and they would symbolically be turned not merely into women, but into "babies." That event would take place on the last day, at the height of the ceremony, when the mothers shaved their sons' head, just as they had first done during the boys' naming ceremony—the first personal ceremony in their lives—when they were two years old. In that ceremony, the boys had received their official names.

Throughout the afternoon, this special dancing continued. The air grew more charged every moment. A sense of intoxication prevailed everywhere. No one was absent. More and more *morans* kept arriving and joining the unique dance.

When darkness came, each *moran* tied his *eleso* to his stick, while the sticks were tied to the doorways of the houses. The *manyatta* assumed a festive air. Colorful flags were waving in the wind, the lion hats were also hung in the doorways of their owners' houses, and everyone was exhibiting signs of excitement. I found an advantage in the display of flags. As the number of *morans* equaled the number of flags, I now circled the *manyatta* and counted the flags: 906 *morans* were present in the Purko tribe's *manyatta*.

~

Dawn. The blowing of the horn of the kudu—a large, stunningly beautiful antelope, its brown body adorned with thin white stripes, and the male's head sporting long horns, curling around themselves and resembling a long shofar, or ram's horn trumpet—woke us up into the chill of the morning. The voice of the *olotonu*, the *moran* elected to conduct the ceremony, sounded soothing in the silence around us. He was praying to God.

This day, Oldabash told me, was called "donkey day." Forty-nine women, the mothers of forty-nine chosen *morans*, loaded their personal possessions on donkeys and departed the *manyatta*, traversing a distance of about sixty feet. They then built a small "village" called *osinkira* ("donkey village"), in which they would stay for the next four nights.

All the mothers of the Ilmeshuki age group now underwent a "morality test": the *morans* slaughtered an immense black ox in the center of "donkey village," which was still being constructed. They skinned the ox and spread its hide on the ground, with the black fur facing down. Around them, hundreds of women, their mothers, stood waiting, screeching, giggling and shoving, each holding an ax and a wooden stake she had prepared in advance. No woman was absent. However, only women who had never had sex with a *moran* could stretch the hide and pound the stake into its edge[29]. The *morans* stood around, tensely examining their mothers. I stood next to the hide in the packed crowd and saw women who bent down, swung the ax… but pounded no stake…

While the women were busy stretching the ox's hide, a group of *morans* departed for the forest. They had to chop down two thick, long and heavy trunks that would serve as foundations, or support beams, for a structure that would be built around them. Despite the length and weight of the trees, as they were chopped down, they were not allowed to fall on the ground and squash any plants or little insects. The logs were only acceptable if during their fall, they were caught in mid-air and then placed gently on exposed ground.

The delegation's return was greeted with much excitement, as these poles would serve as the basis for what I later termed "the temple," the place where the *morans* would receive the elders' blessing.

Each trunk was held by about twenty *morans*, who were surrounded by many more to accompany them and replace those who grew exhausted. When they entered with the logs into the center of the "donkey village," the excitement peaked. Many *morans* entered a trance-like state, their whole bodies shaking, and fell theatrically to the ground, their outstretched arms locked at their sides. Their friends quickly grabbed them and sat them down gently on the ground, waiting for the storm to subside.

The tree trunks were planted in two deep holes dug earlier so they stood tall. The elders, the boys' mentors, marked the required diameter of the structure using small animal droppings. Then, as if a signal had been given, dozens of women holding digging sticks leapt forward. With a harmonious beat, they raised and lowered the sticks, pounding at the ground and creating pits. They inserted thin, long poles into the pits, tying them to each other with more flexible horizontal sticks. Other women inserted green branches into the resulting skeleton, while yet more women applied cow dung to it. I was thrilled by their teamwork.

When evening came, the structure was half-finished. The growing moon suspended in the sky above us cast down its light, and the singing of the *morans* rang out until the wee hours of the night.

The excitement was mounting. We knew this day, just dawning, was the most important in the ceremony, as the heads of the forty-nine *morans* who had moved into the *osinkira* had been shaved in the early hours of the morning. The first of them was the *olotonu*, the master of ceremonies, who served as the "trailblazer."

The head-shaving was a pivotal and very emotional event. I looked at them: *morans* who had been circumcised seven years ago, and ever since then, their very existence had been associated with their long hair, their jewelry and their spears, with roaming the region and with infinite freedom. Shaving their hair for the first time today symbolized shedding this entire lifestyle: the loincloth, the only part of their body covered in fabric, would be removed; the jewelry would be taken off; and the lifestyle consisting mainly of roaming, endless meat celebrations, dancing and fooling around with young girls would end.

Their shaved, exposed scalps were covered with red ochre. As men, they were separate from the rest of their *moran* friends. They even could not eat together now, when only yesterday they had all still been "brothers." Everyone had a hard time adjusting to this new situation. It was hard to recognize the dyed "skinheads" standing on the sidelines. Cries of joy, surprise and recognition rang out from both groups.

Meanwhile, the women continued to build the *osinkira*, and around noon, the "temple" was already constructed. I was impressed both by the size of the structure—about sixteen feet in height and sixty-five feet in diameter—and by the teamwork that had established it within twenty-four hours. The structure was covered in cow dung, with no windows and one very low entryway.

The *morans* were now sent off to slaughter another ox in the *orpul* somewhere within the forest.

Meanwhile, preparations were completed in the "temple." The women had brought hundreds of *kalabashes* inside, some filled with milk, others with beer brewed on site. I bent down and came in. The structure was very dark. Cowhides covered the floor. At the outskirts of the structure, around the walls, the *kalabashes* were piled up. Oil candles were lit on the ground, and the light flickering on the walls imbued the site with a sense of holiness. This sensation was enhanced by the small entryway requiring those entering to bend, to bow down.

Next to the walls of the structure stood traditional four-legged stools made from a single log. In the evening, they would seat twenty elders, four from every Maasai clan. When the time came, the elders told me, the *morans* would enter, one by one. Each *moran* would approach the elders of the clan to which he belonged, and receive a blessing and a *kalabash* containing milk or beer. The *moran* must drink down its contents and leave. This would be the first time, I knew, when the members of the Ilmeshuki age group, as men, could drink beer.

Evening time. The forty-nine *morans* whose heads had been shaved that morning were seen approaching, followed by the rest of the group, in a long column that no one was permitted to cross. At the entrance to the "temple," their sticks were collected from them. The *morans* then went in, sipped from the *kalabash* and exited after several minutes.

Darkness fell.

The last of the *morans* were still waiting to enter the *osinkira*, but the major drama was taking place among those leaving it. It was easy to identify who had drunk milk and who had drunk beer for the first time in his life, gotten intoxicated, and went off to go wild.

"You understand," one elder standing next to me explained, "we knew what would happen, so we left them with no weapons at all, like women. We even took their sticks away. They're not used to drinking. And the ones who drank milk, their job is to watch over the drunks!"

I watched the drunks. They were amusing. I thought about the symbolism inherent even in giving them beer: they were transitioning from the life of *morans*, who were in full control, to a state of losing control. One more layer in returning the boys to society.

∼

Last morning.

Before the black scarf lifted and the first rays of sun broke through, the prayer to God was heard for the last time. The *morans* woke up slowly. The sense of an ending was in the air. One by one, the hides were taken out of each house, and traditional stools were placed upon them. The first of the *morans* sat in the chairs. I followed Tirishe's mother, who had hosted me in her little shelter throughout these days. She was holding a *kalabash* with milk in her hand, poured it over her son's head, and with a razor blade, shaved off strand after strand of hair.

It is not the umbilical cord that disconnect the Maasai boy from his mother but rather this head-shaving, during this ceremony. From this point on, her son became a young adult. He would undergo one more personal ceremony, after which he would take a wife, and she would star in the next ceremonies.

Tirishe sat in the chair. He was trembling uncontrollably. The shaving of his head put an end to a long chapter in his young life. I stood beside him and felt my heart going out to him. I saw how, along with the long red strands of hair falling to the ground, he was slowly being stripped of his power, of his distinction. I thought of one of my childhood heroes, the biblical Samson.

Once the shaving was completed, each *moran* gave the *eleso* which, for the last few days, had served as a flag and as feminine garb, to the mother who had shaved him. Ochre dye was applied to their bare heads. One by one, the young men covered themselves with an *oltshiti* (the men's blanket), huddled together in groups, and prepared for their departure from the *manyatta*, returning to a home from which they had been absent for seven years.

23

Birth Certificate

The *eunoto* ceremony had ended, and now, Samyan and Museré were officially young adults. In honor of the event, I decided to issue them birth certificates. Since they couldn't read or write, I filled out the forms for them, including their father's and mother's ID numbers. In the items asking for the location and date of their birth, I noted "In the village," and sent them off to the government offices in the district's capital.

Late in the evening, they returned excitedly from their trip to the town. We sat watching the sunset together, holding steaming cups of tea. Other friends gathered around us, and Museré began his tale. "We got to Narok and went to a teahouse for some tea. The waiter placed a pitcher of milk, a pitcher of warm water, a teabag and a bowl with sugar on the table. I didn't know what to do with all that, so I tore open the teabag and poured its contents into the water pitcher, and all the sugar too, and I poured the milk into the pitcher as well... All of those liquids overflowed and spilled out. The waiter came and asked, 'What the hell are you doing?' I didn't know what to say, so I gave him a tough look, and answered, seriously, 'I'm drinking tea!'

"I ordered *chapati* as well. They gave me a whole big one on a plate! But I wanted it cut into little pieces. I didn't know what to do, how to eat it. Finally, I found a solution—I took out my long knife and cut it."

"And what about the birth certificate?" I asked.

"Ah," he replied. "That didn't really work out... We didn't understand what that clerk at town wanted from us..."

About a week later, the three of us drove to the town.

We sat down across from the clerk on a wooden bench, the tall Samyan and Museré on either side of me, and me in the middle.

"Why didn't you issue them birth certificates?" I asked. "All the forms were filled out."

"True," the clerk replied. "There's only one piece of information missing: the date of birth!"

"But you know they were born in the village, and no one writes down dates over there."

"Look," the clerk replied slowly, as if I were a dim-witted woman, "I didn't ask where they were born! I asked what their date of birth was!"

I got it. In the presence of the clerk, I asked Samyan, "How old do you want to be?"

He calculated silently and said, "Twenty four!"

"And you, Museré?"

Museré looked at Samyan. "If he's twenty four, I'll be twenty three."

I now turned to the clerk. "Write this down: Samyan was born on October 18, 1983. Museré was born on October 18, 1984."

Both were issued birth certificates listing a date of birth... my own!

24

Capturing Flies

The year 2005 began with a severe drought. For many years now, since the El Niño in the late nineties, the weather had been out of whack. Here, in Maasai Mara, even a two-month cessation of rain causes the grass to dry up. The equatorial sun radiates intensely, sucking up any traces of moisture from the ground, the grass and the plants, whose withered leaves shrivel up, assume an orange hue and are finally shed in a heat-based exfoliation. The cows grow increasingly thinner, until their bones stick out from their loose skin. Every day we raise our eyes to the sky, but fail to find even a tiny cloud that might provide a momentary relief from the blazing sun.

It's late at night. The village women have cooked dinner, each in her own hut, and now they emerge from their homes. We gather in the clearing between the village houses, opposite the village elder's gate, and sing together - each of us waving the hem of her *eleso* - "*Oh, Parsaea, oh, Parsaea...*" *God, don't forget us. Give us rain so the cows may live, give us rain, give us life... Oh, God.*

Engaged in this nocturnal singing, we pass from gate to gate within the village. Across from each gate, one woman leads the singing, and the rest join her in beseeching God. And so we continue to walk and sing until the next gate, circling the houses of the village four times. When our singing weakens, we can hear the women singing in the adjacent villages. All are pleading to God: *Give us rain!* And so we sing for eight consecutive nights.

∽

The Maasai believe in one god named Enkai[30]. Per their belief, God is great, and is very busy taking care of the entire world, and therefore, so long as things are on track—the rain comes when it should, the sun shines on time, the grass continues to grow and there is water in the river—people have no reason to bother Him with their daily affairs. Appeals to God take place only at times of joy or trouble: in ceremonies, God is blessed and thanked for bestowing His bounty, while in times of trouble—droughts, plagues that hurt cattle or people—He is addressed in pleas for help.

However, the Maasai know, and I gradually learned, that staying on track cannot be taken for granted. To ensure that this is the case, humanity is tasked with great responsibility: the responsibility for maintaining harmony in the world.

My illumination came from flies.

Yesterday, it rained. The morning air was jubilant, as was the atmosphere. The sky was blue and clear, there was no dust in the air, and visibility was high. The housework was over. The women were relaxing under the tree, while the children played nearby in the mud. I called one of them by name. He raised his eyes and his face was dotted with dozens of flies circling his mouth, his eyes and his nostrils. The child seemed indifferent to the black, buzzing army engulfing him. He wasn't the only one full of flies. They were everywhere: on the children, in the pots of food, on the cattle. In the days after the rain, they become a true hazard, especially here, in a village built of cow dung, where they had plenty of food and a fertile breeding ground. On such days, I would swaddle myself in fabric from head to foot, and still have to wave my hands to shoo them off. Now, in the shade of the tree, I noticed I was the only one who felt bothered by the flies.

I declared war on them. I clapped my hands stiffly, and two flies fell to the ground. I struck my arm, and another fly bit the dust. The women scolded me. "Nayolang, come on, Nayolang, *tabala* [that's enough]."

Now it was my turn to stare at them and ask, "How are you so apathetic? Don't the flies bother you? Don't you know they spread disease?"

Over time, I got it. The attitude toward a fly reflects the attitude toward the universe. Man is part of creation, and so is the fly. According to the Maasai perception, people are not superior to flies. We are all part of the same creation. And we all have a place in this world.

In the worldview of the Maasai (and other African societies), a person has two main roles in life. One is to serve as a link in the chain of life, a chain that began with his or her ancestors and will continue with children, grandchildren and great-grandchildren. People do not stand alone, in their own right, but rather are a present that cannot exist without the past, and are responsible for the future.

As man is a link in the chain of existence, the decree to "be fruitful and multiply" is very important. Here, someone without children is considered "deficient," and will be treated differently—even upon his or her death—than those who have fulfilled their destiny on this earth. Women without children are an "impossible" phenomenon in terms of Maasai society. Therefore, women devoid of children will raise other women's children. That was why I received children: not just to create a social bond with their parents and with the community, not only to make my life meaningful, but also that I would not be "deficient."

However, every individual has another important role in the world, which consists of maintaining harmony. A person's conduct cannot harm others. Each of us is tasked with preserving the relationship with our friends, our neighbors, with the environment, with nature and the universe around us. This role means that each and every one of us must constantly "tiptoe around" and take care not to sabotage creation, not to needlessly harm other creatures, not to create conflict, express annoyance, anger or negative emotions toward those around us. Perhaps Ecclesiastes meant that when he said, *"Whatsoever God doeth, it shall be for ever: nothing can be put to it, nor any thing taken from it."* (Ecclesiastes 3: 14)

A person can live a long, happy, healthy life if he or she has not disrupted this harmony. But disrupting this harmony the Maasai believe, will cause punishment—malaria, a dead baby, a cow devoured or a fire.

But who can live in this world with no conflict? It's an impossible task! We're all human, and we all sin here and there: chop down trees needlessly, get angry at our neighbor who asks for a cup of sugar for the fifth time, envy a neighbor whose cows are growing plump, etc. The harmony may occasionally be disrupted; however, if nothing is done to bring about a reconciliation, such a disruption will cause punishment as in the case of No'orkishili:

We woke to a hot, cloudy morning. Such a combination usually guarantees rain; however, it didn't come immediately. As the hours went by, the heat increased, as did the humidity, and everyone moaned and clamored for rain to come and bring on a respite from the heat. At four in the afternoon, we felt relief: an immense gray cloud glided down from the hills in the east. The cloud was still distant, but was already raining down. A wide screen of rain approached us swiftly, limiting visibility. The sight was breathtaking, almost primal: in the east, it was gray and rainy, while in the west, the sky was still blue, not even hinting at the deluge to come. I tracked the progress of the cloud, closed the windows, brought home bowls, clothes and various other objects usually strewn about outside, and then, at last, the dam burst and rain poured down , hitting us directly at full force. The air stood still. No wind, no thunder or lightening.

The first rain of the rainy season filled up my water tank.

∾

An hour later, the sky was blue once more. The air emitted freshness, the ground was cleanly washed and the village children ran to play in the mud and puddles. They danced and sang joyfully, and I decided it was just the right time to clean the gutters. I drove my car close to the wall of the house and used it to climb up to the roof. I like to stand up there; here, I feel like I'm on top of the world. The beauty of the place makes me want to sing out loudly, forcefully, and unfortunately, off tune.

I was working on the gutters, but suddenly, I heard loud shouting. I looked up and saw thick smoke rising up from the village. From my spot on the roof, I saw more people had spotted the smoke and ran toward it from all directions.

I leapt off the roof and ran. Inside the village, next to the intensifying column of black smoke, we saw the house belonging to No'orkishili, Larasoi's second wife, going up in flames. Everyone was shocked. About three months ago, his first wife's house had caught fire, and these days, she was busy building a new home!

But there was no time to speculate about this. The fire was eating through the house, which was actually made of dry grass (cow dung), at an immense speed. Within minutes, everyone present set to work. The men held poles and used them to beat at the lower part of the house to dislodge the foundations, dismantle the house and lower the flames, which they feared might spread to the adjacent houses.

The women picked up bowls and containers from nearby houses and ran to the stream to fetch water. The children held little receptacles and gathered water from the puddles that had just formed. We all toiled to put out the fire. The house was gradually collapsing when suddenly, three young goats burst out from it. An adult goat leapt out from a hole on the other side of the house, and two field mice were the last survivors, one moment before the house collapsed upon itself.

We continued to pour water until the fire died out completely. Now everyone fell upon the ruins, picking out pieces of wood and twigs and setting them aside in piles so they could serve as building materials for a new house. I slanted glances toward No'orkishili, a woman who, in mere moments, had lost everything. She had not had a lot of property previously, either, but now she had nothing.

We left the site only once night fell. Where there had been a house there was now only a black pit in the ground. Everyone present was also black and sooty, and now, since it was dark, they gave up thoughts of going down to the stream and washing themselves.

The next morning, Sanguya joined me for morning tea. I asked him what he thought of the fire.

"Something bad is happening with the Olesanduro family. This is the fifth house. We have to fetch an *oloiboni* and find out what is going on."

A few hours later, I met my friend Dr. Anthony, who is not Maasai, and asked him had he heard about the fire yesterday.

"I don't understand it," he said. "Two houses of the two wives of the same man… and he belongs to the Olesanduro family, whose members have lost more homes to fire. We have to get an *oloiboni*!"

Samyan added. "Something's not right with the Olesanduro family. This is the fifth time their houses go up in flames. I was just sitting with the elders, and they say it's a punishment! When Leyan, the elder brother, and the members of his age group were *morans*, they would head out to Tanzania to steal cows. In the course of fighting, they would set the houses of other Maasai on fire. Now they're being punished for it."

"And what needs to be done in order for the punishment to stop?"

"I think we need to call an *oloiboni* to resolve the issue."

The entire region was unanimous about this—the curse must be removed!

∽

Those responsible for restoring harmony, for removing curses or for casting them, are the *oloibonis*.

Originally, the title *oloiboni* was used regarding the Maasai spiritual leaders, who are endowed with "vision," and capable of communicating with the world beyond. They determine the times of ceremonies, opening age groups and organizing prayers in times of drought. In the past, no wars or cattle pillaging campaigns took place without their blessing. As spiritual leaders, the *oloiboni* serve as a counterbalance to the chiefs, who are the social, political leaders.

Today, the title of *oloiboni* is applied not merely to spiritual leaders but also to healers - traditional or alternative doctors—both men and women (they are called "witch doctors" by foreigners, although witchcraft plays no role in their work). Some use plants and various concoctions to heal, some are experts on certain topics only: treating infertility, treating family problems, healing fractures, preparing charms against encountering elephants, bestowing blessings upon pregnant women, and so on. Others, with greater powers, can, in additional to their healing abilities, also communicate with the spirits of family members who have died or with the supernatural world and discover the reason for an illness and how to cure it. As the healer role usually runs in the family, there are well-known families of *oloiboni* among the Maasai.

Most *oloiboni* have only a benevolent therapeutic ability, but a few can also cause harm, i.e., cast a curse on a person or a village. Such cases are very rare, and as Samyan experienced first-hand, the elders have the power of cursing, which serves as a last-ditch measure to restore order. Both groups are treated with mingled respect and awe by those around them.

I have seen many *oloiboni* at work. Each has his or her own method of communicating with the world beyond, but most times, they would mix and shake stones of various sizes and colors in a *kalabash*, then toss them on the ground and "read" the way they fell and assembled. The *oloiboni* repeats the shaking and the casting often, meanwhile learning about the problem and its possible solution.

In everyday life, the people—who live in a small village, in crowded houses in which it is impossible to keep a secret, but in a society that must preserve harmony—internalize and keep frustrations, little jealousies and anger at their neighbor to themselves. Therefore, in most cases, when someone sick, simply getting out of their village and walking to that of the *oloiboni* is enough to ease the patient's distress. Spending time in the healer's company allows the afflicted to discharge the complaints he or she has kept inside for a long time.

Besides listening, the *oloiboni* offers the patient a variety of existing medications: the roots of plants, bark infusions, ground and cooked seeds, and so on. The *oloiboni* serves both as a therapist and as a medical doctor, providing holistic treatment.

∽

However, without the cooperation of those seeking his services, even an *oloiboni* might fail in his healing efforts. This was the case with Kitapo.

One day, about a year after I moved into the village and received the two girls, Lanoi asked me to take a look at Kitapo. As she was eating, she moved her fingers involuntarily, twisting and contorting her hand.

"Kitapo, what's going on with your hand?"

She shrugged her shoulders to indicate she didn't know.

Two days went by, and the contortion had now climbed up her arm, and now both her hands were spasming involuntarily. Within a week, her entire body was moving and contorting in spasms, and her jaw was constantly moving in an odd manner, until we were forced to feed her.

I turned to her mother, a handsome woman of forty, the mother of four children, who had arrived here many years ago as the second wife of the village elder, a blind man of about sixty-five. I had heard many stories about her: as a young girl, she had been forced to marry her elderly husband, whom she has never loved. She tried to run away several times and was always brought back, until finally, after giving birth, she resigned herself to her fate. When I arrived in the village, there was little harmony between them. Her husband constantly lived in the house of his first wife, while she herself had a boyfriend from another village who visited her home occasionally.

I told the mother and the village menfolk that I intended to take Kitapo to the hospital. After a short discussion, they replied: *You can take her, but first, we must try to solve the matter of the disease in our own way. We'll take her to the* oloiboni *to discover the cause for her illness.*

Three days later, Kitapo departed for the *oloiboni*'s house, accompanied by her mother and old, blind father. His diagnosis soon arrived: the relationship between the two parents was not good, which led to Kitapo's illness. The *oloiboni* conducted several treatments, during which a ram was slaughtered and its blood spread on her body, but he explicitly said, "If you want the girl to get better, harmony within the family must be restored." The mother was asked to resume cooking the old husband's meals, washing his clothes and helping his first wife with household tasks. During the week spent with the *oloiboni* she did make an effort, but it did not extend to her heart, or to her spirit. Once they returned to the village, she resumed her old ways.

Without her parents' cooperation, Kitapo could not be cured by the *oloiboni*. She returned home and her entire body continued to contort oddly.

I could now take her to the hospital.

Early in the morning, we boarded the *matatu*, already packed with passengers. The driver hurtled down the bumpy dirt path, raising clouds of dust. The crowding in the bus prevented us from being jostled. It was hard to move or shift from side to side. After two and a half hours, we finally traversed the sixty miles to Narok. From there, we took a taxi to a university hospital, located another sixty miles away, on the upper slopes of the Great Rift Valley, isolated from the heat and dust at the bottom of the valley. The taxi's engine growled angrily as we climbed up the mountain among the podocarpus trees, with black-and-white colobus monkeys leaping between their branches. A pleasant coolness engulfed us, reinforcing the site's Maasai name, Kijabe, or cold.

In the hospital, everyone's eyes were on Kitapo, whose entire body was moving uncontrollably with a rhythm all its own. The nurses, who had never seen such a phenomenon before, brought us quickly into the doctor's office, took her blood pressure and pulse, and hurried to summon him.

After several minutes, the doctor entered the room. He was a young man, dark and tall. He took a quick look at Kitapo, nodded, begged my pardon and said he would return in a few minutes.

He returned with a white doctor. They looked at her, exchanged a few words and departed.

The third time, the doctor arrived with about ten young men, apparently medical students. Only then did he address me.

"Look," he said, "she has a very rare neurological disease called chorea ("dance" in Greek, like in the word "choreography," named after the patients' involuntary gestures). The disease results from an inflammation of the throat not treated, and the bacteria, streptococcus, has entered the nervous system.

"This disease is so rare," he went on, "that it's very important that these students see the girl. They'll never forget the symptoms and will know how to identify them if they encounter them."

We returned home that same day despite the long journey. Kitapo took the medication (one penicillin pill a day for about ten years!) and her condition improved from day to day. When the disease had been suppressed, the smile returned to her face, and she was functioning again—doing the laundry and washing the dishes, cooking, cleaning the house, and playing jacks without her hands shaking—another *oloiboni* finished treating her. He prepared a liquid concoction of herbs for her to drink and placed a mixture of medicinal herbs in a tiny pouch for her to wear as a charm around her neck.

Kitapo recovered. The harmony between her parents remains uneasy to this day.

∽

The Maasai are not dismissive of modern medicine. My impression was that all the "lighter" cases (malaria, typhus, influenza or injuries) are primarily handled by the doctors in each of the small trading centers, whether the clinic is a private or public one.

In more difficult cases, such as infertility, relationships between men and women, recurring fires in the house, or a woman who lost all her sons, one after the other, the *oloiboni* is approached, not only to heal, but mainly to find a cause.

∽

People must conduct themselves in the world without hurting those around them, and will live long, happy lives if they do not disrupt this harmony. But sometimes, the cause for the disruption is not a particular person but society, which has veered away from the traditional social order. Diverging from tradition is considered a threat to the self-preservation and survival mechanisms of society. For disrupting this sort, this society risks a collective punishment from the forces of nature: floods, plagues or droughts.

25

Drought and Tradition

That Friday evening in March 2009 is one I will never forget.

The cows had just returned from pasture, welcomed by the singing women, who started the milking. Suddenly, we heard a dim noise in the distance that gradually increased like thunder. We looked up and saw an unusual sight: a long, strange procession was emerging from a cloud of dust. The milking stopped, the women straightened, and we stood together to watch the gradually exposed scene as the procession drew closer. It was headed by several donkeys, which had been loaded with household possessions and children. They were followed by a group of Maasai women—their clothes stained and faded—prodding the stumbling donkeys to move. A noisy pack of barking dogs scurried around the women. Behind them, calves walked haltingly, while at the end of the column, accompanied by young men, walked skinny, malnourished cows, their skin hanging from their bones.

I felt as if I had gone back in time to the biblical era, watching the procession of Jacob and his sons as they headed toward Egypt.

The procession made its slow way toward us until the two groups, the one milking and the one that had just arrived, stood side by side.

After the traditional greetings, the situation was gradually revealed. These Maasai had come from afar. A prolonged drought had killed off all the grassland in their region, and water had stopped flowing in the rivers. Many days ago, when their circumstances became desperate, they gathered up their meager belongings and lighted out to seek friendlier pastoral land, where their cows could find pasture and the streams provided water. But now, a moment before darkness fell, they merely wanted a place to lay their heads.

I was appalled. By the state of the cows, by the women's helplessness, by their paltry condition. I huddled with the women of our village and suggested that each house host one woman and her children. The village women shushed me, firmly refusing. "If we let migrators into our homes, it will be hard to get them out! We don't know how long they're planning to stay here."

The visitors were shuttled off to a cattle stockade surrounded by a thorn fence, standing empty not far from the village.

The women were right. This group did not merely spend the night with us, but also the months that followed. I felt compassion for them, uprooted from their home and from their country and wandering a great distance away from home, and tracked their acclimation process. That night, their only food was the meager milk supplied by the skinny cows. The families spread cowhides on the ground, covered themselves with more hides and lay down to sleep. The next morning, the energetic women went out to gather wood, and by the afternoon hours, little shacks were already standing at the outskirts of the fence, covered with cowhides. Several more days went by, and cow dung replaced the hides, creating protected enclosures, which provided a roof over the newcomers' heads and a small space to light a fire.

The visitors seemed pleased. Through them, we learned that we were blessed—here, at the outlying areas of Maasai Mara Reserve, water still flowed in the streams, and there was enough grass to feed both the visitors' herds and our own. However, the rumor of this "land of plenty" spread quickly, and more herds arrived in our region.

Too many cows gathered here. Too many people[31].

The heavy heat.

The intense radiation.

The air standing still, making it difficult to breathe.

Every time we hope for a little breeze, it finally arrives hot and dry, blowing fiercely and sucking the marrow from the ground, providing no refuge.

The wilted plants.

The yellow reigning everywhere.

Yellow, yellow, yellow.

In the Talek River, a buffalo sat by the water and did not have the strength to get up. It died where it lay, and we went down with the children to pet its skin, to touch its horns.

The radio announces this is the harshest drought in Kenya since it achieved its independence. We feel it on our flesh.

Cows die. One after the other.

Every day, at least two or three are slaughtered. The women skin them, taking the little bit of meat remaining—sometimes the color is off, sometimes the smell is unappealing—and leaving the skeleton behind.

At first, the dogs enjoyed the remains during the day and the jackals at night, but the predators are already sated, and the slaughtered animals that remain on the ground are stinking.

People grow depressed.

The cows yield no milk and can't be sold, as they are skin and bones, anyway. The only means of making a living is selling the hides of the slaughtered cows: 250 to 300 shilling (about four dollars) per hide. We are in the grips of an intense hunger.

The oldest take the cows down to pasture. They no longer trust the young.

The women tend to the calves. They collect water from the few puddles left in the drying stream into bowls and give them to the calves. Then they go out to gather the branches of plants that the cows can eat.

The rest of us, including me, arm ourselves with thick sticks and stand at the ready to raise cows that fall down and cannot get up. It takes six people to lift up a thin cow. Two poles are inserted under the animal and lifted up by four people. Another person pulls at the horns and a sixth pulls the tail. When we fail and the cow cannot stand—it is slaughtered in the place where it collapsed.

The smell of death.

Tabula, whom I hadn't met in a while, popped over to my house and told me, "I was with the cows for two months in Olmerijo. A person's mind can't relax. He's losing it. Cows die every day, and there's nothing to do. You know how attached we are to our cows. Our brains get all confused when they die…"

∼

One day, still within the dismal atmosphere engulfing us all, I saw all the village women decorated and bedecked with ornaments. They were wearing clean, festive clothes, their bodies adorned with all the jewelry and the symbolic adornments that women are usually required to wear, but these days wear only during ceremonies: the leather belt on the stomach—signaling they are mothers, the earrings in the upper ear, the anklets conveying their married status, the blue-and-white necklace signaling that their children belong to the Ilmeshuki age group, and so on. Dressed in this manner, they went about their everyday activities: going to gather wood, draw water and tend to the calves.

"Hey," I greeted them enthusiastically, "is there some ceremony or celebration happening?"

"No," the women replied indifferently.

The next day, this scene repeated itself, as it did in other villages.

Nesesyay shared the news with me: about a week earlier, in a small, distant village, a woman went to draw water. By the stream, perhaps weakened by hunger, she fainted and fell to the ground. While immersed in deep darkness, she experienced a vision of God.

In her vision, the woman recounted when she woke up, God scolded her. He said, "You women brought this trouble, this drought, upon yourselves. You abandoned Maasai tradition! You wear clothes that are alien to your culture, you don't put on traditional garb, and you no longer carry out the traditional ceremonies. You must return to tradition, and you are the ones who will rescue society from this drought…"

This divine condition—*if you preserve tradition, I'll take care of you*—sounded familiar. I returned home, cracked open that ancient anthropological tome, the bible, and found what I was looking for: "*If ye walk in my statutes, and keep my commandments, and do them; Then I will give you rain in due season, and the land shall yield her increase, and the trees of the field shall yield their fruit.*" (Leviticus 26: 3-4). I kept on reading. God says explicitly: "*But if ye will not hearken unto me, and will not do all these commandments… and I will make your heaven as iron, and your earth as brass…for your land shall not yield her increase, neither shall the trees of the land yield their fruit.*" (Leviticus 26: 14-20).

This speech by God, both to the Jewish people and to the Maasai woman, conveys a clear message to society: responsibility for the fate of the community lies in the hands of its members. Every person must maintain tradition and obey the rules and laws, thus ensuring both personal and collective welfare.

The woman's vision spread like wildfire from village to village. It became the main topic of conversation by the water puddles and on market days. The women took her message to heart[32]. They shed their t-shirts and returned to tradition.

Few weeks later, the drought ended. Fierce rains poured down. The green hues we had forgotten returned in full force. The cows that had survived the drought grew fatter and fleshier, giving birth to calves; the milk resumed flowing, and the land was blessed once more.

26

God Will Help, and If He Doesn't— the White Man Will

During the severe drought of 2009, we were all invited to the school located across the river. Thanks to donations from a Canadian Christian charity organization, the school had undergone a transformation, and from two mud huts, had grown into a long column of stone classes with proper corrugated tin roofs. This year, members of the organization had arrived for a ribbon-cutting ceremony to inaugurate the fancy teachers' residences whose construction had just been completed.

The schoolchildren had been toiling for many days over the songs and dances they would perform before the respected guests. As the event was nearing its conclusion, after the school principal had given an ingratiating speech of gratitude, several heavyset women strolled to the center of the clearing around which we were all standing, carrying immense duffel bags in their hands. To the sound of the parents' and children's applause, they produced pairs of socks, t-shirts and coats, and handed them out to the children.

The ceremony, which had been impeccably organized, ended. I

joined up with the women of my village, who were standing together, comparing the gifts they had received, and together, we made our way slowly toward the trail that would bring us back home. A young Canadian woman named Liz, who had noticed me walking with the rest of the women, stopped me and asked what I, a white woman, was doing here among the parents. The conversation was pleasant, and toward its end, I asked her about her impressions of Kenya.

"Look," she replied, "I only came here for ten days, but that was long enough to form the impression that Kenya is an incredibly beautiful country, very diverse, and that Kenyans are very nice and friendly. One thing bothered me much throughout my visit. The locals, with no exceptions, treated me like a walking wallet. Wherever I visited, they yelled at me, '*Muzungu*, give us money!'"

"Excuse me," I interrupted her. "And what are you actually here for now?"

"To inaugurate the residences we built."

"You mean the residences you built with all the money you brought," I phrased it more sharply.

Liz nodded.

"Well, then, why are you surprised that the Kenyans treat you like a wallet?" I asked. "After all, that's exactly what you're doing here! You brought money, and you're handing it out! You have to understand, every improvement carried out here makes us very happy, but indirectly, there's a problem: you're not only contributing money, but also contributing to the creation of the stereotype of the deep-pocketed white person who comes to Africa to distribute handouts!"

∽

The desolate place where I live is constantly visited by representatives from various organizations: "World Vision," "Better World," "Save the Children" and so on. Some provide food supplies to the "unfortunates": a loaded truck stops near the village, several white men in khaki-colored safari suits disembark, armed with sunglasses and wide-brimmed hats, and unload the merchandise—sacks of maize kernels, wheat flour, oil... The news spreads through the region, and hundreds of women gather, receive their allotted portion and return home happy and satisfied—the white man came, gave, and left.

Sometimes, delegations of doctors arrive. They take up residence in the little school for a few hours. Classes are put on hold. One classroom serves as a "pharmacy," while the rest are examination rooms. The doctors line up all the pupils, and each receives one vitamin pill. Patients and pseudo-patients arrive to get attention and free medication. But who is absent? The patients whose condition is serious, who cannot move from the shade of the tree or from their bed in the hut. They receive no treatment.

In Nairobi, I read in the local paper, a recently conducted study revealed that seventy-seven percent of children in the orphanages built by charity organizations were not orphans at all! Parents preferred to part from their children and deposit them in a place where they were guaranteed a warm bed (a whole bed for every child!), decent meals and free schooling.

I thought about all that, and turned to Liz once more with a touchy question. "Liz, these structures you've constructed—do you really think they help Africans?"

Liz knit her brows in puzzlement, as if she did not understand where I was going with this. In my mind's eye, I envisioned the slim form of Julius Nyerere, a smart, humble man who served as Tanzania's first president. In the 1960s, he tried to disengage from the impossible dependency upon white people, and in one of his speeches, said something like: "The white man talks to us about 'progress.' He wants us to start plowing with tractors that he will sell us, using fuel and spare parts that we will have to purchase from him. The white man wants us to be dependent on him, and does not understand that at this stage, for the African, 'progress' means switching from plowing with a *panga* (machete) to using an ox-drawn plow!"

"Liz," I finally said, "you have to understand. These teachers for whom you've built big, expensive stone houses have lived their entire lives in traditional houses made of cow dung. For them, an enhanced quality of life doesn't require expensive stone houses. Building relatively inexpensive houses made of mud, with corrugated tin roofs, of the kind you can see around here, would be an upgrade for the teachers, and in addition, it would leave you money to provide actual aid!"

"Actual aid? Like what?"

"Like education. You know, it's not enough to build fancy clinics. You have to equip them with medical supplies and doctors. In your case, you invested immense sums of money in a school attended by less than a hundred students—large classrooms, a water well, tanks to collect drinking water, a kitchen… But ultimately, the most important thing is missing here—good teachers! The best teachers prefer the central part of the country, and don't come here, to the periphery. Most of the teachers at this fancy school are locals who have only undergone basic training, and therefore, the level of classes they teach is too low. There are talented, bright children in our region who aren't living up to their potential. We'd be happy if you recruited exceptional teachers by paying them excellent wages. Alternately, you could identify the truly talented, gifted students, and send them to excellent schools, which cost a lot of money (and a Maasai parent who lives here would not pay). They'll study for ten years and then, when they return home, will play a part in moving society forward… That would be real help, rather than stone structures glorifying the name of your organization."

Liz was not frightened off by the criticism I leveled at her. She thought about it, then replied, "Maybe it really is wiser to invest in education and not in structures, but there's a little problem with that.

Our donors want to see some bang for their buck, here and now. They want visible results and they want plaques. Today. Not in ten years. And anyway, if we sponsor kids, could we hang signs on their backs saying, 'Donated by So and So'?"

The women standing beside me and thinking about the household tasks awaiting them urged me to get going. We said goodbye to Liz and walked down the narrow path winding through tangled greenery. I lingered behind, frustrated by my inability to touch upon the heart of the problem of donations—the shaping of African consciousness. Once again, my thoughts drifted back to President Nyerere, who, even back in 1967, instituted a government policy called Self-Reliance[33], intending to establish a state with no dependence on external elements.

Nothing has changed. Nyerere had understood, even then, that such dependence was not merely financial, but mental and cognitive. The generous donations and money streaming in ceaselessly were shaping the Africans' consciousness—and it begins as early as the elementary school tots dancing for Liz—on two levels: The first level consisted of determining their relationship with the white man, which would never be based on mutuality, but rather on givers versus receivers, or rich versus poor. On another level, Africans internalized the perception there was no reason for them to bother acting for themselves: there was no point in banding together and building a classroom, digging a well or damming the river.

After all, God would help, and if He didn't—the white man would.

27

Enkitok Kibor
(The White Woman of Ours)

Finally, the rainy season arrived.

Every day, the clouds pile up on one another, swell and plump, until they can no longer bear their own weight, and free themselves of the excess baggage in cloudbursts.

The air instantly filled with joy and intoxication. The dust settled, and the ground, now enjoying a daily allotment of intense rains, soaked in the profusion of water it had so yearned for. The dry cracks that had formed in its shriveled surface gradually disappeared. Green grass was budding, starting as a delicate fuzz, but within days, already covering the land from end to end. It grew so quickly that I sprawled out on the ground, trying to see if I could witness the moment of growth, like a movie being fast-forwarded. The leaves of the shrubs, which had withered and been shed, were blooming anew. Within a week, the entire meadow had sprouted white flowers that popped up from the ground, looking from afar like bits of paper scattered all over.

The adults heave a sigh of relief and smile. The women climb up to the roofs of the houses every day, applying another layer of cow dung to prevent water from seeping in. The little children scan the sky with their eyes, and when a perfect rainbow is revealed, with all its hues, they station themselves in the rain, jump up and down with their hands held high, and sing: "*Olalai onanyori, panya nkishu ang*" (the green color is mine, for my cows to eat).

It has been years since I first came to live here, in this small Maasai village. Several times a year, especially during special events and ceremonies, when I sit in the little, smoky, crowded huts, participating in lively conversation, I look up and marvel at the way this society has accepted me into its midst. I would like to write "assimilated," but it's clear to all of us, both me and my friends, that no process of assimilation has taken place. I live with them, raise their children, but I am not Maasai!

I am not Maasai in several regards. The most prominent of them is the color of my skin. I am white. My presence shouts out my difference from afar.

In addition, there is the language: the Maa language is distinctly different from every other language I know: Hebrew, Arabic, English, French or Swahili. Not only are sentence structures and grammar different, but the sound and the manner in which the different syllables are "sung" is also significant. In addition, there are two "R"s (regular and emphasized) in the Maa language, while I, as an Israeli, can only pronounce one kind of "R," different from either kind, formed in my throat rather than with my tongue.

I'm often amused to see how those around me, anyone living in the area close to my home, have adapted and learned how to understand my Maa—broken, pronounced with an improper tone and sound, with the syllables being cut off at the wrong time, and the "R"s, oh, those "R"s... frequently, a visitor arriving from afar will sit down in the shade of the tree to converse with the village residents. If I'm there, I may take an active role in the conversation, with the visitor asking, every few minutes, "What did she say?" while one woman takes the time to translate "my" Maa into the generally accepted Maa...

∼

Many children have been born in the village since I arrived. They have accepted my presence naturally. Therefore, I was not surprised when one day, one of the village children clambered up into my lap, played with my straight hair and pulled at it, groped my reddish arms and declared, "Nayolang, you look a lot like the white people..."

Throughout these years, we have learned, my hosts and I, to live side by side. To some extent, the choice regarding how much I want to fit in is mine to make, while they will always see me as something different, other, an adopted foreigner who can be forgiven if, during a ceremony, she did not stand in the right place, if she did not give the elders tobacco as a sign of respect, or if she did not greet them properly.

I have long since realize that culture encompasses a lot more than ceremonies. Culture lies in the countless little details characterizing society. For example, in Maasai society, a man, woman and child walking together will never walk side by side. There are many rules governing in whose company one may eat, and even simple gestures like saying hello are not uniform, and reflect the respect of young people toward their elders, women toward their fathers (and all members of their father's age group), and men toward each other. Thus, for example, all children—uncircumcised boys and girls—must approach every adult (someone circumcised), bow their heads and wait for a hand to be placed upon it, along with a greeting of "*Sopa*" —hello. A circumcised boy who is still not a married adult will be greeted by adults not by placing a hand on his head but by touching his shoulder. He is not enough of an adult to warrant a handshake.

In the first months, I was constantly vigilant when trying to properly greet people correctly, identifying which adult belonged to my father's age group, requiring me to bow my head and wait for a touch of his hand, and which were my peers, and therefore would be greeted with a light handshake. I even had to examine the boys, to determine which ones had been circumcised and therefore would receive a handshake, and which ones should be greeted with a hand on their heads.

But more than anything else—beyond skin color, language and cultural barriers, my greatest variance is invisible, but will always separate me from my Maasai friends—I am not circumcised!

As circumcision is the key for admission into Maasai society, and the very act of circumcision transforms a girl into a woman and a legitimate member of society, how should they define me? This time, the dilemma belongs to my hosts—I am an adult in one regard, still a child in another!

I took advantage of my special status. As I was not circumcised, and therefore not fully a woman, I could be admitted to and participate in ceremonies intended for men, from which women usually keep their distance.

One such ceremony was the circumcision of "my" sons.

28

Water Cannot Climb Uphill

Miton, who was younger in age than Lemein and Leporé, exhibited signs of puberty before them. He grew taller, his voice became deeper, and he even grew one facial hair, which he nurtured faithfully. He felt he was already mature, and applied pressure on his father to begin the process that ultimately led to his circumcision ceremony.

The circumcision of a boy, like that of a girl, is one of the two most important personal rites that Miton would undergo in his lifetime, one that would make him a part of both the Maasai people and of his age group, and endow him with many rights: he could have sex with a circumcised woman and greet those younger than him or be greeted by those older than him in a different manner than previously. Most important, he would become a man!

The decision on when a boy is circumcised is made by his father, and depends upon his assessment of his son's maturity and ability to carry out the tasks allotted to him. Training is gradual, and the tasks include relaying messages from the father to distant relatives (the boy is tested on his ability to remember information and convey it accurately, while also getting to meet additional family members) or sending him out to collect a debt such as a goat or ram (a test of his ability to communicate with elders, to hold his own, and so on). When the boy is ready, the father asks him to collect birds—the task signaling the circumcision—as an indication he acknowledges his maturity and fitness.

Miton, who was about seventeen and considered himself mature—an entire hair was already sticking out of his chin—was frustrated by his father's being taking his time issuing the instruction to collect birds. When no such instruction arrived, he began to hunt birds and collect them of his own accord.

∽

Every day, on their way back from school, he and his friends ran around in the dense thicket of shrubs surrounding the path on both sides. Based on his bouncy movements, his body language and the immense smile lighting up his face, I could see from afar whether he had succeeded, and whether he would produce a colorful bird from one pocket of his pants.

After changing out of his school uniform, he sat down on the bench outside and began "taxidermy": gently, he held the bird between two fingers, and with a knife in his other hand, slit open its stomach vertically. He then removed the skin, along with the feathers, from the bird's body (which was tossed to the dogs), placed it carefully on a small, light wooden cylinder he had prepared in advanced, and "sewed" the skin around the cylinder using acacia thorns. Once he was done, he properly straightened the feathers, wrapped his creation in a piece of cloth and placed it in a sack hanging from one beam of our house.

He didn't always have time to kill the bird. I remember one night when I simply could not fall asleep. Strange murmurs and rustles whose source I could not figure out were emerging from the large room where the children slept. Around dawn, as the children woke up and got ready for school, I finally discovered the source of the rustling: a superb starling sporting blue metallic hues and a rusty breast, now helpless and exhausted, lay drained at the bottom of the school bag, not knowing that its fate had been sealed.

I tracked the progress of the hunting task, sometimes joining the children as they ran around in the thicket, gripping weapons (stones, *rungu* and sticks; I was amazed to discover that slingshots were not used at all), pointing out frightened birds and trying to hit them. Huffing and puffing, I concluded that this was by no means an easy task: birds recognize danger and fly high, finding shelter in the thicket of trees, and most of them fly solo rather than in large flocks. The children could spot some large, relatively slow birds easy to hit, but the desirable ones—colorful and unique, or rare, with a high "value"—were small and elusive.

∼

Besides collecting birds, Miton had to prepare for the circumcision ceremony in other ways; at the height of the ceremony, as the foreskin was being cut, he must avoid making a sound, batting an eyelash or moving a finger. He had to steel himself against the pain. One day, the boys lit a bonfire near the house and knelt around it. I approached them and watched, horrified, as they passed around a burning firebrand from hand to hand. Each grabbed hold of the stick with the red-hot ember at its end and placed it against his thigh without letting out a moan of pain or moving. Miton and his friends' legs filled with burns, which, once they'd healed, left behind round, symmetrical scars.

The sack of birds was gradually swelling. When Miton's father acquiesced and finally instructed him to collect birds, he already had quite a few at his disposal. Now he had only to wait for the end of the school year, for the long break that would allow him to be circumcised and recover before the new school year began.

Our village came to the decision to circumcise Miton along with two other boys from other families. The consideration was financial: many guests would arrive for the ceremonies, and food and drink would need to be provided for them; therefore, it was better to combine the celebrations and shoulder the burden together.

About two weeks before the school year ended, emissaries were sent in all directions in order to collect the required items: giant tanks to brew beer, black, purple or blue sheets of cloth in which the boys would wrap themselves during and after the circumcision, *kalabashes* for the ceremonial beer, and so on. The time when the beer would be brewed had to be carefully considered, so it would be ready both when the school year ended and during a "white" moon period, i.e., while the moon was shining in the sky above us.

~

Brewing the beer for the guests is an event in its own right, keeping the men and women of the village busy for hours and even days, depending on the beer being prepared: the simple, cheap and less-tasty beer is made from the bark of a certain type of acacia tree. Its preparation depends on the work of men who go out to the bush, locate those acacia trees, and use knives to peel off the bark, whose inner layer comprises white fibers with a unique aroma. The fibers are separated from the external part of the bark, taken to the village and laid out to dry.

People of means skip all this trouble and purchase "sausages"— oblong bulbs from one variety of aloe plants—so named (by foreigners, as the Maasai in the bush had never seen or tasted a sausage) due to their shape. Purchasing them is a long-term investment, as they can be used repeatedly, multiple times, and brew a tasty beer much in demand.

Every house in the village hosted giant tanks of twenty gallons, twenty-five gallons, and even a few fifty-gallon tanks. The women's role was to fill these tanks with water, and once enough "sausages" or acacia bark had been accumulated, they were stuffed inside the tanks along with sugar or honey. The tanks were carefully sealed for the fermentation process. Once it ended, two weeks later, the result would be a sweet, tasty beer that could be sipped like juice, but was intoxicating.

As the beer ripened, the village gradually teemed with visitors. Men huddled in groups, "tasting" beer and expressing their opinion as to whether it had matured. Once they were satisfied, and the time of the circumcision grew near, a batch of ceremonial beer, used for blessings and prayers, was brewed in a giant *kalabash*. It required the use of "sausages" and honey, but could be brewed in a mere five days.

～

The eve of the circumcision. A round moon glided slowly through the sky, tinting the rounded hills with silver and illuminating the silhouettes of giraffes moving outside the village. Within the village, guests were thronging together. The houses were full of them, and many sat outside the village fence, enjoying the moonlight protecting them from surprises with wild animals.

The immediate family gathered in the house of Miton's mother. He was sitting on one bed, flanked on either side by older men, the members of his mentoring age group. One of them was holding a little box containing white powder in one hand, and a knife in the other.

The room grew silent.

The old man drew a white line across his forehead—from the bridge of his nose, between his eyebrows and up to the roots of his hair. He explained to Miton he would now be asked an important question he must answer honestly. Anyone who sins by lying would be cursed and punished! The knife would execute the punishment, tomorrow, during the cutting!

The old man paused briefly, took a deep breath, stared at Miton and asked, "Have you ever slept, even a single time, with a circumcised woman?"

The question, like the answer, was crucial.

According to the rules of Maasai morality, since a boy who has yet to be circumcised is not considered a man, if he slept with a circumcised woman (who is entirely a woman—although she can be the boy's age, circumcised before he was and arriving in the village as a bride), he has "leaped over" his age group, and violated a very severe prohibition, according to which children shouldn't fool around with adults (as defined by their social status). Answering this question in the affirmative would bring shame to the family, which has raised a boy who cannot exhibit restraint. As the boy behaved like a "man" even though he was not one, he would have to prove he is indeed a man during the circumcision—which would be carried out with no one holding him from behind.

Could Miton lie[34]? No! The Maasai believe that "the knife knows." If a boy has lied in response to this question, some disaster will take place during the circumcision: lethal excessive bleeding, or an infection that will cause trouble.

The tension mounted. Everyone waited silently for Miton's answer.

Finally his voice, somewhat hoarse from excitement, was heard. He answered with the expression "Water cannot climb uphill." *I did not sleep with a circumcised woman; that would be impossible.*

A sigh of relief was heard, and all at once, everyone present, all of whom had been holding their breath talked, giggled and sang.

Suddenly, heartbroken cries echoed from outside. We ran out and discovered that one of the other two boys about to be circumcised along with Miton had admitted that he had slept with a circumcised woman. His family members burst out of the house as if they had all lost their minds. If they had hair, they would have been tearing it out. They whimpered and wailed, cried and yelled as if they were in a state of deep mourning that had caused them to lose control.

Those left in that house demanded an explanation, and the boy apologized. "I went into the hut... It was totally dark... I couldn't see... I didn't mean to sleep with her, but with a different girl..."

～

In our family, unlike most Maasai families, which circumcise their sons at dawn, circumcision takes place around noon, when the sun is blazing in the sky. It is a very difficult trial, as that same evening, immediately once the questioning had ended and after they had eaten and drunk, the three boys took the cows out to night pasture, which would continue until noon of the following day, when they would return to the village tired, thirsty and hungry. They would then undergo circumcision.

The next morning, while the boys were still out with the cows, the preparations for the ceremony continued: two old men passed through the village, from gate to gate and at the entryways to the boys' homes, provided a blessing. Simultaneously, as with female circumcision, a delegation comprised of women, girls and young men set out to fetch wild olive branches to serve as a soft pallet for the circumcised boys' beds. The rest of us, who had stayed at the village, relaxed until they returned, about two hours later.

The sun climbed to the zenith, sending blazing rays at those of us waiting. Everyone sought shelter. The men sat in the small foyers at the entrance to the houses, holding plastic bottles full of beer and chatting with each other. Others sat in the shade of the houses, wandering from side to side as the sun moved across the sky. Many, swooning in the heat, fell asleep in the shade of the trees. Everyone was waiting for the boys to return from pasture.

Noontime. The preparations had been completed: the man performing the circumcision, a Ndorobo, arrived, wild olive branches were placed on the beds of the boys undergoing circumcision, and those waiting occasionally gazed into the distance, to check whether the boys, who had been herding the cows since the previous evening, were already visible on the horizon.

Two p.m. One woman pointed out the boys and the cattle, finally appearing at the top of a hill. Everyone woke up at once, and the boys' friends set out toward them. We saw the two groups approaching each other. Once the friends reached the herd, they grabbed hold of the three boys and ran with them to the village. On their way, as they ran, the three were stripped of all their clothing and childhood jewelry. The cluster containing Miton and the two other boys drew closer and closer.

Naked as the day they were born—and this is not merely a metaphor, as symbolically, the boy must die to be reborn as a man (and in both cases, birth and death, a person enters the world and leaves it with no clothes or possessions)—the boys were led to the calves waiting, along with the menfolk of the family, close to the village. They were accompanied by their recently circumcised friends (called *olaibartani*), who were distinguished from the rest of the attendees by the colors of the cloaks they were wearing, black or purple, and by the bird "crowns" towering from their heads. Each was holding a pair of sticks, which were beat to create a major commotion, adding to the tension and the excitement. I waited at the village gates. The group drew closer. Judging by their manner of walking and their slumped shoulders, I could imagine how tired the three boys were. They mingled with the calves, which hid their nakedness. The *olaibartani*, who surrounded the calves like a protective wall, urged them to run toward the village.

A hubbub.

People yelling. Excited.

Men falling in ecstasy to the ground. Fainting. A commotion.

Tumult.

The group had reached the village. Each boy entered his mother's home, while the calves were taken to the central cow stockade. All at once, the tension was discharged, and a temporary calm took hold.

Quiet.

~

Miton, who had entered the house in his 'birthday suit,' put on a black cloth sheet, was treated to a glass of milk, and rested while one of the old men dipped into the large ceremonial *kalabash* for some of the beer brewed five days earlier and blessed him and the members of his household. A few minutes later, Miton, draped in the black cloth, exited the house,, sat down on a sheet of cowhide and surrendered to his mother's hands as she shaved off his hair and eyebrows (earlier, he had shaved off his pubic hair). Shaving symbolizes his transformation into a smooth baby. I stood by his side along with the *olaibartani*, who never stopped beating their sticks in order to "chase his fear away."

Three members of his mentoring age group kneeled at Miton's feet. They prepared a pair of sandals for him, which I privately thought of as "King David sandals": an appropriately sized sole was cut from cowhide, holes were punched in its circumference, and laces, also cut from the hide, were inserted.

The three boys, freshly shaved and wearing cowhide sandals, went out to the bush again, this time accompanied by all the men, to return the cattle, which had been left behind, back to the village. The other attendees—family members, friends and guests—waited outside the village gates, watching them wander off while the sun bore down at full strength.

The lowing of the cows separated yesterday from their calves tore through the space and at the heart, signaling the boys' return. This time, the three boys walked slowly, their head bowed down and their eyes staring at the ground as if they were about to be sacrificed. As they approached, I thought of another form of symbolism I had grasped: about an hour earlier, as children, they led the calves to the village, while now, as they went through becoming men, they were returning to the village with the cows.

The lowing of the cows.
The calves bellowing, seeking their mothers.
The constant rattle of the sticks.
The deafening noise.
The mounting tension.

More men swooned and fell upon the path in a dead faint, while others jumped in the air, raising their sticks and yelling. The boys and the cows approached the village, each entering through his father's gate. The boys would undergo the circumcision ceremony from the oldest to the youngest, and Miton was the second in line. The first boy, naked, took a sheet of cowhide from his mother's house. Similarly to the symbolic purification in the girls circumcision, he stopped briefly to have water poured over his head from a clay jar prepared in advance, and then—with slow steps, his head bowed—he continued to drag the hide into the cow stockade.

The cowhide was placed on the ground . The boy sat on it, stretched his legs out before him and leaned back against a mentoring man who supported his back. Dozens of men huddled around him, waving their sticks, jumping and yelling.

The circumciser declared the beginning of the cutting.

The boy "died." He lay sprawled out, without making a sound, moving a fingertip or batting an eyelash.

The men surrounding him examined him carefully, seeking signs of "running away from the knife": that twitch that would indicate his failure and weakness; that movement that is a great insult to the boy and his family. In the past, the old men recounted, such boys would be ousted from society, and sometimes, even stoned. These days society was much more tolerant, and a boy who twitched could redeem himself by paying a cow to each of the age groups and to the *Ndorobo* performing the circumcision; those around him would then never mention his humiliation again. I thought of the expression "lip service"...

I stood close to the inner circle and watched the excited, yelling men. I felt they were experiencing their own circumcision again, letting out that same shout they could not let out.

I glanced at my watch. The cutting lasted less than a minute, and its ending was marked by the call, "Bring milk, bring milk, quick!" The circumciser had cut the foreskin, but had not separated it all. A small part of it had remained hanging on the penis as a reminder of the circumcision.

The first boy was carried out of the stockade on the cowhide and brought into his mother's house, and now came Miton's turn. Much to my relief, he went through the circumcision without shaming his family. Later, he told me that the call of "bring milk" was important to him, as it penetrated through the "swoon" he was experiencing, indicating that the cutting was over. He still did not move even then, but could feel the milk being poured over his wound and how he was carried on the cowhide into the house, and onto the pallet of wild olive branches prepared for him in advance.

Now came the turn of the third boy, who had slept with a circumcised woman. Two men thrust a tree branch into the ground so the boy could lean back against it, as no one would hold him. Naked, the boy dragged the sheet of cowhide on the ground, and entered the clearing upon faltering legs. A moment before the cutting, fearing he would move and that the spectators' reaction would escalate, I got out. I sought the women with my eyes. Most were ensconced in their doorways, peering out into the commotion, their eyes moist.

At my back, I heard calls of "Bring milk," and knew that the third circumcision had ended successfully.

The village's honor had been maintained.

∼

While Miton rested in the hut on a soft pallet of wild olive branches, the men hurried out to catch a calf from the herd. Sanguya wrapped a leather band around the calf's neck, probed the artery, which now protruded somewhat, took a few steps back, kneeled, drew back his bow and shot out an arrow. A stream of blood burst out, straight into the *kalabash* held by one woman.

The blood-filled *kalabash* was quickly taken to Miton. His extended family gathered around his bed, urging him to drink. He kept silent, watching them with piercing eyes. My gaze bounced between him and them as I tried to understand what was going on. Several minutes went by.

His brother was the first to break the silence. He approached Miton's bed and promised him a heifer. His mother came over and offered him a young goat. One by one, the family members approached, promising him sheep, goats and calves. Only after he had "accumulated" enough gifts and created a future herd for himself did Miton consent to drink the blood and allow the last part of the ceremony to take place.

In the cow stockade, the mentoring "elders" sat down in three groups, one for each circumcised boy. They produced the traditional fire sticks, one flat and one rounded, and rubbed the rounded stick over the flat stick until a spark was formed. Gently, they put the spark inside a dry donkey turd cut in two. They repeated the process three more times. They blew lightly, and a thin spiral of smoke signaled the growth of a flame. Three fires were lit. "The torch" is passed on—the tradition continues!

Guests continued to stream to the village throughout the day. I enjoyed watching as the women approached. They arrived in groups, wearing their best finery, bedecked and adorned. As they drew closer to the village, they sang and danced, lingering outside until the women of our village, singing and dancing, came out to greet them, and together, all entered the village.

While the men, sitting together in the shade of the houses, belted out drunken songs, clasping plastic bottles filled with the intoxicating yellow beverage, the women helped themselves to a proper meal: rice, potatoes and the meat of the sheep slaughtered in advance to feed the celebrants.

∾

The dawning morning found the village partially abandoned. Most guests had dispersed. The villagers themselves, exhausted from the massive ceremony, slowly restored the village to its former condition: pots and plates were washed; the "sausages" were placed on the roofs of the houses to dry; the beer containers, empty now, were washed out and sent back to their owners in the adjacent villages.

The three newly circumcised boys, wearing black cloth sheets[35], sat together in the shade of the tree, wrapped in a thin blanket, with the *surutya*—an adornment made of two copper spirals, indicating the boys' new status as *olaibartani*, or newly circumcised—fastened tightly around their temples.

The time had now come to prepare the birds crown. This was an intricate task performed by two men. Miton, sitting next to them and observing their progress, gave them a sack stuffed with thirty-five birds, all breathtaking in their multitude of colors: rollers, starlings, shrikes, weavers and even one cuckoo. The men connected four sticks to one another and used them as a base to link the birds to one another until a colorful, stunning, heavy headdress was formed.

After several days of recuperation, the three *olaibartani* embarked on their travels, wearing their black cloth cloak and their leather sandals, while proudly sporting their heavy bird crowns on their heads. I saw these crowns as a double expression of the "handicap principle": they displayed the young men's abilities at bird hunting , and now, like the horns on the heads of the male impalas, also exhibited their fitness to carry the weight of the crown on their heads. They traveled to different villages where circumcision ceremonies were taking place, encouraging the boys undergoing circumcision. They huddled with their girlfriends and female peers, who gave them rings from colorful beads, and received gifts from the elders at the different villages.

The month after the circumcision flew by. The new school year was about to begin. Miton's hair was shaved, the *surutya* was given to me, his mother, and I was tasked with making *issuri*, a long chain in shades of blue and white, indicating my status as the mother of a circumcised boy who had joined his age group.

The shaven-haired Miton, no longer an *olaibartani* but holding a new title, *ilikiliani* (young adult), was facing a difficult dilemma: should he abandon school and join the many friends embarking on the next stage of the age group and becoming *morans*?

He chose school.

29

Life Is a Miracle!

One rainy afternoon, I was winding slowly through the meadow surrounding the village, and suddenly heard a commotion. I hurried toward some women huddling together and heard them whispering and talking in low voices. "Lesiton died... Now... At home..."

Lesiton? It couldn't be! I had just seen her that morning, safe and sound, talking to some women!

I ran to her village, about 200 yards away, and noticed the people thronging from afar: men, women and children were huddling at the entryway to her home. I approached them. Lesiton was laid out on the ground, her upper body exposed, a flowery skirt at her waist, her eyes open and her mouth full of vomit. I stormed into the circle of people surrounding her. "What happened to her?"

"She's dead!"

"Did you call a doctor?" There was a rural clinic located just a short distance away.

Everyone turned their faces toward me. "Nayolang, she's dead!"

I immediately took control. "You, run get the doctor, and you, bring me a flashlight."

I kneeled over Lesiton, cleaned the vomit from her mouth and opened up the airways. I placed my hand on her pulse and felt a weak beat. Had she fainted while throwing up? I loosened the thick leather belt securing her flowery skirt and gave her mouth-to-mouth resuscitation.

The doctor came to relieve me. I directed the flashlight just delivered at Lesiton's eyes. The pupils did not react to the light. Was she truly and irreversibly dead? When does death become irreversible? Apparently, the doctor was uncertain, and kept trying. She gave Lesiton several injections, to no avail.

~

I recalled an event that had happened twenty years earlier, when I had taken part in an attempt to save a man's life. It happened on the Sinai Peninsula, already returned by Israel to Egypt. I arrived at Dahab Beach with a group of tourists. We settled down on the beach, opposite the majestic coral reef of the Blue Hole, a well-known diving spot. I was standing with my back to the sea and the group of tourists across from me, teaching them how to place the diving mask and how to use the snorkel. I turned my face to the sea, and right in front of me, saw a diver floating on the water face-down. He was wearing a diving suit, with an oxygen tank on his back, but something seemed odd. His weight belt was not at his waist, and his arms were rising and falling with the waves as if he had no control over them.

I called out to him but he did not react. I walked toward him carefully on the reef, pulled his hand, and he floated toward me as if he had no volition of his own.

The man was dead.

I turned him over, tore off his diving suit and began a cardiac massage. Every time I pressed down on his lungs, water burst from his mouth and nose—lots of water. Followed by blood… I knew the man was dead, but I didn't want to give up…

~

Lesiton was dead.

I left her home, heartbroken. I couldn't understand how a woman who, just hours ago, had been walking around hale and hearty could die like that, apparently suffocating, with so many people around her—and no one had lifted a finger to help her. Who knew how long she had lain like that, choking, until I arrived, several minutes too late.

Evening came. Red rays reached me as I sat watching the view. I buried my face in my hands. One question beat at me again and again. Why hadn't anyone done anything? Why? Why did the Maasai give up so easily?

To the Maasai, death is an integral part of existence, while life is a miracle that takes place every day[36]. Death is so incontestable—and would arrive anyhow—that fighting it seems ludicrous. If Lesiton's day had come now, what good would it do to put it off by another day, week, month or ten years?

And no, this should not be interpreted to mean that when a person is sick, no effort is made to save him or her. The patient's family members will try to cure him or her with natural medicine or at local clinics or larger hospitals. But it is all done out of a deep internal understanding that these efforts might be in vain.

~

One afternoon, Nashelu came to my home holding her little son, a baby, who was burning up with a fever. As the mother of four girls, she had yearned for a boy. Several years ago, she had given birth to a boy, but he had passed away. Her new baby was only two months old, and now had a high fever and his body stiff. Yesterday, she told me, she had walked with him down to the regional clinic, located nine miles away. The doctor gave him several injections and sent them home. Now that the baby's temperature had climbed up again, she asked me to drive her, along with her husband, his mother and a friend, to a nearby clinic.

The nurse laid the baby down on the treatment bed, moved his arms from side to side, examined his eyes, which were gazing at a fixed spot. She thought for a moment, then shook her head mournfully. The signs, she said, indicated this was meningitis. *You have to rush to Narok. To the hospital.*

It was evening time. The family was not prepared for the long drive down the bumpy dirt road. However, Nashelu would not give up, and wanted to consult another doctor. We drove on to a private clinic.

The doctor hooked the baby up to an IV, but while on the treatment bed, he expired.

Nashelu uttered a cry of pain.

We all returned to the vehicle, surrounding Nashelu from every direction as she held her dead baby in her arms and wept.

Everyone present immediately addressed her, silencing her. "Nashelu, stop it! Nashelu, why are you crying?"

I drove the vehicle toward the village as darkness gradually enveloped the earth. Behind me, I constantly heard Nashelu trying to stifle her sobbing. Suddenly, her husband asked me to stop. I veered off the path winding through a thicket of greenery and parked on the sidelines. The entire family disembarked and wandered about sixty feet into the thicket.

There, in the thicket, the baby's head was shaved by his grandmother. Nashelu wrapped the baby in his thick blanket, thrust him deep under one bush, and returned to the vehicle, supported by her husband.

We returned to the village.

Burial in a pit is a relatively new process that began in our area about twenty-five years ago. Until then, after the ceremony of saying goodbye to the dead - which consisted of shaving their head, slaughtering a ram and applying the fat of the ram to the body - the Maasai would go down at nighttime to toss the body outside the village gate, so the hyenas would eat it (hyenas eat not only flesh, but bones as well). This fulfilled the Maasai's perception of themselves as an integral part of the natural world, the Maasai version of "ashes to ashes, dust to dust." The next morning, there was usually no sign of the dead. If the body had not been eaten, the family members knew that such a heavy sin lay upon the dead that even the wild animals avoided him or her. If this was the case, the family of the dead had to conduct a "purification ceremony" that included slaughtering another ram, this time covering the corpse not just with fat but with blood.

In the late 1990s, the El Niño phenomenon led to a change in the burial process: it had rained heavily for many weeks. Maasai Mara was flooded. Rivers and streams overflowed, their color becoming reddish-brown because of massive soil erosion. The Maasai huts were slowly falling apart, and the rain that infiltrated soaked the hides serving as mattresses. Despite the fire burning in the hut, the floor did not dry, and neither did the clothes; the cow stockade turned into a bog of dung and mud that came up to people's knees. There was no refuge from the wetness.

Along with the rain, the wetness and the mud came diseases: cholera, typhus and malaria claimed many victims. Every night bodies were tossed beyond the fences of the villages. The dead were so numerous that not only hyenas but lions as well joined the party of those feeding off human flesh. The wild animals grew used to the smell of man, as if it were the smell of edible meat, and attacked live people.

A plan needed to be formulated. The solution ultimately found was burying the dead in the ground and piling stones on their graves.

∼

When we returned to the village, the women saw Nashelu's empty hands and did not require an explanation. Supported by them, she walked slowly home, accompanied by wailing and crying.

One woman put a kettle on the fire, another brought water, while others peeled potatoes. They were very skilled in helping one another. I knew there was not a single woman around me who hadn't suffered a loss, and imagined the intensity of their feelings swelling with the death of the baby that evening.

Several days later, Nashelu was still lying in bed, with no energy, but the women no longer flocked around her. They had stopped visiting her.

"It's true that she's sad," they replied in response to my question, "but we want her to get back to normal life as soon as possible. As long as we take care of her, she'll allow herself to stay in bed and feel sad. That's why we stay with her in the first days, help her take care of the kids and do the housework, but then we leave her alone, so she'll go back to routine quickly. Her adult children or her husband's mother will be the only ones helping her with the cooking—no one else…"

∼

No'oltualan, one of our two village elders, was about seventy years old. The constant tremor in his hands hinted that he might be suffering from Parkinson's disease. I was raising his son Miton and his grandson Lemein. At least three times a week, he would hobble down to my house, sit with me in the shady veranda, drink tea and bless me. One Saturday, he arrived under his usual habit. The kids, already teenagers, were home, and Lemein was cooling the tea for him by pouring it from cup to cup. No'oltualan was talking to the three of us. He explained how he would like his land to be divided after his death, expanding on his herds.

At the end of the conversation, I told my children, "It's odd, what he was saying sounded like a will to me. I think the man is planning to die..."

I had harbored this suspicion for many months now, as ever since one of his wives had died two years ago, he seemed to fade away.

A few days later, after sitting with him in the shade of the tree outside the village gate, I went home and wrote in my diary: "His eyes are extinguished; it seems that his will to live is gone."

Sadly, I was not wrong.

The next morning at dawn, unmistakable wailing sounded from the village. I ran toward the voices and found him sprawled out outside his home, rattling out his last breaths with his eyes wide open, held by his children.

The preparations for the burial began. His wife shaved his head and his jewelry was removed. Then, wrapped in his blanket, he was brought inside the house and laid out on the bed while shovels and hoes were gathered outside, and digging the pit began outside the village, across from his personal gate.

Traditionally, a person is not buried in the morning (sunrise means life) but in the hours when the sun is tending westwards, and we had a few hours to go before his burial. It was hot and dry, the ground was as hard as concrete, and digging the pit took hours. All the men were present. While some were digging, others rested in the shade of the tree. The sweat flowed and the silence was heavy.

Notice was sent out to No'oltualan's family members, a rented motorcycle was sent out to fetch his oldest son, who had headed out to the market the previous day, and two men were delegated to pick a plump ram, which was taken to the cattle stockade, slaughtered, and its meat cooked and eaten by the attendees, while its fat was gathered to anoint the dead.

I offered to go get his son Miton from school but to my surprise, the family members refused. "The father's already dead—why interrupt his studies?"

That entire morning, I walked around restlessly. I had a hard time believing in the death of the village elder, in the death of No'oltualan. I had seen him breathing! Perhaps the family had given up on him too early? I went into the house, sat down across from the bed on which his body was laid out, and for about an hour, stared at his feet. I waited for him to exhibit any sign of life. Move a finger. That same finger he could not move during his circumcision—perhaps he would move it now...

Two p.m.

His sons gathered in the house to start the burial process. They approached the bed on which their father was lying, gave each other final instructions, and then—silence. From the moment they tended to their father and until he was buried, they could not speak. I saw them communicate wordlessly, with silent hand gestures. The eldest son scooped up fat from the ram slaughtered earlier and applied it to his father's head. The other son covered his shoulders and chest with fat, and in this manner, each of his circumcised sons applied the fat over a different part of his father's body, with the youngest tending to his feet. They wrapped their father in a blanket serving as a shroud, wrapped the blanket with the cowhide from his bed, and carried him to the pit, its floor already covered with green leaves as a pallet for his head. The sons cast the first clods of dirt and returned to the hut to help themselves to some milk.

At that moment, the realization that his death was final hit me. A friend, and a protector, had died.

I wept bitter tears.

I was the only one crying, and everyone standing next to me scolded me: "Nayolang, be quiet! You could have cried earlier. Now is not the time to cry."

One woman berated me, "Nayolang, his death is God's will. Are you challenging God? Shut up."

The grave was filled with dirt. Heavy stones were placed on the clods of dirt, and the attendees dispersed silently.

His family brewed beer—a final farewell to the dead.

I returned home, mentally reconstructing the burial rites. I thought about the way the body was anointed with fat. , When the body of the deceased was tossed in the bushes, the fat attracted the hyenas to it. However, what role does it fill now? I recalled another funeral held a year earlier in a nearby village. There, the old man had passed away in the hospital, and in the town, they had been unwilling to release his body without a casket. The family purchased a coffin and transported his body back to the village. Across from the open grave, a dilemma ensued: his family was wary of opening the coffin and looking at the old man, who had died several days ago, but wanted to carry out the ceremony according to custom. After a short discussion, a solution was found: the lid of the coffin was covered in ram fat[37] by the oldest son, and only then was the coffin lowered into the open pit.

About a month after No'oltualan's death, the family performed a small ceremony to distribute his property and say a final farewell. Although his offspring did not have to attend the burial, this current gathering required all his sons and daughters.

No'oltualan had prepared for his death. He had chosen a memento for each of his children in advance: his personal knife, his shepherd's staff, the *rungu*, his tobacco can, and so on. Each son received an iron bracelet carved with crosshatching, to be worn on the right arm, symbolizing he had been orphaned of his father. The eldest received his father's bracelet, which had been passed on from father to son, from generation to generation.

No'oltualan also determined exactly how his property would be divided: the cows, the goats, the sheep and the plot of land under his name.

∼

In his life, old No'oltualan had begat many children, grandchildren and great-grandchildren, thus fulfilling his role as a link in the chain of life. His name would remain engraved among his children, among his friends and those who cherished him. However, this was not the case with everyone who passed away. I witnessed this many months later, when I was sitting with several other women in Simaloi's hut. Simaloi, lively, giggly and noisy, had just cooked lunch. The house was hot and smoky. From her trunk, she produced a photo album and handed it to us. We gathered around the album, head touching head, and tried, in the house's faint illumination, to look at the photos and identify the people in them. The pictures all resembled one another. All showed women or men wearing their finest clothes, displaying many necklaces, and standing frozen in front of the camera.

I looked closely at one photo. Suddenly, with no warning, Simaloi snatched the album from my hand, took out the photo, and with no hesitation, threw it straight into the coals at the center of the house.

"Hey, Simaloi, why? That was a nice photo!"

"Ah, because one of the women in the picture died a few weeks ago…"

"So?"

"You can't leave anything of her behind," she replied, "because if any of her family members see her photo—they'll grow sad."

How the Maasai remember or forget the dead depends on whether that person has fulfilled his or her destiny. And self-fulfillment means having descendants.

A young person who dies—such as the woman in the photo, who had yet to have children—is buried with all of his or her jewelry, and erased from the collective memory[38]. Not only are any photos in which they appear burned, but any people in the vicinity who shared the deceased's name must change their names, so as not to cause sorrow to the parents and family members of the deceased.

I listened to Simaloi's explanation, and my thoughts instantly leaped to that different world from which I had come. I imagined my own death: my family members and friends would mourn deeply, would cry. Would feel sorrow. Would want to know why, and how, and what was done to save me. They might turn my life into a "shrine"—a corner of their home that would serve as a memorial site, along with a burning memorial candle and large photos of me. They might establish a memorial site for me online. Perhaps they would found a charity bearing my name? Their lives would never again be the same. They would live in the shadow of my death.

Here, in Maasai Mara, people live their lives, and once dead, are removed from the collective memory to make way for the living.

30

The Zebra Carries Its Stripes with It Wherever It Goes

For over ten years, I was busy mostly with "doing nothing at all," as my friends put it. But then, one day, after years of resisting, I succumbed to temptation and brought a laptop to Maasai Mara. I did not do so wholeheartedly, as more than anything the computer represented the individualism of the Western world, individualism in the sense of sitting one on one, man across from machine, in total contradiction to the way of life here.

The entry of technology into my life, in the form of laptop, required me to reorganize my schedule. Twice a week, I had to cruise in my vehicle to the nature reserve and spend a few hours in one lodge, working on the laptop and recharging it. I got used to it, enjoyed hanging out, it wasn't too much bother, but... what about village life?

The presence of the small, black, silent object was actually most prominent in its absence. I had continued my life in the village as usual, and every day I sat down in the shade of the tree with the women—listening to their chatter, waving away the flies and stringing beads. However... I had a toy at home. A private toy. And that toy tickled at my fingertips. I was sitting beneath the tree, yet felt a sense of dissonance, as the whole world was now at arm's reach!

I casually got up, shook the dirt off my pants, put on my sunglasses, snuck-walked home slowly, closed the door behind me and… connected!

In a society in which people were constantly in each other's company, closing the door behind me made me feel bad. However, much to my surprise, I had no quandaries at all! I had opened a little crack, and "my" world, the world I'd left behind, with all its significance, thrust a foot through that crack and worked its way in at full force.

The computer became my most important companion. It took up more and more of my time, consistently decreasing my "do nothing" time. It raised doubts in me—did typing away while ensconced in my room, with only the jangle of the cowbells sounding from afar, mean "doing something"? Was the way I once spent a significant part of my life "there" —work, movies, cafés, TV—meaningful? What is it that is supposed to bring me satisfaction?

I don't always close the door behind me.

Sometimes I sit outside and raise my eyes to the rolling hills and the gray clouds floating across the sky. But when I look down, I see my reflection in the screen. In this mirror that the computer places in front of my eyes, it becomes clearer than ever to which world I truly belong.

∼

Once again, the women were busy from morning to evening.

Since 2001, the year I moved to Maasai Mara, the village built at the same time as my home has been relocated once, and now it was relocating once more. I calculated the time and confirmed: it had been over fourteen years since I got here. As always, I continue to be moved by the beauty of nature around me and feel blessed.

The years that have gone by have left their mark on me. The African sun has beaten at me mercilessly, and the wrinkles on my face are no longer merely expression lines. I needed these years, and the dimension of African time, in order to "steep" in Maasai culture. To accept it, to understand it, and to some extent, to internalize it.

∽

The afternoon hours. I'm sitting on the veranda of my home. The cowbells around me are jangling in their unique tune. Only yesterday, I had learned that a Maasai can recognize any herd solely based on the sound of the bells. Each herd has its own bells and its own melody. Two boys join me in the shade, ask for a glass of water, sit down on the bench next to me and stare out at the view. I look at them, thinking, *after all those years, could I have more fully fit in within society?*

A spotlight of thought flashes through me: the social network. Have I fitted in? I consider Maasai women. Throughout their life, they live in crowded conditions alongside many other women—some nice, some not so nice, and some not nice at all. But whatever the women's characters are like, all will always maintain good relationships with everyone else. They will help each other out—always.

And what about me? Although, thanks to the children I've adopted, I've created the basis for a social network, I have continued being a distinct product of Western society: I have carefully selected the few women with whom I have "good chemistry," and they have become my friends. The rest of the women live in physical proximity to me, we greet each other every day, but I have not included them in my circle of friends—my social network has remained limited. I have failed.

Another spotlight flashes: "the patron" ("Big Man"). Over the years, I have realized that the African social system is built of concentric circles around one or more members of the village or the region who have achieved success: grown rich in cows, grown rich in money, accumulated political power and so on.

The "Big Man" —and this does not apply solely to the Maasai— enjoys displaying his wealth in public. He builds a bigger house, buys a vehicle, or daily parades his hundreds of cows. However, to win the devotion of those around him, he must share his wealth: he opens his house to his neighbors —i.e., slaughters a goat or a ram and invites those around him for a celebration of meat (and the more livestock he slaughters, the more people will arrive to huddle around him). He frequently hands out small gifts to the people around him: tobacco offerings to the elders, bottles of beer for the younger generation, and so on. His social network gradually expands, and people will mention their association with him with pride. The return on his investment will arrive quickly: he will be invited to serve as an arbitrator when disputes occur or to serve as an "elder" in traditional ceremonies. Many will want to marry off their daughters to his sons, and he will also be invited to join as a partner in more businesses, thus increasing his wealth.

I understand now, that the family that adopted me as a white friend hoped I would be their "Big Man." That I would exhibit my "wealth," distribute it like every other "Big Man" does, and that their very proximity would enhance their social status. In my ignorance, I did not understand the social system at the time. They expected me to build a house with a generator, an electric fence and a television, a house that would be a source of pride for the entire neighborhood... But what I had wanted was to fit in: like the rest of the women, I gathered branches and cooked over a fire, washed my clothes in the stream, sat in traditional chairs rather than recliners. For many years, the children did their homework by the light of a lantern, and to this day, there is no running water in my house.

The Maasai provided me with chances to become a "patron" by

repeatedly requesting gifts of or a little money to buy beer or to fund their children's schooling, but I said no to some. I was afraid that they were turning with such appeals because I was white. I wanted to be like everyone else, and therefore, I gave selectively. I did not understand that by not giving, I had stopped being like everyone else.

And here is a third spotlight: my place in society. Had I become, as I'd initially hoped, one of them? The negative answer, much to my surprise, pleased me. I had maintained my selfhood, expressed my opinions, and suggested more options besides the existing ones. Other than during ceremonies, I continued wearing my usual clothes.

Three spotlights. The illumination is already bright, and by its light, I observe my children: I had, after all, learned and internalized that in Maasai society, children pass from family to family. Don't get attached! Meanwhile, I had gotten attached to these children—whom I had loved with every bit of my heart, each with his or her own unique character—and would not let go. Even to this day, when they all have already children of their own, and some are already passing their children on to others, I still cling to them as "mine."

~

Can a leopard change its spots? I had asked myself that question often in my life here. Today, this question is much more than skin deep. It encompasses an entire culture, a worldview, a full perception of life.

The answer, apparently, is no. The Maasai say, "The zebra carries its stripes with it wherever it goes." Even after many years, it's hard for people to change their skin, to shed their culture.

31
The Zebra Does Not Deny Its Stripes

As I had realized, I carried my stripes with me wherever I went, but what about the Maasai? How did they "carry their stripes" as a society? And as a people?

I came across a thin booklet written in Tanzania about forty years ago, containing a collection of Maasai proverbs. In the introduction, the author recounted a short story: an elderly, venerable Maasai summoned his youngest son and both embarked on a journey to the "Mountain of God" (Ol Doinyo Lengai—a smoking volcano in northern Tanzania, in the heart of Maasai country). After two days' journey, they reached the foothills of the mountain and sat down in the shade of one of the ancient acacia trees with their knotty trunks. The old man talked to the boy: "My child, hear the words which I speak. Hundreds of years ago, our ancestors left their country of origin and slowly migrated until they reached the place where we are sitting today. They managed to survive in various places and climates and to overcome plenty of obstacles. Were we not once the most courageous warriors[39] in the region, warriors who inspired fear in others?

"My child, I lived my life like my father and like his father before him, but it has been many years since the time when I wore the lion's mane headdress! Now, my son, I have grown old, and I'm afraid of the future: what is the power of the *morans* these days? They are no better than women! Where has our greatness disappeared today? Without wars, how can we distinguish between the brave and the cowardly?

"Old men do not understand change. My days are numbered and the future no longer matters to me. I am not afraid. I will die like a real Maasai. But my children—I can't even imagine how they will grow up."

~

A common Maasai expression states, "The zebra does not deny its stripes." And what about people? Can they deny their tradition?

Sunday morning. Sounds of drumming are heard from the small trading center next to us. I walk up to the tiny mud structure with its two doors, enter through the back door and join the audience of women and children whose singing and offerings of praise to God can be heard from afar. The walls of the structure are covered with cloth. Two rows of benches and a variety of plastic chairs in different colors are crammed into the small space. At the anterior, near the front door, is a table with several men dancing and singing around it. The collective singing dies down gradually, and each attendee begins "speaking in tongues,"[40] communing with God, in his or her own way: some kneel, shedding tears, some wipe off their sweat, some raise their hands in the air, their whole bodies trembling, mumbling incomprehensibly. A group of girls now steps forward, leading another song with a dance. Their voices are melodious and the singing coalesces into great music.

This weekly gathering fascinates me. Until recently, singing and dancing were part of daily village life, but they gradually faded away. Seeking the "togetherness" that had melted away, society found a contemporary solution to this need.

Is it really togetherness, though? As churches are popping up like mushrooms after the rain, whereas previously there had been a sense of unity, now the local people are divided. Each person attends his or her own church.

Churches have become agents of change in an important way: they create new opportunities for social mobility. Young teens, some of whom did not finish elementary school and would otherwise have spent their lives as cattle shepherds, have become spiritual shepherds as church pastors. They open meetings with church prayers, subverting the elders' authority.

In the era of technology and the global village, the agents of change are numerous. The reason churches are so appealing to the Maasai is that they seem modern; it is one way for the Maasai to connect with global society.

Modern life has not skipped over Maasai society, and tourism is another important agent of change. In recent years, Kenya has experienced an unprecedented surge of tourism. The tourists traveling between the national parks stop for a visit in one of the Maasai villages, and an entire show is put on in their honor: they watch *morans* exhibiting their ability to jump to great heights and women singing while adorned in their finest outfits and jewelry. The visitors learn how to light a fire in the traditional manner, by rubbing sticks together, are invited in to enter a house, and at the end of the visit, purchase mementos in the small market built at the edge of the village. Tourism, more than any other factor, transitions the Maasai in our area to a market economy. Money is now available.

The availability of money has naturally increased expenses: new clothes are purchased more frequently, plastic housewares are replacing traditional ones, and the diet has expanded—it includes not just *ugali* but also rice, potatoes, cabbage, onions and various spices. The changes in eating habits have resulted in weight gain.

The extra funds are routed into purchasing additional commodities, which also serve as agents of change: for the price of three cows, young men buy motorcycles, which are used as taxis transporting brides to their new homes, sick people to the clinic, or women to the market. Distances have grown shorter, and fewer people walk. I watch these young men in amusement: the motorcycle has replaced the spear as a symbol of masculinity.

Every man or woman has a cell phone, which has changed their life: the phones are used to warn the shepherd in the park of approaching rangers, to inform a beloved boyfriend that the coast is clear—i.e., the husband is not around, to listen to music, to convey news about ceremonies, births or deaths. There is no longer a need to come to market to hear the news.

The change is also apparent in the traditional ceremonies, which, just a few years ago, were considered an unmissable event. Guests came from afar. The ceremonies were filled with joy and jubilation, accompanied by singing and dancing. Similarly to market days, ceremonies were an opportunity to meet friends from all over the region and get caught up on news from every village. Today, cell phones have replaced these gatherings as a source of information. Fewer guests come to ceremonies, and even fewer of them dance as they once did. The only ones who have not changed are the elders: they arrive in the village before the ceremony starts, and leave it only when there's not a single drop of beer left to squeeze from the vats.

∽

Tourism and the availability of money have wrought an essential change in the definition of a man's obligations: in the past, a man would marry two or three wives, and maintained them. He would sell a goat, a ram or an ox, and fund his household needs with the money. Today, as women manufacture beaded souvenirs, selling their handicrafts and receiving cash —many men see themselves as released from the obligation to provide for the family. Modern life has created a situation where, besides women's traditional roles— gathering wood, fetching water, cooking, washing clothes, giving birth and taking care of the children—they are also tasked with obtaining cash to buy food or pay tuition. The older men spend their days drinking[41], while the livestock continued to multiply.

The money on hand from tourism attracts members of other ethnic groups: Kikuyu, Luo, Kisii and Kamba. While the men work as handymen—carpenters, mechanics, or masons—the women open bars, hair salons, food stores, pharmacies and so on. Other ethnic groups' encounters with the Maasai are fruitful, in both senses of the word. The Maasai men see the advantage of marrying these women: most are educated, know how to engage in business, support the family, and as important—their extended families are not in the vicinity, and therefore, seemingly, the burden and obligation toward the extended family is limited. For the women themselves, marrying a Maasai man signifies receiving a seal of legitimacy, meaning there is someone to protect them.

The privatization of land also plays a major role in change. In recent years, the Kenyan government has granted every household title to a plot of land, changing these people's lives forever. Families that had lived together for decades in a certain area received land elsewhere. They were forced to leave a place where they had lived for many years and relocate to their new land. Moreover, the fact that every man within a household received a plot of his own caused a dismantling of the traditional villages, as many young men move to their own private plots of land. Most plots are surrounded with a fence, and stone houses or new, larger mud houses are constructed. Life within the familial clans loses its value, and the collective grazing area of the herds is decreased.

Receiving ownership over land signaled an extreme change regarding worldview: if, until recently, land had been shared territory on which cattle—viewed as the most important resource—would graze, currently, *land* has become the most important resource, which can be sold or leased (to establish lodges and camps for tourists, or to create "wildlife conservancies"). The economical, emotional and social value of cattle is gradually decreasing—today, fathers are interested in marrying their daughters off to a person who owns land, and not to an owner of cattle.

Many lodges are being built on private land, and the nature of the entire area bordering the national reserve has changed. The money a person receives for leasing or selling lands is usually spent on buying more cows, while simultaneously, his pasture areas are lost. During my first years in the village, in the rainy seasons, the grass would sometimes rise to my knees. The grass was so high that one day my brother, who came to visit me, walked the thirty yards to my bush toilet, and was surprised by a cheetah lying in the grass. Today, the grass no longer grows so high, an indication of overgrazing. Selling or leasing the land has led to overcrowding among livestock and people. The area cannot sustain them all.

Schools also play a significant role in the change that Maasai society is undergoing. In 2002, Kenya instituted free mandatory education in elementary school. Ever since, with very few exceptions, all children go to school and study in English—Kenya's official language—which hastens their entry into global society, but, to the same extent, depletes the wealth of their mother tongue. The children encounter values and a culture different from the ones they learn at home; for example, there is a prohibition on piercing ears or extracting the middle bottom tooth, two traditional Maasai characteristics.

The schools encourage the children to adopt Western names: Robert, Dan and Andrew have replaced the traditional names.

Religious studies in school do not include the traditional religion with which the youths grew up at home, but Christianity, taught both via formal lessons and through singing and dancing.

While learning science, nature studies, social studies, math and geography, it is indirectly conveyed to the children that in contrast to the traditional Maasai perception—which places them and their values at the center of existence—they are no more than a trivial marginal group in the world. The same customs that were a source of pride and a distinct identifying characteristic—scarring the body, going out to the bush for a few years as *morans*, or drinking cow's blood—are all perceived by others as primitive. Because of such changing attitudes, killing wild animals—lions, ostriches or birds—by the *morans* is now strictly forbidden.

The children, who up to this point had divided their time among multiple mothers, playing creative games in which no one is better than anyone else, are currently evaluated based on their achievements: who received higher grades, or what each child's position in the class is in relation to others. As they do anywhere in the world, schools encourage achievement in children, which naturally increases competitiveness, highly uncommon within Maasai culture, at the expense of other children in the class, their friends.

Schools are agents of change affecting life beyond classroom hours, as I witnessed regarding my children: if, several years ago, personal ceremonies were spread out over the entire year, today, the timing of ceremonies is aligned with school vacations: April, August and November-December. In addition, children do not want to waste their time going to and staying in the ceremonial villages, plus leaving for the bush for seven years as *morans*. For experience, some youths will join the *morans* for the length of one school vacation (Morans are still roaming the land, but most arrive from remote locations where the pace of change is slower). Most youths are tempted by "real" life: high school, college, finding a lucrative tourism job and starting a family. The term 'age group' increasingly refers to their class in school, rather than to recruiting members for a network of mutual responsibility.

The attitude toward female circumcision, one pillar of society, has been influenced by the conversation in the global media, but mostly by the schools, which repeatedly condemn it—and this sermonizing is sinking in. In some Maasai areas, female circumcision has ceased completely, while in others, the cutting is symbolic, or is expressed as a token bloodletting.

The Kenyan government is encouraging women to give birth in clinics, tempting them with gifts: a mosquito net for the mother and child. The more sterile delivery reduces mortality rates. The women are encouraged to use birth control, and the average number of children per family is decreasing

During school vacations, the children no longer feel proud to wear their traditional outfits. A pair of pants and a t-shirt are just fine. Ear piercing, extracting the bottom tooth or scarring their bodies no longer serve as a source of tribal pride.

∽

The modern age has not skipped over my home: Samyan, Museré, Leporé and Lemein work in tourism, earning handsome salaries. They are married and fathers of children. Miton finished his senior year of high school in a boarding school, and will also soon join the world of tourism. All have smartphones and Facebook friends from Kenya and all over the world. As part of the global village, they watch TV shows in real time, and their desires and dreams has expanded. In contrast to the "social network" that has thus far kept them hewing close to society, these days, individualism appeals to them and tempts them.

How can I explain to them that their search for individuality is taking place when Westerners, excessively individualistic, are feeling lonely? Westerners seek a way to return to the bosom of their "extended families," doing so by establishing charity organizations focused on helping others, participating in social networks online and in real life—or as I did, by adopting an entire family.

Can you sever strands within the social network and still leave it whole? Is it possible for individuality to develop without harming the infrastructure of society?

I look at my children and feel a twinge of sadness within my heart. Not due to the very fact of change, which stems from inside them and takes place at their own pace—as it should. The twinge in my heart is because I'm aware that this inevitable process entails loss and relinquishment: losing a tradition of many years and relinquishing values—both societal and moral—that constituted cornerstones of Maasai society.

As I've witnessed in recent years, Maasai society in this little village at the outskirts of the Maasai Mara Reserve is facing an important crossroads. In order not to fall apart and remain solely a nostalgic memory, it must redefine its boundaries: the boundaries of the individual, the village, the society and the people.

End

Epilogue

Orkiteng Loorbaa

"The team" had left home. Fifteen years have gone by, and once again, I found myself alone, like on the day I arrived here.

But not for long. Samyan's little girls, who were born straight into my arms, left their mother's bosom and moved in with me. A new cycle began. Nanetya, the oldest, exhibited an immense thirst for stories. She was too young for me to tell her stories in English or Swahili, and no one from her father's age group remembered any stories in Maa. As I watched Nanetya grow up and go to school, I realized that the process of contemporary Maasai youth disengaging from tradition was not expressed merely by adopting new customs and a new religion, but also in forgetting. Forgetting traditional customs, mythological stories and folk tales, and often, switching from speaking in their mother tongue to the official state language. A small study I conducted clarified that this pattern exists in many African societies sucked into globalization, and thus losing their distinction.

That was how the "Nanetya Foundation" was established[42]: helped by friends and volunteers, missionaries, anthropologists and linguists, we collect myths, proverbs and folk tales from different ethnic groups, all written in their original language—so the language and the stories will be preserved—and upload them to the Internet.

∼

The village continues its daily routine. My relationship with No'oltwati is now back on track. She lives in the village and we meet often. Today, she is the mother of two daughters, and thanks to her fluent English, works as a teacher in the local school, and also contributes stories in Maa to the Nanetya Foundation. Her husband Kitipai has taken another wife, and divides his time between the two.

Nesesyay, my good friend and the mother of Samyan, Leporé and Lanoi, experienced a cardiac event and became the first Maasai in our region to undergo open heart surgery[43].

The rest of my friends go on with their lives, dealing with another drought in late 2014 and asking themselves what caused it that time.

∼

Barsoinkan, my good friend, is growing older. Sialo, his oldest daughter, is growing up. Her budding breasts are visible through her shirt, her body has grown lanky, and she is showing signs of femininity. She will be able to undergo the circumcision ceremony only after he himself undergoes the last personal ceremony in his life, a ceremony signaling the completion of the cycles of childhood and maturity, and entering the respectable circle of elders.

To be worthy of this ceremony, Barsoinkan had to carry out two important tasks. The first of these was technical: to finally seal his marriage to his wife. They have been living together for many years, and she has borne him eight children. But her status as his wife was considered temporary if the full bride price—meaning the cows he had committed to paying when he took her as a wife—had not been conveyed to her parents or family. The Maasai system enables those who own little property to get married, and the cows are conveyed in several payments, but these must end before the eldest child is circumcised. Meaning the groom has a period of about fifteen years to pay the bride price.

The second task, social, is the impressive and moving one, which makes this ceremony the most significant one for a Maasai man: Barsoinkan can only undergo the ceremony once his heart is clear and pure. By the time of the ceremony, he must make up with any rivals, pay off his debts, deal with anger and resolve misunderstandings. Only thus, in a state of harmony with everyone around him, can he enter the society of the elders. The ceremony is called "*orkiteng loorbaa*," "the ox of wounds," named after the wounds left open and unhealed in relationships.

I imagine the stop sign. The barrier. The moment when everyone must stand, look in both directions, see what went wrong and with whom it went wrong, fix what requires fixing, and only then keep going.

Here, people sail on into old age only once they have reconciled with those around them.

~

Sheep and goats are slaughtered fairly frequently here; however, there are only two occasions when a man must slaughter an ox[44]—a large, heavy animal, but mostly very expensive. The very act of its slaughter indicates the importance of the ceremony.

Barsoinkan began the preparations. I knew he was not concerned. He was almost done conveying the bride price, and was now busy walking among the villages and meeting the elders and his peers to make sure there was no resentment against him and that his debtors would come to collect their debts. In addition, he was seeking an appropriate ox (possessing a particular color, with horns not broken, healthy and with good eyes), finding a companion who will be by his side during the ceremony, finding two elders from his mentoring age group to run the ceremony, collecting containers to brew beer, buying sacks of sugar to ferment the beer and other technical matters.

Two days before the ceremony, the guests streamed into the village, including the two mentoring elders who would conduct the ceremony. They sat in his home, holding glasses of local beer, and interrogated him: *Since your daughter was born, have you severely beaten a man? Have you broken anyone's bones? Have you killed a man?* Only when Barsoinkan replied with a "no" to all questions did the two bless him, thus signaling the beginning of the ceremony.

∼

Early in the morning. Dozens of village residents and guests left the warm houses, exiting into the cold wind blowing outside, raising clouds of dust. The black ox had been taken out of the stockade in which it had been closely watched over and stationed next to Barsoinkan's entry gate.

Nabaru, his first wife, whose wedding day I had witnessed at a time that now seemed like ages ago, came out of the hut. She was wearing an *orkela*, her face was tinted with red ochre, and she was holding a large *kalabash* in her hand. She slowly approached the immense ox, whose back sported a hump. Slowly, she poured milk over it[45], starting with its head and ending with the tail. Leading the ox, all the men exited through the village gate, walking deep into the bush, where the slaughter would take place.

I joined them on their way to the place of the sacrifice, which had been determined days in advance. I was impressed by the teamwork: some men brought wood for the fire, others chopped down branches, from which they created a grill, another group dealt with slaughtering the ox, while others chopped more branches and used them to build a low enclosure used to eat the meat.

At noontime, after the meat had been roasted and all preparations were done, came the highlight of the ceremony. Barsoinkan was the first to enter the enclosure, its rounded shape and single opening symbolizing the village. He was followed by his companion. They sat down, while a select portion of the roasted meat, including the ox's heart, was placed in front, on a stack of branches. Barsoinkan's friends and family members now also entered the enclosure. Not all of them could enter. Only the ones whose heart was pure: they had beaten no one, not broken bones, not killed.

I went in. I felt very moved. Not by the very fact of my presence there, as my heart, too, was pure, but due to the very existence of a custom honoring those who maintain a respectful relationship with others, and respect the rules of society. I looked around me. Sounds of laughter and hushed speech accompanied the eating of the meat. The men were sitting on the ground, large hunks of meat clasped between their teeth; using the long knives drawn from their sheaths, they cut them into little pieces. Every few minutes, I was offered a piece of meat, which I gratefully accepted.

Sitting inside the enclosure and eating the meat was a peak experience for Barsoinkan. In the next few days, he would circumcise his daughter and enter the final stage of maturity in his life. I felt this was a peak experience for me. I had come a long way in his company and with his family, and I felt this enclosure symbolized a closure for me, the culmination of a path on which I had embarked many years ago.

Commentary

Chapter 1: African Princesses
(1) **Spitting out the beverages on the ground**: Like other African societies, the Maasai believe that man is a link in the chain of existence, and the dead are part of the same chain (see Chapter 24). The Maasai do not engage in ancestor worship, but their ceremonies commemorate those who have recently died, allowing them to participate in the celebration. Here, they are offered drinks of beer and milk, thus indirectly receiving their blessing for the ceremony.

This resembles the custom of lighting a memorial candle in Jewish culture, signaling to the dead (and those who have outlived them) that they are remembered. During the Passover ceremony, a glass of wine and an empty chair are left for the Prophet Elijah, who thus "takes part" in the celebration. Similarly, on Christmas Eve, milk and cookies are often left for Saint Nicholas, or Santa Claus.

In other places in Africa, mainly in its western regions, the souls of the dead have a larger presence in everyday life. They accompany life. This is one more meaning of the famous saying, "In Africa, you are never alone." Each person is endowed not merely with many mothers who raised him or her throughout their life, and not merely with many fathers (anyone in the father's peer group) but also with the spirits of ancestors, who are with them at every single moment, and making sure that the rules of society are preserved.

(2) **Accumulating gifts from the women**: Every girl has seen brides arriving in the village dozens of times, and therefore, knows what to expect. This reception should ensure the new bride will not be arrogant or vain. The bride will never enter the village gates before receiving gifts of livestock from the women of the new village, which will be the start of a future herd of her own.

Chapter 2: No'oltwati
(3) **The parasite seizes control of the nervous system, enters the brain, and ultimately kills**: Medicine recognizes this strain as cerebral malaria, in which the parasite invades the brain, initially causing twitching and spasms, followed by loss of consciousness and death.
(4) **Witchcraft was always brought up in social and religious systems**: Most societies in Africa (south of the Sahara Desert) believe in witchcraft. This belief fulfills several social functions:

First, casting a spell is perceived as a force, punishing those diverting from the social norms. Many societies believe that a person may be born, live a full life and die at a ripe old age if he or she has not diverted from society's system of values and rules. However, subverting the social norms, even unconsciously, will cause punishment (injury, illness, death, a curse). Therefore, when people experience any calamity, they will immediately seek the reason for it, searching for answers to "why" questions (why did this happen? Why now, of all times? Why did No'oltwati become ill?) rather than "how" questions (the question of how No'oltwati got ill, or what form her illness took, was obvious to all). With No'oltwati, the villagers claimed that she used her fluency in English to receive gifts (for the village's children) from tourists visiting the village, but was too prideful and selfish, and kept them for herself.

Another function of witchcraft is to explain events or occurrences that cannot be explained scientifically, thus resolving an unconscious need to find a reason and a cause for everyday problems. For example,

Nashelu gave birth to six children. The four girls stayed alive, but every time she had a boy, he died (see Chapter 29). In response to the "why" question (*why were my boys the ones who had to die?*), she claimed that her husband's first wife, who was jealous of her, had cast a spell on her. A purification ceremony was conducted, and happily, her next child, a boy, survived.

Spells don't cast themselves, and many societies have witches and wizards, people who can use their powers in various ways to change an existing situation (for evil—to hurt or kill a person, or for good—to protect someone from a different spell).

Judeo-Christian religions acknowledge the existences of witchcraft, but forbid it: "*Thou shalt not suffer a witch to live*" (Exodus 22:18). Witch hunts or purges were a common phenomenon in early modern Europe and Colonial North America—between 1450 and 1750—resulting in about 35,000 to 100,000 executions.

Similarly to African witchcraft, magic as described in the Jewish Kabbalah is based on the power of the word, or combinations of words, to create change in the physical world.

Chapter 4: Samyan

(5) **These crazy ideas**: Homosexuality does not exist in Maasai culture. I'm not claiming there are no homosexual tendencies among the Maasai. However, social conformity is still stronger than individual tendencies. The custom of parents matching up and arranging marriages for all young men and women practically prevents young people from choosing mates according to their natural tendencies. A married man with homosexual tendencies who rarely engages in sexual relations with his wife would probably have children (considered his) via his wife's lover.

Chapter 6: When the Child Is in the Belly— It Is Yours. When It Is Out—It's Everyone's!

(6) **A deep perception essentially stating, don't get attached**: We must distinguish between principle, i.e., the social edict not to get attached to children, and actuality: in real life, a deep bond exists between parents and their children, brothers and sisters, friends of both genders, and so on. There is a gap between survivalist wisdom and reality.

Chapter 7: Black-Ear

(7) **This unique breed, called Zebu**: One of the sub-breeds of Zebu cattle is called Brahman or Brahma, and was first bred in United States from cattle breeds imported from India.

(8) **A sharp, clear distinction between the "cultural" world where people made a living off their manual labor (raising cattle) and the "natural" world, where people fed off what they found**: Duality is a major topic in anthropology, including whether duality is universal. Most societies have dualistic worldview creating a distinction between spirit and matter, good and evil, God and Satan, darkness and light, or culture and nature. This dualistic system is usually necessary for social order, to set up an instructive mirror and sharpen the distinction between 'do's and 'don't's. Sometimes the duality is also a feature of the society's organizational apparatus: between men and women, the young and the old, and so on. Duality should not be perceived as dichotomous (i.e., two opposing ends) but as two parts of the whole.

The dualistic idea poses a challenge to Judeo-Christian religion: Is there someone (Satan) or something that can stand beside or opposite God? If the answer is yes, then God is not supreme. Therefore, the devil is subordinate to God: "*Now there was a day when the sons of God came to present themselves before the Lord, and Satan came also among them. And the Lord said unto Satan, Whence comest thou?"* (Job 1: 6-7).

For an interesting discussion on the question of duality, see the book *The Attraction of Opposites*, by Uri Almagor and David Mayberry-Lewis (see bibliography).

Chapter 8: The Water Tank Births a Lamb

(9) **What could I do to minimize my impact as much as possible?**: Dozens of studies have addressed the place of the anthropologist in the society he or she is researching. Can they be merely "a fly on the wall," with no impact on those around them? It's clear that the answer is no, as even a stone placed gently in the water creates ripples. It's true that I did not come to the Maasai as an anthropologist, yet this dilemma—to what extent I should express my opinion, whether or not to create change—accompanies me to this day. As you'll read, I committed fully to expressing my opinion about circumcision and the pain accompanying it, AIDS, and so on.

Chapter 9: Your Blood Is Happy

(10) **Implications for her life in the long term**: Naturally, society has created a set of 'rules' (culture) that cause a woman want to desire to be circumcised. As the chapter clarifies, an uncircumcised woman cannot get help from her friends while she is giving birth. In addition, a woman who gives birth before her circumcision (i.e., has subverted the social order and given birth while still a girl and not a woman) cannot fill the role of a mother in her children's future ceremonies (shaving a daughter's head, managing the ceremony, shaving her son's head during the *eunoto* ceremony, and so on).

This topic brings up questions of freedom of choice. As prisoners of our culture, are we free to choose? In a culture idolizing thinness, are women dieting out of free choice?

Every culture has sets of rules or a social order integrated into the society's cultural containment, sometime making its members do things that are inexplicable to other societies. Examples might include male circumcision or Israel's mandatory military service (not serving in the Israeli Army impacts the chance of working in certain jobs, and eliminates some tax benefits).

I share the opinion of Dr. Nnamuchi (see bibliography), who claims that the basis for the strong objection to female circumcision, and the sweeping warnings against it, is shaky. He claims that not a single study has measured the implications of female circumcision using objective measures, or proven that circumcised women have a higher prenatal or postpartum death rate, or that they suffer more complications during pregnancy and birth compared to women who have not undergone circumcision. Dr. Nnamuchi believes that existing studies serve "political correctness," and are actually a tool of cultural imperialism directed against societies that the Western world perceives as inferior.

Chapter 10: Operation Mom

(11) **Share the food prepared for each one of us**: I believe this habit led some mothers to cook less, hoping their son would eat more at another mother's house. Within this group of boys—as among lion cubs—there were always those who swallowed quicker and ate more, and those who were not satisfied.

Chapter 13: An Old Groom

(12) **Almost no damage, either in the short term or the long term**: Contemporary medicine classifies female circumcision into four varieties. In the first kind, only the clitoris is removed. In the second kind, the clitoris and the labia minora are removed. The third kind consists of removing the labia minora and sewing the labia majora shut (Pharaonic circumcision), while leaving a small opening for fluids to be expelled. The fourth kind includes any other form of marking the female genitalia (piercing, cutting, burning and so on).

The first and second kinds constitute over 90 percent of circumcision operations. Pharaonic circumcision is performed mainly in Somalia, Sudan and Egypt. It should be acknowledged that the great majority of circumcised women who have come out in opposition to the custom have experienced Pharaonic circumcision, meaning they do not belong to the majority.

(13) **An American anthropologist of Sierra Leonean origin who had undergone circumcision**: Fuamabi S. Ahmadu's article is titled "Disputing the Myth of the Sexual Dysfunction of Circumcised Women"; it is cited in the bibliography and can be found online.

Chapter 15: One Round

(14) **To perpetuate his dependence upon them**: From an evolutionary perspective, men and women obviously have different goals in life: men are interested in passing on their genes to as many offspring as possible (having multiple wives and girlfriends therefore fulfills this impulse), while women are interested in maximizing their offspring's chances of survival. Therefore, women need a man's help and protection, and seek ways of ensuring his proximity. The fact that in Maasai society only women have houses of their own is one of several circumstances increasing men's dependency upon them.

(15) **The number of girls born has always exceeded the number of boys**: In a sample which is by no means statistically controlled, I kept track of 24 women living in my vicinity. In twelve years, they gave birth to 33 girls and 28 boys.

(16) **Perhaps there is nothing wrong with polygamy**: I smile when I think about the way we, as products of Western culture, are seemingly averse to a man having multiple wives, while it also exists among us, in a different form: a man marries a woman, has children with her, divorces, marries another woman, has more children with her, and so on. By the time they reach old age, many men have been married to and had children with several women. Odd, but according

to our moral and cultural laws, the man must first part from one woman, with all this entails—pain for the children, financial battles and so on—in order to live with another...

Chapter 18: Morans

(17) **You can't refuse**: Boys recruited to be *morans* but are attending school and want to continue their studies may redeem themselves (paying with livestock). Some boys go to school but still want to be *morans*. They join the *morans* for brief periods during school vacations.

(18) **Receive instructions from the elders, our mentors**: Every age group has a mentoring age set, older than it by two phases (meaning the two groups, mentors and mentees, are separated by two grades: "right hand" and "left hand"). It is important to understand the distinction between age groups (which open every seven years) and age sets (which combine two age groups every fifteen years).

(19) **Our society relies mostly on "vertical" mutual responsibility**: in real life, responsibility of both types, vertical and horizontal, exists: in our society, other horizontal connections can also be found, such as the fraternity of high school or army friends. Among the Maasai, vertical responsibility (grandfather—father—son) also exists to the extent possible.

(20) **The boys may have sex with almost any woman**: The difference between boys and girls cannot be ignored. From their circumcision on, during the liminal period of being *morans*, boys may have sex almost without limitation. From the moment of their circumcision until their marriage about six months later, girls must entirely abstain from having sex.

Chapter 19: The Nose Does Not Precede You

(21) **Ceremonies will take place during this period**: As stated in the chapter regarding the perception of time and the year, and as the

seasons are not fixed anyway, traditionally the Maasai do not have fixed holidays related to the seasons (such as a "harvest festival"). However, currently, fixed external holidays, such as New Year's Day, have been added to the calendar. The personal and collective ceremonies—traditionally conducted during the "white moon"—are now also conditioned upon school vacations, which take place at predetermined times.

Chapter 20: Maasai Justice

(22) **Marked with a branding iron**: Every Maasai cow is branded with the symbol of the sub-clan, and the tips of its ears are clipped off in a pattern specific to a certain family. Therefore, anyone can identify to whom a cow belongs if it is lost (goats and sheep, however, rarely are marked).

(23) **A fine of five cows**: It is surprising to discover the extent to which the Maasai system of rules and penalties resembles the biblical one. An identical penalty can be found in the book of Exodus: *"If a man shall steal an ox, or a sheep, and kill it, or sell it, he shall restore five oxen for an ox, and four sheep for a sheep."* (Exodus 22: 1)

(24) **The number forty-nine**: This number combines the Maasai's two lucky numbers: four (an even number that is not the smallest one) and nine, the number of orifices in the human body.

Chapter 21: Children Are a Shining Moon

(25) **Emptied her stomach and cleansed it using natural means**: Odd as it may sound, studies have shown that elephants do not eat all plants, but are selective in their diet. In Tsavo National Park (Eastern Kenya), fourteen main types of plants, including medicinal herbs, were documented as their preferred sustenance. It is therefore logical that their dung contains a 'cocktail' of medicinal herbs. The Maasai knew which animal's droppings to choose; since both elephants and donkeys (mentioned later) are not ruminants, they excrete a major

part of their diet, comprised of plants, as a softened, non-digested material.

(26) **All day long, they sing**: In a society with no radio or TV, the children and women sing constantly. They sing while playing, sing while milking, sing during ceremonies, sing when they're walking in the bush and sing in the houses, around the fire. Some ancient songs praise the age groups or important historical events, and there are also well-known ballads by Maasai singers. Usually, however, the songs comprise existing melodies and contemporary lyrics, which change according to context. Thus, for example, in the period after the *morans* were wounded following the encounter with the lion, people were singing about "the green car with the white roof that that took the *morans* to the clinic and saved their lives." A while later, this song was cast aside for songs about other incidents. Today, when women have cell phones enabling access to songs by established singers, they are less inventive, and merely accompany the singers with their voices.

Chapter 22: Eunoto

(27) **The handicap principle**: The Handicap Principle is a phrase coined by the Israeli zoologist Amotz Zahavi, who studied the behavior of a tiny bird named the Arabian babbler. Inspired by his observations, Zahavi reached some far-reaching conclusions about animal behavior: the male places various burdens on itself (large horns on its head, a prominent color scheme, or… getting a pilot's license) to impress the female and prove to her that its genes are better than those of other males, i.e., that it is fitter and stronger, and therefore, that the female would do well to choose it.

(28) **Disarming them had turned them symbolically and temporarily into "women"**: the *moran* phase is actually an interim period, a liminal time, in which the age group is exiled outside many aspects of the Maasai social order. Its members may behave differently

(growing hair, lack of social commitment, and so on). During the *eunoto* ceremony, the *morans* (already subject to a seven-year interim period) enter another liminal state, their transformation into women, before they are returned to society as adult men.

For more on the concept of "liminal state," refer to the theories of British anthropologist Victor Turner, who studied ritual processes—particularly rites of passage—and claimed that society can exist only in the tension between structure (social order) and anti-structure.

(29) **To stretch the hide and pound the stake into its edge**: This moral edict is clear as day—if a woman has had sex with one of the *morans*, it is as if she had sex with her own son! The test, of which every adult woman is aware, is intended to warn her away from violating the moral rules of society.

Chapter 24: Capturing Flies

(30) **In one god named Enkai**: The prefix "En" in a name is feminine; therefore, the Maasai's sublime creator is a goddess, feminine, who gave birth to all the things in the world: trees, rocks, water, animals, people and so on. During storms, the elders tell their children, "Mother is angry." The meaning of the word "woman" (*enkitok)* is "the powerful one."

Chapter 25: Drought and Tradition

(31) **Too many cows gathered here. Too many people**: The concentration of so many Maasai in a small area led to the overcutting of trees for firewood and overgrazing. During this drought, one limitation of modern life—arbitrary political borders—caused the Maasai to suffer. Severe droughts had occurred in the past, starting with the biblical Jacob heading for Egypt, and including the Maasai's own tale of migration. But back then, the shepherds could migrate hundreds of miles with their herds until they found pasture and water. Today, national borders block them, making it harder to find a solution.

(32) **The women took her message to heart**: A consistent element can be discerned in the Maasai faith—the responsibility for maintaining personal, social and cosmic order lies firmly upon the shoulders of the individual. It is not passed on to the police or the courts, or blamed on global warming. This is a heavy burden, requiring each and every one of us to behave properly all the time, to do some soul-searching, and to make amends if something goes wrong.

These days, when the Maasai have become a part of the "global village," many (and members of other African societies) wish to shake off this burden. The easiest escape route is to convert to Christianity (along with the forgiveness offered by Christ) and turn their backs on traditional beliefs.

Chapter 26: God Will Help, and If He Doesn't— the White Man Will

(33) **A government policy called Self-Reliance**: I'm a big fan of Julius Nyerere, Tanzania's first president, who was one of the only African leaders to display unique, independent thought toward overcoming the hurdle of turning the 120 ethnic groups within the artificial borders of the country into one nation. As part of his Self-Reliance policy, he declared Swahili, at the time a language that was only spoken, rather than written, to be the country's official language (as opposed to the rest of the African countries south of the Sahara, which adopted the languages of their colonial rulers), established a Swahili language academy to determine grammar laws, and translated Shakespeare into Swahili. As part of his efforts to create a unified nation, he issued an edict of "population mingling," dislocating entire villages, a process that raised the ire of the Western countries against him. The Self-Reliance policy failed, and in the 1980s, Nyerere swallowed his pride, requested assistance from the World Bank and the International Monetary Fund, and resigned from the presidency (he was one of the few presidents at the time to willingly resign).

Chapter 28: Water Cannot Climb Uphill

(34) **Could Miton lie**: There is no ignoring that now, responsibility for the success of the circumcision has been transferred from the person performing it to the initiate. If something went wrong during the circumcision, the blame would fall upon the young man who "lied."

(35) **Wearing black cloth sheets**: Wearing dark-colored clothes (black, dark blue, dark purple) symbolizes a person's separation from society (a woman who has given birth, boys after their circumcision). In this condition, he or she is considered closer to God than to human society, and therefore, may not be touched. Wearing black comes with growing out hair. In addition, the dark colors symbolize wisdom and maturity: the Maasai chiefs are distinguished by their black *rungu*. After children are circumcised, each man receives a necklace of dark blue beads, and so on. This custom is linked to the Maasai belief that God has two faces: the divine black face and the terrestrial red face. One expression of the terrestrial face may be seen in the ochre dye with which the face is tinted during ceremonies, and the red cloth cloaks—the traditional Maasai garb. This symbolism may also be linked to the two moieties of Maasai society: the "red ox" and the "black ox" (see Appendix 3).

Chapter 29: Life Is a Miracle!

(36) **Life is a miracle that takes place every day**: The Jewish morning prayer (Shacharit), which begins, "*I offer thanks to You, living and eternal King, for You have mercifully restored my soul within me*," hints that Judaism also views life as a daily miracle.

(37) **The lid of the coffin was covered in ram fat**: This is a classic example of one way tradition evolves or is created. After several more corpses are returned from the hospital in a coffin, being buried in a casket or covering the coffin with fat (or both) will become the norm, a new tradition.

(38) **Erased from the collective memory**: Perhaps Ecclesiastes meant *"There is no remembrance of former things; neither shall there be any remembrance of things that are to come with those that shall come after."* (Ecclesiastes 1: 11).

Chapter 31: The Zebra Does Not Deny Its Stripes

(39) **The most courageous warriors**: Over eighty years ago, Isak Dinesen wrote in her book *Out of Africa* regarding the Maasai: "The tragic fate of the disappearing Masai tribe… could be followed from year to year. They were fighters who had been stopped fighting, a dying lion with his claws clipped, a castrated nation." (Isak Dinesen, *Out of Africa*, Modern Library, 1992)

(40) **"Speaking in tongues"**: This is mostly (but not exclusively) a characteristic of the Pentecostal Church, in which the course of the prayer includes several minutes dedicated to a personal appeal by the believers to God. Human language is not a worthy medium for conversing with the Holy Spirit; therefore, each congregant mumbles his or her prayer in an incomprehensible "tongue."

(41) **The men spend their days drinking**: Drinking alcohol is not a new custom. I don't know of even a single African society that does not brew alcohol out of anything they can get their hands on: natural plants, sorghum, maize, bananas and so on. This is one way for adult men and women to spend their days together companionably. These days—and this is the problem—many are no longer satisfied with the homemade beer in which the alcohol content is negligible, and buy bottled beer, or, even worse, spirits with a high alcohol content, leading to addiction.

Several years ago, while I was sitting at home and reading a book, I heard a commotion and shouting from the village. I ran toward the small "trading center" comprised of two stores and three bars, and watched an unbelievable sight: a group of enraged women was gradually drawing closer, holding sticks and waving them around.

Wordlessly, they attacked the three bars and shattered all the liquor bottles! The men, and the bar owners, all fled. Later, when the frenzy died down, the women explained that they had tired of their drunk husbands, until they took action…

Epilogue: *Orkiteng Loorbaa*

(42) **That was how the "Nanetya Foundation" was established**: the Nanetya Foundation tries to preserve stories and myths in various mother tongues, and contribute to preserving those languages. Stories are uploaded to the Web (and in certain special cases, books are published in their original language) to allow members of small ethnic groups to read them in their mother tongue. Discover more about the foundation at www.nanetya-foundation.org.

(43) **The first Maasai in the region to undergo open heart surgery**: As part of the changes in worldview taking place these days, I was moved to see how Samyan and his family fought for their mother's life, rather than resigning themselves to losing her to heart disease. They raised a fortune by selling cows and taking out loans (about $20,000) and saved her life.

(44) **There are only two occasions when a man must slaughter an ox**: The first time a man must slaughter an ox is the time between his return from *manyata eunoto* (marking the end of the *moran* period) and the time—while already married and a father of children—he undergoes a personal ceremony of "eating meat." Many men from the same age group leave for the *orpul*, i.e. the bush, far from any village, for a period of several days to a week, slaughtering oxen in an enormous meat celebration.

At the end of this ceremonial *orpul*, before parting ways, all the men go to everyone's villages, carrying meat with them as a gift for their wives.

(45) **Slowly, she poured milk over it**: This resembles certain rules in the Bible, where, before an animal is slaughtered, it must be blessed,

i.e., symbolically transported from an everyday secular state to one of holiness. This was usually done by laying hands upon it and saying a blessing.

Appendix 1

Where Did the Maasai Come From?

Night. It is pitch dark outside. Out there, a pesky rain is falling, but inside the hut, a warming fire is burning, infusing those present with a sense of security. Next to me on the hide-covered pallet are several adults, while across from us, on the other bed, several teenagers, boys and girls, are huddled together. Everyone is talking to everyone else, and I toss out an innocent question: "Who are the Maasai?"

Baffled faces turn toward me.

"You're all Maasai?"

They nod and hum in confirmation.

"How was the first Maasai born? Where did he come from?"

Although the young people snicker, they are the first to respond, making up answers, one after the other:

Meteur: "God created two first—Man and the snake. Man, when he reaches old age—dies. But the snake sheds his skin every time and renews…"

Netito: "God had three sons. The first received cows—that's the Maasai. The second received a drinking glass—that's the white man. The third received a *panga*—that's the Kikuyu (another ethnic group), who went on to become farmers…"

Kitango: "God first created man and the donkey. The donkey had a short penis and man had a long penis. One day, man was invited to a party, but didn't want to be burdened by his long member, so he asked the donkey to switch. They did, and at the party, everyone admired man with his short member, and he decided to keep it…"

Mayu: "God created the man and the woman in a fertile valley. They ascended from the valley, climbing a long rope, and decided to settle. They had five boys and four girls who married each other, and that's how the Maasai were born…"

These odd answers make me burst out in laughter, and I refer the question to a woman of fifty or so.

"Look," she replies, "God created the first Maasai along with the cow. One day, the Maasai tied a leather belt to her tail and followed her. During his travels, he met a woman, and together they went on a journey to find more cows. Then the man discovered that the woman had different sex organs, and slept with her. That's how they had children… Then God created the white man and gave him a drinking glass. Then he created the Kikuyu, with a different, incomprehensible language, and gave him women of his own, and a hoe, so he would farm the land…"

Now it was my turn to tell them a mythological story I had read in a book written by a Maasai, though none of the attendees had ever heard of it:

"In the distant past, the Maasai lived in a sprawling valley, surrounded by high, impassable cliffs. One time, the rains were late to arrive, and a drought fell over the land. People had no water, cattle had no grass, and both began to die. In the yellow landscape stretching all around, the only green grass was brought from a faraway place by birds, which used it to build their nests. The elders saw these birds carrying green grass and sent scouts to discover where it came from.

"With great effort and much courage, the scouts climbed the walls of the cliff. When they got to the top, they marveled at what they saw: before them stretched a green land, its soil fertile, with many springs and streams, a multitude of trees, shrubs and fruit. The scouts toured the land, and when they returned to their families in the valley, they carried back samples of the bounty they had found all around them.

"When they returned to their land, they assembled the elders and told them about the great plenty up above. The elders heard them and decided they must emigrate there. But how would they leave their current location? After many efforts, they managed to build a "bridge," and once it was ready, the migration began: women, children, cows, sheep, and donkeys… But alas, during their exodus, the bridge tore, tossing about half the people down…

No solution was found. The council of the elders decided they must carry on. The half of the population left behind became "foreigners" (those who are not Maasai), while those departing, the Maasai, settled down for many years in their new land, where the cows could graze."

~

I wondered where this valley was located. What was the origin of the Maasai? I turned to academic literature.

Linguistic research—tracking the development of languages and their distribution—indicates that speakers of the Maa language, including the Maasai (for whom the language of Maa is also the source of their name), apparently originate somewhere north of Lake Turkana, where the borders of current-day southern Ethiopia and South Sudan intersect. Fifteen hundred years ago, the ancestors of the Maasai left this area, characterized by meager soil, high temperatures and limited sources of water, and began their migration south, seeking a more hospitable land. On their way, they assimilated other ethnic groups within their ranks, and about a thousand years ago, they entered the area of the Great Rift Valley—within the territory of modern-day Kenya.

Hundreds of years went by before some of the Maa speakers specialized in raising livestock and cattle—a sophisticated, unusual form of economical specialization—which became possible thanks to the ongoing relationship of these groups with both other Maa speakers (and other ethnic groups) who had transitioned to farming the fertile highlands, and hunters-gatherers living in the forests at the outskirts of the Great Rift Valley. Cattle herders depend entirely upon farmers and hunter-gatherers for supplying them with non-animal food and necessary equipment, such as pottery jugs, metal spearheads and ritual objects. The neighbors' help was also essential during natural disasters, such as floods and droughts, in which the shepherds are the first casualties.

Therefore, it was in the pastoralists' best interest to maintain relationships with members of neighboring ethnic groups, and they did so by creating a broad, flexible cultural framework that could encompass them all. They absorbed women from other tribes, integrated societies defeated in battle into their ranks, and created marital bonds with the members of other economical societies.

About 400 years ago, the Maasai identity emphasizing cattle as a value, and the Maasai as the caretakers of all cattle, grew more cohesive. They continued migrating south, while several groups turned east, disengaging from the main force and eventually coming to be called Samburu and Laikipia. About 200 years ago, the Maasai expansion peaked, and they settled throughout the region that eventually became southern Kenya and north-central Tanzania.

∾

Hundreds of years of migration. I'm not surprised. The carrying capacity—meaning the number of residents or herds a land can support, as a function of the soil, climate, precipitation, flora and so on—of most parts of the African continent is low. Therefore, if in a certain location, the population has multiplied beyond the carrying capacity of the area, many families were forced to leave and search for new pasture. The Bible has told us about this: "*And Abram was very rich in cattle… And Lot also, which went with Abram, had flocks, and herds, and tents. And the land was not able to bear them, that they might dwell together: for their substance was great, so that they could not dwell together.*" (Genesis 13: 2-6).

A severe drought can also trigger migration: "*And there was a famine in the land: and Abram went down into Egypt to sojourn there; for the famine was grievous in the land.*" (Genesis 12: 10), like the ones in Maasai Mara in the years 2005, 2009 and 2014. These days, the Maasai migratory journey would have had to stop once they reached international borders. How about in the past, however?

Many ethnic groups roamed the African continent over the years. Each tried to improve its life in this harsh, unforgiving continent, sometimes by taking over the turf of other ethnic groups, and sometimes by assimilating a weak group into a stronger one.

∼

About a hundred years ago (in the late nineteenth century), the Maasai experienced disasters: a drought that lasted several years killed off thousands of livestock, and those that survived suffered from rinderpest and pneumonia. As the people were overcome by smallpox, colonial expansion in East Africa was at its peak, further weakening local societies.

The Maasai—who were inspiring the European myth of the "noble savage," herding his cattle in the endless planes—tried to prevent Europeans or other Africans from invading their turf, to no avail. East Africa was divided with a ruler-straight line between Britain and Germany, thus splitting the Maasai people in two.

When colonialism ended and the African states were granted independence (in the 1960s), the borderline persisted, perpetuating the division of the Maasai between Kenya and Tanzania. African politicians were a lot less romantic than the British, and hungry for more land. The Maasai once again found themselves forced to defend against the confiscation of their lands into agricultural farms or to create nature reserves.

And thus, ironically, the Maasai who, about 150 years ago, were a dominant force throughout the East African region, have today become a marginal group in current economic, social and political terms.

Appendix 2

Who Are the Maasai?

From its earliest days, Maasai society has been known for its tolerance and its willingness to integrate foreigners into its ranks. The hundreds of years of Maasai migration have come with constant wars with other societies. Mostly, these wars ended in Maasai victories, and assimilation of the losers into the ranks of the Maasai: Maasai men married foreign women.

It's interesting, I thought to myself: for thousands of years, my people, the Jewish people, attributed the secret of their longevity as a nation to Judaism's isolationist approach, the fear of integration and assimilation. While here was a society that attributed the secret of its ongoing existence and survival precisely to assimilation. According to the Maasai perception, the only way to imbue society with fresh blood is to integrate outsiders into its ranks.

Maasai tolerance has allowed the assimilated societies to preserve their ancient customs, while also adopting Maasai customs. To this day, different families celebrate ceremonies in differing ways. There is no requirement to "obey to the letter." Therefore, the question arises—who is considered Maasai?

Until recently, the answer to this question was complex, but clear:

It entailed adopting a new identity as a pastoralist, speaking the Maa language, piercing the ears (a slow process, which begins with inserting a thorn into the lobe and then slowly expanding it by inserting wooden "corks"—initially, their diameter is small, but as the lobe stretches, the diameter increases; some of the cartilage in the lobe is also removed), extracting the middle bottom tooth (both from a child's baby teeth and from an adult's permanent teeth. The background for this custom is when many Maasai contracted tetanus, which causes the muscles in the body, including those in the mouth, to contract, until the patient dies. Extracting the bottom tooth enabled inserting a straw into the mouth, and feeding patients until they died), and wearing typical garb: two sheets of red cloth for men, two sheets of colorful cloth for women, covered by a blanket, also in a shade of red. This outfit replaced the traditional manner of dressing, which existed eighty years ago—goatskins dyed with red ochre.

But beyond these external characteristics, there are two essential cornerstones in Maasai culture: both men and women must undergo circumcision (the admission pass into adult Maasai society) and fit into the social apparatus of age groups and age sets—a social and cultural mechanism that affects all areas of life, including law and morality.

If a foreign outsider will accept these terms, the fact that he or she belongs to a different ethnic or racial group becomes meaningless, and that person is invited to join Maasai society.

∼

Many of these characteristics have lost their meaning these days: the children go to school and no longer pierce their ears. They are vaccinated, and therefore do not extract the middle bottom tooth.

Traditional Maasai outfits are being replaced by cheap secondhand clothes, or ones made in China. For many years now, Maasai who live on the fertile planes no longer migrate by following a cow's tail. They live in modern stone houses, have converted to Christianity and no longer celebrate private or collective ceremonies. As life becomes increasingly individualistic, the significance of the age groups decreases, and circumcision of girls is also disappearing.

Today, the Maasai are left with their language, the Maa language, as a main indicator of identity, and a day will come when they will be assimilated into general Kenyan society, just as many societies were once assimilated into the Maasai.

Appendix 3

The Maasai Social Network

When a Maasai child is born, he or she enters a "social network" that defines the person's place in society.

Museré, for example, belongs to his nuclear family, which gave him his last name, the cattle and livestock that will serve as the point of origin for his growing herd, and will ensure his part in the family inheritance. Belonging to an extended family will require him to honor that family's unique customs: what clothes and jewelry his sister will wear as a bride on her wedding day, how the groom's family will pay her bride price, and so on.

He was born to one of five clans (*ilgilat*, or *olgilata* in singular form), which define broader blood relations (encompassing tens of thousands of people). Membership in the clan defines whom he might marry, payment obligations to the victim's family if one of the clan members commits an act of murder, and so on.

The five clans are divided into two 'halves' (moieties) in accordance with the following myth:

In the distant past, the forefather of the Maasai (named Naiteru-kop) married two wives. He gave the first wife a rust-colored ox.

Therefore, the elders gave her the name Nado-mong'i (owner of the red oxen). She built her house on the right-hand side of the gateway to the village. Nado-mong'i had three sons, who were the progenitors of three clans, which are named after them. The second wife built her house on the left side of the gateway, and got a black cow; therefore, she was given the name Narok-kiteng (owner of the black cow). She had two boys, who were the progenitors of two more clans.

The Odomong'i (rust-colored oxen) moiety—called the "right hand" (since the mother built her house on the right-hand side of the gateway)—has three clans:

- Ilmolelian
- Ilmakesen
- Iltaarrosero

Two clans belong to the Orok Kiteng (black oxen) moiety—the "left hand":

- Ilaiser
- Ilukumae

Over the years, additional clans joined the five original Maasai clans, including Ildalalekutuk, Ilwasinkishu, Ilmoitanik and Samburu. Besides the nuclear family, the extended family and the clan, Museré also belongs to the Purko tribe (section), one of fifteen tribes (*iloshon, olosho* in singular form), which are geographically distinct from one another.

Membership in a tribe defines the place where Museré lives, the style of jewelry he wears, his clothing, the dialect he speaks, and his grazing rights in the region.

The Maasai Tribes (*Iloshon*) In Kenya:
Ildalatlekutuk (Ilkankere), Ildamat, Ilkaputiei, Ilkeekonyokie, Ilmatapato, Ilmoitanik, Iloilai, Iloitokitoki, Iloodokilani, Ilpurku, Isikirari, Isiria, Ilwasin-kishu.

In Tanzania:
Ilkisongo, Serenget.
Besides these fifteen tribes, more tribes speak the Maa language. Some, like the Waarusha tribe in Tanzania, have transitioned to an agricultural lifestyle, and no longer share the Maasai way of life.

In every tribe's territory—for example, the Purko—families from all clans (blood relations) mentioned above live side by side.

Age Groups and Age Sets
From the moment he is born, Museré becomes a part of these membership circles. When he grows up and becomes a youth, he will enter another social circle, that of the age group (*ol-porror*), which includes all the boys circumcised within five to seven years from the time the group was established. Membership in the age group defines who will undergo shared ceremonies along with him, who will host him when he travels to a distant village, and so on. When they mature, every two age groups will be united into a single age set (*olaji*). Therefore, for convenience, they are usually called "right hand" and "left hand."

Age groups and age sets are an important historical marker. In historical memory, for example, "the great flood" took place one year after the Ormegoli age group underwent the *eunoto* ceremony.

In the course of their lives, the members of each age group will gather four times in ceremonial villages (*manyatta*) for collective rites of passage that serve as transitions from one stage of maturity to the next:

First Collective Ceremony: Manyatta Emowo or EnKipaata

This *manyatta* is conducted before the boys are circumcised. When a "right hand" age group opens, the *manyatta* is called *Manyatta ya Emowo* (the *manyatta* of the horns). Two unique ceremonies will take place in this *manyatta*. The first, "grabbing the bull by the horns," requires the boys to approach the ceremonial bull chosen for this purpose, one by one, and grab his horns without the bull rebelling. The second ceremony unique to this *manyatta* is having the elders light a fire the traditional way, by rubbing two special sticks against each other, symbolizing the initiation of a new group of *morans*.

About seven years later, this age group will be closed, and the "left hand" will be opened in a *manyatta* called *Manyatta ya EnKipaata*. In this first *manyatta*, the elders will choose the boy who will become a ceremonial chief, a role assigned for life. The boy must be peaceable in nature, physically intact and to have no scars on his face. The chosen boy is marked with a long scar over his right knee, and he receives an *orinka*, a black wooden club. From this moment and until he dies, he will convene his age group for discussions and will be the arbitrator in any dispute within his age group.

The closing time of an age group is fluid. There is no closing event or ceremony. The closing will usually result from pressure from an older age group to mentor the younger ones, a mentoring that will be immediately expressed in holding the boys while they are being circumcised.

Second Collective Ceremony: Manyatta Eunoto

This is the second collective *manyatta*, built toward the end of the *moran* period, as described at length in the book.

Third Collective Ceremony: Manyatta o Nngusidin (the *manyatta* of sticks).

It is also known as *Manyatta Elashe*, the *manyatta* of calves. This *manyatta* takes place in "mid-life," and signals that the members of an age group are becoming full-fledged members of society. As proper grown-ups, they bring their wives and children with them (while the previous *manyatta* was attended by their mothers). In honor of the wives, many cows and sheep are slaughtered (during *eunoto*, when they were still *morans*, they could not eat meat with women).

Fourth Collective Ceremony: Manyatta o Lorikan (the *manyatta* of chairs). It is also known as *Manyatta o lngesherr*. This is the last collective *manyatta*, symbolizing the transition from a physical peak to a political peak. At this stage, the men are already forty or older. All are married and have children. In this *manyatta*, two age groups—the two hands, "right hand" and "left hand"—unite into one body, one age set, in which the age gap between the youngest and the oldest is about fifteen years. During the *manyatta*, the men receive the traditional chair: a low stool with four legs made from a single log. From now on, the men will earn more respect and political status, and soon, will become the mentors of a new age group.

Following are the age groups and age sets in the twentieth century (these are the names accepted within the Purko tribe. Other Maasai tribes sometimes use different names). The names are listed from the oldest to the youngest:

>   Age set: Irpeles—no longer alive.
>   Age set: Terito—opened in 1926; no longer alive.
>   Age set: Ilnyan'gusi—opened in 1942.
>   Age set: Ise'uri—opened in 1955.
>   Age set: Ilkitoip—opened in 1968–1979.
>   Age set: Orkishero—opened in 1980. Comprised of two age groups united in a ceremony held in 2004.

Age group: Ilmeshuki—right hand (opened in 1995).
Underwent the *eunoto* ceremony in 2004.

Age group: Orkimunyak—also known as Elkemayana—left hand (opened in 2007). Underwent the *eunoto* ceremony in 2012.

Age group: Ilturenkop/Ilmirisho—right hand (opened in 2015). Currently open.

Within the social network described above—the extended family, the tribe, the clan, the age group—these are pre-determined for Museré. As an adult, he will continue developing his personal social network: giving heifers, goats or sheep as gifts and marrying several women. The broader the network is, the more his chances of survival improve.

Museré's wife belonged to a tribe, a clan and her father's extended family. While still a baby, she underwent the first personal ceremony, "name giving," and in her youth, underwent circumcision. Several months after her circumcision, she was married to Museré, and from that moment on, became a member of his extended family, clan and even his age group. She will be the one to accompany him in the personal and collective ceremonies he will undergo from now on.

Appendix 4

Names, Latin Names and Uses of Plants Cited

The residents of the village where I live use natural medicine often, particularly infusions of plant roots intended to strengthen the body, which are given to babies daily. Adults, too, brew concoctions from nature besides receiving public medical aid. The uses of plants are not confined to medical purposes, as reflected in this short list, comprised of plants mentioned in this book:

Acacia (Acacia Gerradii): The bark of this tree is used to brew the local beer (the bark is peeled off the tree, and the inner white fibers are peeled off and dried. During preparing the beer, these fibers are placed in a container with honey or sugar. The container is sealed and left for about two weeks). Its branches and those of other varieties of acacia trees are used to build the fence surrounding the village.

Agave (Agave sisalana): A plant with thick, thorny leaves originating in Central America. It was exported to Africa to be used to manufacture rope (sisal rope). In Kenya, it is primarily used as a divider separating plots of land. The Maasai use its leaves to make ropes, serving to reinforce the skeletons of their homes.

Esunguroi (**Aloe volkensii**): A variety of the aloe plant. The local beer is made from its subterranean bulbs ("sausages"). The fluid in its leaves is used to heal external wounds.

Juniper (Juniperus procera): A tree that grows in the high mountains of semi-arid areas. As it is resistant to termites, it is much in demand for building houses or fences, and is subject to deforestation. Two of its trunks were chopped down by the *morans* to create the "temple" in the *eunoto* ceremony. Its common name in Kenya is *mutarakwa*, a name adopted in Swahili from the Kikuyu dialect.

Oleleshwa (**Tarchonanthus camphoratus**): Wild camphor. Its soft, velvety leaves are used as toilet paper. The branches of the shrub, with their pronounced scent, are used as deodorant, and are commonly tucked into the armpit.

Olokirdingai (**Croton dichogamus**): A variety of croton, a very hardy shrub that resumes growing after a wildfire and is responsible for the great quantities of firewood the women enjoy. Its branches are resilient against termites and are used to build huts and the fences surrounding villages.

Oltakurkurite (**Gardenia volkensii**): The branches of this tree, which grows slowly, are strong and forked. They serve as a "door" (*oltim*) closing over the village gate at night and dragged outside it during the day.

Oseki (**Cordia monoica**): Known as "sandpaper tree," thanks to the coarse roughness of its leaves. During ceremonies - when a new bride arrives or during a 'naming ceremony' - its branches are placed on the *oltim* (the wood serving as an entrance gate to the village) and on the gates, as a blessing upon anyone who enters the gate. The *orkiteng loorbaa* ceremony—the last personal ceremony in a person's life, signaling the transition to old age—must be conducted between two *oseki* trees. During every ceremonial slaughter, the meat is roasted on a grill made from the fluid-filled branches, which burn slowly. Its leaves are used to produce medication against eye ache (after the leaves are shredded and soaked in water, the solution is used to wash out the eyes).

Podocarpus: An evergreen with very dark leaves, which grows in the high planes of Africa. The tree might reach a height of nearly a hundred feet. Its leaves resemble asparagus, and its trunk is twisted in shape, as if it had been wrung out.

Oloirien **(Olea Africana)**: Wild olive. A tree with hard wood that grows slowly. Its branches and leaves are used in many ceremonies, mostly as a pallet laid over the beds of those circumcised. The bark of the tree is used to prepare medicine against intestinal worms.

Appendix 5

Glossary

Bush—a dense thicket of shrubs and trees, which is not dominated by any particular plant.

Chapati—a pancake made of wheat flour.

Eleso—the outer layer of fabric worn by the women over the two inner cloth sheets. This is a colorful cloth adorned with various patterns (in Swahili: *kanga*).

Enkai—Meaning "God," and "sky."

Enkela—a sheet of cowhide from which the hair has yet to be removed. Thick and heavy, it is used by men during ceremonies.

Enkepai—the Maasai name for the Mara River, crossing the Maasai Mara Reserve.

Enkiteti—a broad leather belt worn around a woman's waist and indicating she has given birth.

Eunoto—the closing ceremony of the *moran* period, marked by building a ceremonial village (*manyatta*) in which all the *morans* gather. Some are wearing a lion's mane or ostrich feather headdress. At the height of the ceremony, the young men's hair is shaved, and they return to society as young adults.

Ilikiliani—a young man at an interim stage, in the period between the time of recuperation after his circumcision (*olaibartani*) and becoming a *moran*.

Issuri—a long necklace in shades of blue and white worn by every woman whose son has been circumcised and has entered an age group.

Kalabash—a type of gourd shaped like an elongated, hollow bottle, which serves as a receptacle for liquids: milk or blood (in Maa: *olkurkurto*). Some African societies cut the *kalabash* in two and use its parts as spoons or drinking bowls.

Manyatta—a special village built to conduct collective ceremonies. The village's houses are so close to one another that from the outside, they seem like one reinforced wall. At the end of the ceremony period, the *manyatta* is set on fire.

Matatu—public transportation van in Kenya, usually very durable, which drives down every conceivable path, transporting the tightly packed passengers to their destinations.

Moran—a boy who has recovered from his circumcision, entered an age group, and goes out to the bush for a period that might last up to seven years, during which he grows out his hair and dyes his skin with ochre. Many taboos apply to him. The *moran* phase ends with a ceremony called *eunoto*.

Muzungu—a Swahili nickname for a white person (plural, *wazungu*).

Narok—the central town about sixty miles from the Maasai Mara Game Reserve. It houses government offices, the district hospital, a photography studio, high schools, a supermarket and a mall. Generally, it is a grimy roadside town, while during the rainy season, the dust turns into mud, and the river crossing the town, after which it is named Narok ("black water") overflows, flooding and sometimes drowning people.

Ndorobo— Ndorobo is a mispronunciation of the original name, *torroboni,* which mean "a poor man with no cattle." A Maasai term for a subgroup among them, whose members lost their livestock in the distant past and turned to hunting, an occupation treated with disdain. Men from the *Ndorobo* sub-clan circumcise the boys.

Ochre—a natural dye made of chunks of soft rock. Its color maybe mustard yellow, but is usually red. The chunks are ground into a powder and sold in the markets in this form. The powder may be mixed with water and used to adorn the body, but in ceremonies, it is always mixed with fat and applied to the head and face.

Olaibartani— newly circumcised boy. The healing period lasts about a month. At the end of the recuperation period his head is shaved and he becomes an *ilikiliani*.

Oloiboni—a man or woman with the ability to heal, bless or curse. Some can communicate with the spirits of ancestors and the forces of nature, which they use to discover the reason for a disease and how to heal it. Most *oloiboni* are members of the Laiser clan (and the Inkidongi subclan). They are the spiritual leaders of the Maasai people.

Oltshiti—a light blanket for men, checkered mostly in shades of red.

Orinka—a wooden club with a rounded knob at one end. Also known to tourists by the common name *rungu*.

Orkela—a sheet of sheepskin processed until it grows soft, adorned with colorful beads and dyed with red ochre. Used in ceremonies.

Orkiteng loorbaa—the last personal ceremony a man undergoes in his life. To undergo the ceremony, he must finish paying the bride price for his wife and cleanse himself from previous sins. The name means "the ox of sins," or literally, "the wounds."

Orpul—a shady place among the shrubs, close to a river but far away from the village, to which men or *morans* go to slaughter a goat or a ram.

Osero—the Maasai name for the Maasai Mara Game Reserve.

Osinkira—a "temple" in which the *morans* are blessed, built during the *eunoto* ceremony (marking the end of the *moran* period). It is built in only one day, used one evening and then set on fire.

Panga—a machete, the women's knife. Thick and long, they use it when they go out to chop wood.

Purko—A Maasai tribe (section) residing south of Narok town, toward the Maasai Mara Game Reserve in Kenya (read more about the Maasai tribes in Appendix 2).

Segera—cowrie shells. They were imported to Africa from the Far East, and in the distant past served as currency. In many African societies, they are a symbol of female fertility, as their shape resembles the female sex organ. The Maasai incorporate these shells in female artifacts, especially a girl's tiara, worn immediately after she is circumcised, which is therefore termed *segera* as well.

Sukuma wiki—kale. Its green leaves, resembling coarse spinach, are similarly cooked. The name literally means 'provides a week-long push,' i.e., grants strength.

Surutya—a spiral made of copper thread, worn by a boy over his temples immediately after being circumcised and throughout his recuperation period. A woman wears a *surutya* on her neck after her husband had paid off the cows that constitute her bride price.

Swahili—Tanzania's official language, and the lingua franca of Kenya and throughout east Africa. Created by Arab merchants who blended into the local population on the east African coast (*sahel* means 'coast' in Arabic), it is a mixture of words in Arabic and Farsi along with African words and grammar. English words for modern terms have been incorporated into the language in the last hundred years.

Ugali—Kenya's national dish: maize flour and a pinch of salt are added to boiling water and stirred well until a solid mixture is formed. Less maize flour in the pot will cause a softer dish called *madida*. Even less maize flour and no salt will create a liquid porridge called *olshoro*.

Bibliography

The African Worldview

Mbiti, John. *African Religions and Philosophy*, U.K.: Heinemann, 1969.

Mbiti, John. *An Introduction to African Religion*, U.K.: Heinemann, 1975.

Ray, Benjamin C. *African Religions: Symbol, Ritual and Community*, New Jersey: Englewood Cliffs, 1976.

Sabar, Galia. *We're Not Here to Stay: African Migrant Workers in Israel and Back*, Tel Aviv: Tel Aviv University, 2008.

> This academic study opens a window into the African "social network," and providing a mirror reflecting Israeli society, in the way it is perceived by "the Other," for better and worse. (Hebrew)

Schwartzman, Ori. *White Doctor, Black Gods: White Psychiatric Medicine in the Jungles of Africa*, Tel Aviv: Aryeh Nir Publishing, 2007.

> This fascinating book describes additional aspects of the African perception of death and religious beliefs, including the spirits of deceased ancestors. (Hebrew)

Aid Organizations

Hancock, Graham. *Lords of Poverty: The Power, Prestige and Corruption of the International Aid Business*, New York: Atlantic Monthly Press, 1989.

> One of the first books to openly expose the negative aspects of aid organizations.

Maren, Michael. *The Road to Hell: The Ravaging Effects of Foreign Aid and International Charity*, New York: The Free Press, 1997.

> The author was a volunteer in a large aid organization, and writes about the surreal, unexpected consequences of Western aid, primarily in Somalia.

Polman, Linda. *The Crisis Caravan: What's Wrong with Humanitarian Aid?* New York: Picador, 2011.

> An intense book describing the damage caused by aid organizations in Africa, especially during times of war.

Female Circumcision

Fuambai, S. Ahmadu. "Disputing the Myth of the Sexual Dysfunction of Circumcised Women," in *Anthropology Today*, vol. 25, no. 6, pp. 14–17 (2009).

Nnamuchi, Obiajulu, "United Nations' Resolution on Elimination of Female Genital Ritual: A Legitimate Response to a Human Rights Problem, or What?" in *Medicine and Law*, Dec 2014, vol. 33, pp. 61–114.

Folk Tales and Mythology

Kipuri, Naomi. *Oral Literature of the Maasai*, Nairobi: East African Educational Publishers, 2002.

> A fascinating book with a collection of stories, proverbs and witticisms in English and Maa.

Massek, A. ol'Oloisolo and Sidai, J.O. *Wisdom of Maasai*, Nairobi: Transafrica Publishers, 1974.

African Politics

Chabal, Patrick and Daloz, Jean-Pascal. *Africa Works: Disorder as Political Instrument*, Bloomington: Indiana University Press, 1999.

> An important academic book investigating political trends in Africa and exploring the phenomenon of "the patron."

General Literature about the Maasai

Amin, Mohamed, Willets, Duncan and Eames, John. *The Last of the Maasai*, London: Bodley Head, 1987.

Bentsen, Cheryl. *Maasai Days*, New York: Anchor Books, 1991.

Brunner Edward M and Kirschenblatt-Gimblet Barbara. "Maasai on the Lawn:

Tourist Realism in East Africa," in *Cultural Anthropology* 9, no. 4 (1994), pp. 435-470.

Dinesen, Isak. *Out of Africa*, New York: Modern Library, 1992.

OleSanken, S.S. *The Maasai*, Nairobi: Kenya Literature Bureau, 1995.

Spear, Thomas and Waller, Richard (eds.). *Being Maasai: Ethnicity and Identity in East Africa*, Athens: Ohio University Press, 1993.

> An important anthology of academic articles about the origins of the Maasai in the past and their identity today.

Spencer, Paul. *Time, Space, and the Unknown: Maasai Configurations of Power and Providence*, London: Routledge, 2003.

Spencer, Paul, "The Maasai Double-Helix and the Theory of Dilemmas," in David Maybury-Lewis and Uri Almagor, *The Attraction of Opposites*, Ann Arbor: University of Michigan Press, 1989.

The Dietary Habits of Elephants

Bax, P. Napier and Sheldrick, D.L.W. "Some Preliminary Observations on the Food of Elephants in the Tsavo Royal National Park of Kenya," in *African Journal of Ecology*, vol. 1, issue 1, pp. 40–51, 1963.

Acknowledgments

When I first settled down among the Maasai, I was convinced there was a great difference between the Maasai worldview and logic and that of the "modern" world in which we live.

Today, eighteen years later, as I finish writing this book—after sharpening both my pen and thoughts, after describing the difference in clothing, customs, rites and language—I grin at the mad discovery that essentially, deep down inside us, we are so very similar! Happiness, sadness, laughter, anger, bliss, pain, compassion—the way we express all these is culture-dependent, but they always exist and serve as a bridge. A bridge that allows us, all humans, to communicate with one another easily.

This insight, that similarity does exist invariance, has opened up the gates of the world to me. I now cruise and fit in easily among the members of various societies. I might err in the way I greet someone, but I'll never err by smiling warmly at those around me. They will understand.

This similarity also applies to social systems. Even in our modern, individualist life, with our rapid pace of living in the technological era, we cannot exist without the social network that envelops us in its own way. That network is the one that encouraged, supported, criticized, pushed me, and helped to create this book.

Without my dear friends Yossi Baidach from Yavniel and Ori

Tabenkin—who sowed the seed and prodded me to write the book—I'd be sitting to this day, staring at the savanna with a blissful expression on my face.

The tedious task of reading the shoot as it began to sprout—the first drafts—fell to my family members: my father Dudu, my mother Hava, my brothers and sisters. They, for years enthralled listeners as I recounted my tales of adventure, now suffered again and again from this baby's growing pains.

Anat Shaul, Ami Even, Hila Raz, Ofir Drori, Ori Tabenkin and Galia Sabar read, reacted, critiqued, enhanced, fine-tuned and complimented.

A special thanks to Orit Bahat and Shachar Moses, who not only read the contents several times, commented and scolded, but also allowed me to seclude myself in the "ivory tower" —their charming guest room in the heart of a blooming garden—and bring this book to its final version.

Dorit Weissman from Abirim not only read the book—now a full-fledged tree—critiqued it and expressed her enthusiasm but was the one to pick the fruit and serve it to the publishing house. If it wasn't for you, Dorit, the fruit would have rotted…

I was amazed to discover how many hands embrace and nurture a manuscript until it ripens completely. Editing, linguistic editing, cover design—these were sensitively done in the Hebrew edition by Navit Barel, Sigal Geffen, Vered Zinger, Yifat Hareven and Dana Tziviak.

The English translation of the book was done with plenty of patience and sensitivity by Yael Schonfeld Abel, who swam elegantly and successfully in an unknown sea of phrases, habits, and culture. Thank you, Yael.

Thanks to Joseph Healey, an American Catholic missionary priest - who has many African names and has eaten a lot of salt (over 50 years!) in East Africa – for his friendship, advice, proofreading and accompaniment.

In Kenya, the home of Hillel and Lydia Oron was always open for what I called "recovery." I especially needed this recuperation period after being bitten and swelling up at Barsoinkan's wedding. Hillel helped me find my car, and with countless pieces of advice.

I've experienced the most mature, best and happiest years of my life in the little village in Maasai Mara. Here I was privileged with insight about generosity, tolerance, pluralism, accepting others and giving. I cherish and appreciate it in every single moment of my life.

Thank you, my Maasai friends.

Printed in Great Britain
by Amazon